LOT VIEWING
Orange County Convention Center
North Concourse, Level 2
Room 220 D, E, F
9400 Universal Boulevard • Orlando, FL 32819

Monday, January 4, 2010 • 10:00 AM - 7:00 PM ET
Tuesday, January 5, 2010 • 8:00 AM - 7:00 PM ET
Wednesday, January 6, 2010 • 8:00 AM - 7:00 PM ET
Thursday, January 7, 2010 • 8:00 AM - 7:00 PM ET
Friday, January 8, 2010 • 8:00 AM - 7:00 PM ET
Saturday, January 9, 2010 • 8:00 AM - 6:00 PM ET

View Lots and Video Lot descriptions Online at HA.com/Coins

LIVE FLOOR BIDDING
Bid in person during the floor sessions.

LIVE TELEPHONE BIDDING *(floor sessions only)*
Phone bidding must be arranged on or before
Tuesday, January 5, 2010, by 12:00 PM CT.
Client Service: 866-835-3243.

HERITAGE Live!™ BIDDING
Bid live from your location, anywhere in the world,
during the Auction using our HERITAGE Live!™ program
at HA.com/Live

INTERNET BIDDING
Internet absentee bidding ends at 10:00 PM CT
the evening before each session. HA.com/Coins

FAX BIDDING
Fax bids must be received on or before Tuesday,
January 5, 2010, by 12:00 PM CT. Fax: 214-409-1425

MAIL BIDDING
Mail bids must be received on or before
Tuesday, January 5, 2010.

*Please see "Choose Your Bidding Method" in the back of this
catalog for specific details about each of these bidding methods.*

This auction is subject to a 15% Buyer's Premium.

Extended Payment Terms available. See details in the back of this catalog.

*Lots are sold at an approximate rate of 200 lots per hour, but it
is not uncommon to sell 150 lots or 250 lots in any given hour.*

LIVE AUCTION
SIGNATURE® FLOOR SESSIONS 1-5
(Floor, Telephone, HERITAGE Live!,™ Internet, Fax, and Mail)
Orange County Convention Center
North Concourse, Level 2 • Room 230 B
9400 Universal Boulevard • Orlando, FL 32819

SESSION 1 *(see separate catalog)*
Wednesday, January 6, 2010 • 7:00 PM ET • Lots 1-958

SESSION 2
THE BOCA COLLECTION, PART I
Thursday, January 7, 2010 • 6:30 PM ET • Lots 2001–2071

SESSION 3 - PLATINUM NIGHT *(see separate catalog)*
Thursday, January 7, 2010
Immediately following Session 2 (Approximately 7:00 PM)
Lots 2072-2646

SESSION 4 *(see separate catalog)*
Friday, January 8, 2010 • 12:00 PM ET • Lots TBD

SESSION 5 *(see separate catalog)*
Friday, January 8, 2010 • 7:00 PM ET • Lots TBD

NON FLOOR/NON PHONE BIDDING SESSIONS 6-7
(HERITAGE Live!,™ Internet, Fax, and Mail only)

SESSION 6 *(see separate catalog)*
Saturday, January 9, 2010 • 2:00 PM CT • Lots 7001–8490

SESSION 7 *(see separate catalog)*
Sunday, January 10, 2010 • 2:00 PM CT • Lots 8491–10201

AUCTION RESULTS
Immediately available at HA.com/Coins

LOT SETTLEMENT AND PICK-UP
Room 220 D, E, F
Thursday, January 7, 2010 • 10:00 AM - 1:00 PM ET
Friday, January 8, 2010 • 10:00 AM - 1:00 PM ET
Saturday, January 9, 2010 • 10:00 AM - 1:00 PM ET
Sunday, January 10, 2010 • 9:00 AM - 12:00 PM ET

THIS AUCTION IS PRESENTED AND CATALOGED BY HERITAGE NUMISMATIC AUCTIONS, INC.

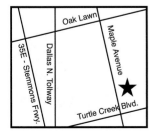

Heritage World Headquarters

HERITAGE HA.com
Auction Galleries

Home Office • 3500 Maple Avenue, 17th Floor • Dallas, Texas 75219
Design District Annex • 1518 Slocum Street • Dallas, Texas 75207
214.528.3500 | 800.872.6467 | 214.409.1425 (fax)
Direct Client Service Line: Toll Free 1.866.835.3243 • Email: Bid@HA.com

Heritage Design District Annex

FL licenses: Heritage Numismatic Auctions, Inc.: AB665; Currency Auctions of America: AB2218; FL Auctioneer licenses: Samuel Foose AU3244; Robert Korver AU2916; Mike
Sadler AU3795; Shaunda Fry AU3915; Jacob Walker AU4031; Andrea Voss AU4034.

Steve Ivy
CEO
Co-Chairman of the Board

Jim Halperin
Co-Chairman of the Board

Greg Rohan
President

Paul Minshull
Chief Operating Officer

Todd Imhof
Executive Vice President

U.S. Coin Specialists

Leo Frese
Vice President

David Mayfield
Vice President,
Numismatics

Jim Stoutjesdyk
Vice President,
Numismatics

3500 Maple Avenue, 17th Floor • Dallas, Texas 75219
Phone 214-528-3500 • 800-872-6467
HA.com/Coins

DIRECTORY FOR DEPARTMENT SPECIALISTS AND SERVICES

COINS & CURRENCY

COINS – UNITED STATES
HA.com/Coins

Leo Frese, Ext. 1294
Leo@HA.com
David Mayfield, Ext. 1277
DavidM@HA.com
Jessica Aylmer, Ext. 1706
JessicaA@HA.com
Diedre Buchmoyer, Ext. 1794
DiedreB@HA.com
Win Callender, Ext. 1415
WinC@HA.com
Bert DeLaGarza, Ext. 1795
BertD@HA.com
Chris Dykstra, Ext. 1380
ChrisD@HA.com
Sam Foose, Ext. 1227
SamF@HA.com
Jason Friedman, Ext. 1582
JasonF@HA.com
Shaunda Fry, Ext. 1159
ShaundaF@HA.com
Jim Jelinski, Ext. 1257
JimJ@HA.com
Katherine Kurachek, Ext. 1389
KK@HA.com
Bob Marino, Ext. 1374
BobMarino@HA.com
Mike Sadler, Ext. 1332
MikeS@HA.com

RARE CURRENCY
HA.com/Currency

Len Glazer, Ext. 1390
Len@HA.com
Allen Mincho, Ext. 1327
Allen@HA.com
Dustin Johnston, Ext. 1302
Dustin@HA.com
Michael Moczalla, Ext. 1481
MichaelM@HA.com
Jason Friedman, Ext. 1582
JasonF@HA.com

U.S. COINS
PRIVATE TREATY SALES
HA.com/Coins

Todd Imhof, Ext. 1313
Todd@HA.com

U.S. COINS
PURCHASED
HA.com/Coins

Jim Stoutjesdyk, Ext. 1310
JimS@HA.com

WORLD & ANCIENT COINS
HA.com/WorldCoins

Warren Tucker, Ext. 1287
WTucker@HA.com
Cristiano Bierrenbach, Ext. 1661
CrisB@HA.com
Scott Cordry, Ext. 1369
ScottC@HA.com

COMICS & COMIC ART
HA.com/Comics

Ed Jaster, Ext. 1288
EdJ@HA.com
Lon Allen, Ext. 1261
LonA@HA.com
Barry Sandoval, Ext. 1377
BarryS@HA.com
Todd Hignite, Ext. 1790
ToddH@HA.com

FINE ART

AMERICAN & EUROPEAN
PAINTINGS & SCULPTURE
HA.com/FineArt

Edmund P. Pillsbury, Ph.D., Ext. 1533
EPP@HA.com
Ed Jaster, Ext. 1288
EdJ@HA.com
Courtney Case, Ext. 1293
CourtneyC@HA.com
Marianne Berardi, Ph.D., Ext. 1506
MarianneB@HA.com
Ariana Hartsock, Ext. 1283
ArianaH@HA.com

ART OF THE AMERICAN WEST
HA.com/WesternArt

Michael Duty, Ext. 1712
MichaelD@HA.com

FURNITURE &
DECORATIVE ART
HA.com/Decorative

Tim Rigdon, Ext. 1119
TimR@HA.com
Meredith Meuwly, Ext. 1631
MeredithM@HA.com
Nicholas Dawes, Ext. 1605
NickD@HA.com

ILLUSTRATION ART
HA.com/Illustration

Ed Jaster, Ext. 1288
EdJ@HA.com
Todd Hignite, Ext. 1790
ToddH@HA.com

MODERN &
CONTEMPORARY ART
HA.com/Modern

Frank Hettig, Ext. 1157
FrankH@HA.com

SILVER & VERTU
HA.com/Silver

Tim Rigdon, Ext. 1119
TimR@HA.com

TEXAS ART
HA.com/TexasArt

Atlee Phillips, Ext. 1786
AtleeP@HA.com

20TH-CENTURY DESIGN
HA.com/Design

Christina Japp, Ext. 1247
CJapp@HA.com
Nicholas Dawes, Ext. 1605
NickD@HA.com

VINTAGE & CONTEMPORARY
PHOTOGRAPHY
HA.com/ArtPhotography

Ed Jaster, Ext. 1288
EdJ@HA.coms

HISTORICAL

AMERICAN INDIAN ART
HA.com/AmericanIndian

Delia Sullivan, Ext. 1343
DeliaS@HA.com

AMERICANA & POLITICAL
HA.com/Historical

Tom Slater, Ext. 1441
TomS@HA.com
Marsha Dixey, Ext. 1455
MarshaD@HA.com
John Hickey, Ext. 1264
JohnH@HA.com
Michael Riley, Ext. 1467
MichaelR@HA.com

CIVIL WAR AND
ARMS & MILITARIA
HA.com/CivilWar

Dennis Lowe, Ext. 1182
DennisL@HA.com

HISTORICAL MANUSCRIPTS
HA.com/Manuscripts

Sandra Palomino, Ext. 1107
SandraP@HA.com

RARE BOOKS
HA.com/Books

James Gannon, Ext. 1609
JamesG@HA.com
Joe Fay, Ext. 1544
JoeF@HA.com

SPACE EXPLORATION
HA.com/Space

John Hickey, Ext. 1264
JohnH@HA.com
Michael Riley, Ext. 1467
MichaelR@HA.com

TEXANA
HA.com/Historical

Sandra Palomino, Ext. 1107
SandraP@HA.com

JEWELRY & TIMEPIECES

FINE JEWELRY
HA.com/Jewelry

Jill Burgum, Ext. 1697
JillB@HA.com

WATCHES & FINE TIMEPIECES
HA.com/Timepieces

Jim Wolf, Ext. 1659
JWolf@HA.com

MUSIC & ENTERTAINMENT
MEMORABILIA
HA.com/Entertainment

Doug Norwine, Ext. 1452
DougN@HA.com
John Hickey, Ext. 1264
JohnH@HA.com
Garry Shrum, Ext. 1585
GarryS@HA.com
Jim Steele, Ext. 1328
JimSt@HA.com
Kristen Painter, Ext. 1149
KristenP@HA.com

NATURAL HISTORY
HA.com/NaturalHistory

David Herskowitz, Ext. 1610
DavidH@HA.com

RARE STAMPS
HA.com/Stamps

Harvey Bennett, Ext. 1185
HarveyB@HA.com
Steven Crippe, Ext. 1777
StevenC@HA.com

SPORTS COLLECTIBLES
HA.com/Sports

Chris Ivy, Ext. 1319
CIvy@HA.com
Peter Calderon, Ext. 1789
PeterC@HA.com
Mike Gutierrez, Ext. 1183
MikeG@HA.com
Lee Iskowitz, Ext. 1601
LeeI@HA.com
Mark Jordan, Ext. 1187
MarkJ@HA.com
Chris Nerat, Ext. 1615
ChrisN@HA.com
Jonathan Scheier, Ext. 1314
JonathanS@HA.com

VINTAGE MOVIE POSTERS
HA.com/MoviePosters

Grey Smith, Ext. 1367
GreySm@HA.com
Bruce Carteron, Ext. 1551
BruceC@HA.com
Isaiah Evans, Ext. 1201
IsaiahE@HA.com

TRUSTS & ESTATES
HA.com/Estates
Mark Prendergast, Ext. 1632
MPrendergast@HA.com

CORPORATE & INSTITUTIONAL
COLLECTIONS/VENTURES
Jared Green, Ext. 1279
Jared@HA.com

AUCTION OPERATIONS
Norma Gonzalez, Ext. 1242
V.P. Auction Operations
Norma@HA.com

CREDIT DEPARTMENT
Marti Korver, Ext. 1248
Marti@HA.com
Eric Thomas, Ext. 1241
EricT@HA.com

MARKETING
Debbie Rexing, Ext. 1356
DebbieR@HA.com

MEDIA & PUBLIC RELATIONS
Noah Fleisher, Ext. 1143
NoahF@HA.com

HOUSTON OFFICE
Mark Prendergast
713-899-8364
MPrendergast@HA.com

CORPORATE OFFICERS
R. Steven Ivy, Co-Chairman
James L. Halperin, Co-Chairman
Gregory J. Rohan, President
Paul Minshull, Chief Operating Officer
Todd Imhof, Executive Vice President
Leo Frese, Vice President

The Boca Collection of Proof Sets, Part I
An Introduction

The present offering represents an achievement we believe to be unprecedented in modern times. Collecting diligently, over a period of decades, the consignor has accomplished the incredible feat of completing three runs of U.S. silver and minor proof sets, covering the years 1856-1916. The last record we have uncovered of anyone completing even one run of proof sets covering this entire time period was in the legendary John Story Jenks Collection (Henry Chapman, 12/1921), lots 6302-6364. The circumstances that enabled Jenks to complete his magnificent collection no longer exist today, as intact proof sets from this early era are seldom encountered in dealer offerings. The consignor purchased intact sets when they were available, but he was often forced to assemble the yearly sets one coin at the time, sometimes requiring years to complete a particular set. Because of this experience, he has instructed that his first collection is to be offered as intact proof sets, enabling collectors to secure an example of each yearly set with a single bid. We are honored that he has favored us with the opportunity of auctioning his first run of proof sets on this memorable occasion.

Popularity of Proof Sets in the 19th Century

Collecting runs of proof sets was quite popular in the 19th century, and the enthusiasm for this mode of collecting is easily understood. In an era when mintmarks were not considered important, the most efficient way for a collector to acquire a high quality example of every current denomination was to order a proof set from the Philadelphia Mint every year. While proof coins were produced in this country as early as 1817, proof sets (and singles) from that era are extremely rare. The collector base was not large enough to justify yearly commercial offerings from the Mint until the late 1850s. The exponential increase in the number of coin collectors occasioned by the retirement of the old copper large cents in 1857 made an annual production of proof sets for collectors economically feasible. Mint Director James Ross Snowden published standard prices for proof sets and outlined ordering procedures for the collecting public in 1858. Collecting runs of intact proof sets became extremely popular immediately afterward and, within 10 years, W. Elliot Woodward considered it more important to feature complete proof sets in his auction catalogs than to offer complete date runs of silver coinage. In his introduction to the Mickley Collection (Woodward, 10/1867), Woodward reflected, "Owing to the arrangement of the Silver into Proof sets, many additions in the regular lines of silver might well have been made, to fill the spaces made vacant by the Proofs removing; …" In lot 1706 of the catalog, Woodward actually paired an 1827 proof quarter with a proof dime and half dollar of that date to form a silver proof set. The 1827 quarter is a classic rarity and the coin would have undoubtedly attracted spirited bidding if offered individually. Woodward refrained from filling in the gaps in the date runs with coins from his stock because he wanted to preserve an accurate record of the silver portion of the Mickley Collection.

Virtually all major collections formed in the second half of the 19th century included runs of silver and minor proof sets. In the 1890s, super-collector Virgil Brand had a standard practice of ordering 10 silver proof sets and 20 minor sets every year, along with selected gold proofs and extra specimens of favorite denominations. In 1894, he is known to have doubled his order of silver and minor proof sets. The practice of collecting runs of proof sets continued well into the early 20th century. The Chapman brothers' sales from this period are particularly rich in these items. The George Earle Collection (Henry Chapman, 6/1912), featured 15 gold proof sets with dates between 1860 and 1910, and lots 3699-3754 were all silver and minor proof sets from the years 1857-1906. Henry Chapman seems to have made a specialty of proof sets, acting as an agent for Robert Garrett, Dr. Christian Allenburger, and others. Chapman was by no means alone in his formidable proof set offerings during this era. In the Peter Mougey Collection (Thomas Elder, 9/1910), lots 1247-1269 were gold proof sets from 1882-1906, missing only the years 1904 and 1905. Lots 1270-1329 were silver proof sets dated 1842-43, 1846-48, 1850, 1852-1902, and 1903-06. Other collections of the period, e.g., Parmelee and Winsor, had similar runs. Proof sets were plentiful through the first decade of the 20th century. In fact, later date proofs from the 1860s and 1870s were common enough at the time that they were often group lotted. But the popularity and availability of proof sets began to diminish after the Mougey Sale.

The Popularity Wanes

Beginning in 1907, a true Renaissance in U.S. coinage design occurred. During the next 14 years, every circulating denomination of U.S. federal coinage underwent a design change. The new designs were beautiful, innovative, and usually featured high relief devices. Unfortunately, these designs were not suitable for production of traditional proof coins with brilliant surfaces. The Mint tried several different finishes for proof coins over the next nine years, including sandblast and Roman proofs, but no style succeeded in winning the approval of contemporary collectors. Orders for proof sets declined each year until the Mint finally stopped production in 1916. The following year the United States entered World War I, and public attention was focused on the war effort. By the time the war was over, proof sets seem to have been largely forgotten by the collecting public. A few appeals were made to resurrect the proof set program but the issue was generally out-of-sight and out-of-mind until the 1930s.

With the decline in proof set collecting, coin dealers began to reverse Woodward's practice of assembling proof sets from individual coins, and began breaking them up instead. A dealer's primary function is to sell coins, and there was no market for intact proof sets, instead there was constant demand for high quality specimens to fill date and mintmark runs of all denominations of U.S. coinage. The pressure to break up silver proof sets was too great for most dealers to resist. Henry Chapman continued to offer intact proof sets in his catalogs into the 1920s (see the aforementioned Jenks sale), but this practice was unusual. In the James Ten Eyck Collection (B. Max Mehl, 5/1922), Mehl offered many gold proof sets intact, but he disassembled the silver sets because of the popularity of those lower denomination coins, and cataloged the coins individually. Collecting large denomination gold coins did not become popular until the late 1930s, so there was little pressure to break up a proof set to satisfy collector demand for a rare date eagle or double eagle. As a result, gold proof sets continued to be offered intact for another 15-20 years. However, by the time of the Dunham Collection (Mehl, 6/1941), all the gold sets were parted out as well. Mehl specifically mentions breaking up the gold proof set of 1875, purchased intact by Dunham in 1906, in the lot descriptions for the proof coins of that date. The practice of breaking up proof sets became nearly universal and has persisted to the present time, with the result that an intact original proof set from a date before 1916 is an extremely rare item today.

The Depression Years

The Depression had a profound effect on the survival of intact early proof sets. The 1930s are a numismatic Dark Age as far as auction catalogs are concerned. Dealers like Mehl, Bolender, Kosoff, Elder, Bluestone, and Wayte Raymond continued to hold auctions, but they were much smaller affairs. There was not a single blockbuster sale during the entire decade. The great collections that were dispersed during that era (Newcomer, Brand, and Col. Green) were all sold privately. The proof holdings from these collections were, for the most part, sold in a haphazard, piecemeal fashion that encouraged the breaking up of sets. Collectors of more modest means, finding that their proof sets brought small premiums, often broke them up and sold, or even just spent, the individual coins. It is likely that the total number of intact proof sets was greatly reduced during this period.

One large hoard of proof sets did surface in 1935, when M.H. Bolender auctioned the A.M. Smith Collection. Andrew Mason Smith was a coin dealer/wine merchant living in Philadelphia from 1875 to 1886. He served in the Civil War and was acquainted with dealer John W. Haseltine and Mint Superintendent Oliver C. Bosbyshell through their membership in the G.A.R. Smith is best known as the author of the Visitor's Guide and History of the United States Mint, and thus worked closely with Mint personnel for some years. He later moved to Minnesota where he died in 1915. He apparently acquired a huge supply of proof sets during his association with the Mint, as Bolender reported his collection included more than 1,000 proof sets, mostly dates in the 1870s and 1880s. Bolender offered the collection in a series of five sales in 1935-1936. Fewer than 300 proof sets were actually cataloged in these sales, with the majority representing only minor sets. It must be assumed that the other 700+ sets referred to by Bolender were sold privately, wholesaled to other dealers, or broken up and offered as individual coins over a series of years.

Bolender also sold the proof set collection of Martin Luther Beistle in his 100th Auction Sale on November 30, 1935. Beistle was the author of the Register of U.S. Half Dollars, and his collection included proof issues from 1858-1914. Unfortunately, the proofs were offered exclusively as individual coins, with no intact proof sets cataloged.

Of course, the modern era of proof set collecting also began in this decade. The practice of collecting coins from circulation had become popular for the first time in the 1930s, and the number of new coin collectors increased dramatically in this time period. The Mint responded by resuming its annual proof set offerings in 1936. Initially the program attracted little attention, but the sets soon became popular, and business was booming again by 1940.

The 1940s and 1950s

The nicest public offering of proof coinage in the 1940-1950 time frame took place in the Royal Sale (Mehl, 3/1948). This catalog featured the collection of Dr. Christian Allenburger, which contained a complete run of proof sets from 1854-1904, and also had a large number of earlier proof coins. In his description of lot 1277 Mehl disclosed, "Dr. Allenburger purchased all these beautiful proof coins from the Chapmans many years ago. They were all purchased in complete sets and haven't changed hands since the date of issue, probably more than two or three times." The coins were primarily offered individually, but Allenburger had duplicate sets from many years and, for those dates, Mehl offered one set as individual coins and the other set as an intact proof set. This is the only instance found in our research when a cataloger had a chance to offer these items in such a fashion.

The decade of the 1950s was relatively uneventful in terms of proof set offerings and the unfortunate trend of breaking up original proof sets continued. A substantial collection of proof coins was featured in the Mrs. Henry Ford Collection (Stack's, 12/1951), with proof examples dating back to 1849, and the fabulous collection of King Farouk of Egypt contained many wonderful proof coins. Farouk purchased these coins privately, from the estates of Virgil Brand, Col. Green, and F.C.C. Boyd. Unfortunately, we have no record of these transactions. When the collection was cataloged as The Palace Collections of Egypt (Sotheby's, 2/1954), the coins were sold in group lots by denomination, and any original proof sets were broken up. Much of the history of these important coins was obscured in this process.

The 1960s and 1970s

The remarkable collection of Howard D. Egolf was offered at public auction by the Stack's firm on May 5, 1961. Lots 778-833 of the catalog consisted of intact proof sets, dated from 1859-1915. Each lot contained an original proof set, including the original wrappings from the Philadelphia Mint. Where Egolf obtained these sets is a mystery, since he was born in 1893 and did not begin collecting until the early proof set era was ending. The catalogers noted Egolf's father was interested in coins prior to the Civil War, and had preserved a small collection which he passed on to his son. Perhaps the early proof sets were part of this ancestral collection. The Egolf sale was a rare opportunity for collectors to purchase intact early proof sets, four decades after most dealers had ceased to offer them.

Of all the collectors of early proof sets, from the time of John Story Jenks until the present day, the man who most closely matched the feat of our present consignor was Charles Jay. His collection was auctioned by Stack's on October 28, 1967 and lacked only the 1916 proof set to complete the run. The catalogers reported:

"The collection contains an example of virtually every proof coin in silver, copper, and nickel issued by the United States Mint commencing in 1856.

"The series was literally assembled piece by piece from numerous pedigree collections sold during the past decade, with quality the prime factor governing their selection and purchase. This is without doubt one of the finest groups of Proof Coins ever offered."

Following the usual practice of the times, the coins were offered individually.

Prominent coin dealer Harry Forman told the story of an outstanding collection of early proof sets formed by Washington Augustus Roebling. Roebling was the famous civil engineer who helped design the Brooklyn Bridge with his father, John Augustus Roebling. When his father was killed in an accident during the construction of the bridge, the younger Roebling took charge, and supervised the project through its successful completion. Forman related that Roebling's grandson sold his collection of early proof sets, dating from 1858-1915, to New Netherlands Coin Company sometime during the 1950s. When Forman became aware of this transaction, he arranged to purchase the entire collection for $75,000, for his own holdings. The sets were all original proof sets from the Mint, and the quality of the individual coins was extraordinary. Forman consigned the collection to the S.S. Forrest Sale (Stack's, 9/1972), and estimated the collection realized about $200,000.

Recent Times

Collecting early proof sets in recent times has followed the pattern that began in the early 20th century. A small group of dedicated collectors, including the present consignor, has endeavored to piece together runs of early sets from widely disparate offerings, usually one coin at the time. Occasionally, an older collection containing original early proof sets will unexpectedly surface. A case in point is found in the Century Collection (Superior, 2/1992). The proof sets in the Century catalog were collected by an old-time collector, a Mr. Campbell, in the usual manner. He ordered sets from the Mint every year from 1880 -1914, and they were preserved by his heirs in a safe deposit box until 1991. Superior sold the collection in February 1992, using an unusual cataloging scheme. The coins were offered individually in separate lots, and collectively in a single lot for each set, if the bidder was willing to bid more than the total the lots in the set had realized separately. This approach enabled some lucky collectors to obtain entire original proof sets. Another important opportunity occurred in the Carl Zelson Collection (Stack's, 10/1985). Zelson's collection consisted of a run of complete silver proof sets from 1858-1891, missing only the 1876 dated set. In an extremely unusual move for a modern auction company, Stack's offered the coins in complete proof set lots.

Probably the most important opportunity for collectors of early proof sets in recent times was found in the Floyd Starr Collection (Stack's, 10/1992). Starr was a lifelong resident of Philadelphia, and an early collector of U.S. proof sets. He is known to have purchased some of the coins in the John Story Jenks Collection, and was at his collecting height in the 1940s. Starr died in 1971, leaving a fantastic collection that was dispersed by Stack's in a series of famous auction sales. Starr is the numismatist who most nearly matched this consignor's feat in recent times, as his collection included a run of silver proof sets from 1858-1916, along with examples of many earlier proof coins. Walter Breen studied Starr's collection, and it was a major inspiration for his Encyclopedia of United States and Colonial Proof Coins. Breen discretely referred to Starr's holdings as a "Philadelphia Estate" whenever he mentioned them in his text. The Stack's catalogers noted his collection of early proof sets was "perhaps the largest and most comprehensive ever to cross the auction block in modern memory." Of course, that distinction will now pass to the present collection. Much useful pedigree information was included in the catalog, but the coins were offered individually, and many sets were dispersed.

Other modern sales with significant proof coin offerings include Garrett, Eliasberg, Norweb, Pittman, and Hetrich. Garrett included a run of early proof sets offered as intact sets. The Eliasberg, Norweb, and Hetrich coins were offered individually, but probably came from original proof sets that were broken up for the sale. Pittman's sets were probably assembled from different sources, except for a few early complete sets.

The completeness of this collection, and the opportunity to purchase intact proof sets in single lots, makes the present offering an extraordinary opportunity, nearly unique in recent times. The last time a significant collection of early proof sets was cataloged to be sold as intact sets was 24 years ago, in the Zelson Collection. The last time a run of early proof sets was offered that approached the completeness of this collection was in 1992, in the Starr Collection. It is unlikely that a similar collection will surface in the foreseeable future. Please keep these considerations in mind as you peruse the catalog, and plan your purchases accordingly.

The Boca Collection Part I

Floor, Telephone, HERITAGE Live!™, Internet, Fax, and Mail Signature® Auction #1136
Thursday, January 7, 2010, 6:30 PM ET, Lots 2001 - 2071
Orlando, Florida

A 15% Buyer's Premium ($14 minimum) Will Be Added To All Lots

Visit HA.com to view full-color images and bid.

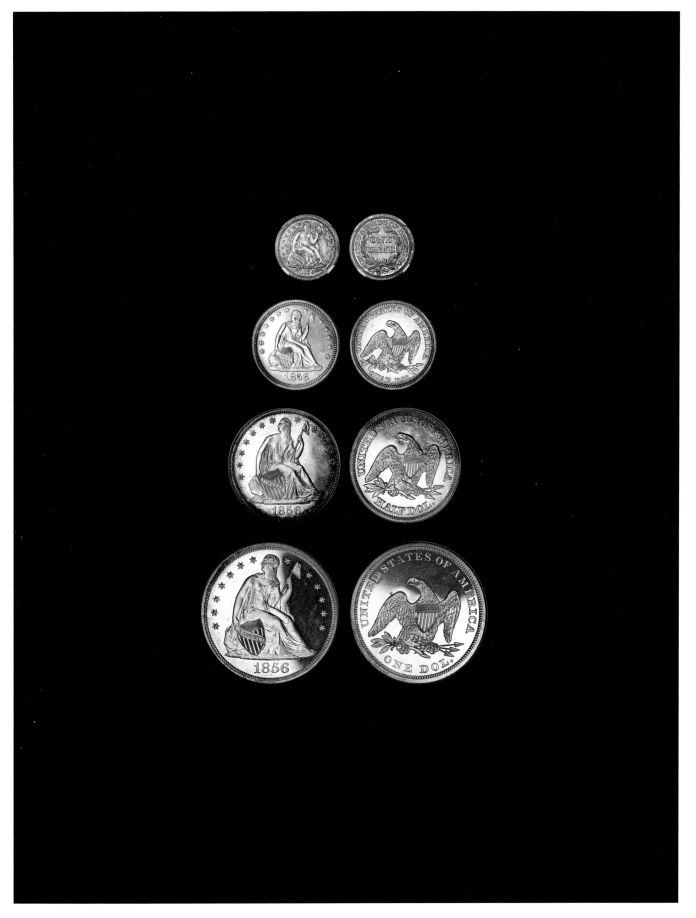

Important 1856 Proof Set with PR65 Flying Eagle Cent

2001   1856 Nine-Piece Proof Set NGC. The Flying Eagle small cent is perhaps the most notable of the 1856 silver-minor proof coins. It was produced as a pattern coin to help influence Congress to replace the large copper pieces with a small copper-nickel coin. Richard Snow (2009) estimates the 1856 proof small cent mintage to be at least 1,500 pieces, a very large quantity for the era.

With respect to 1856 silver three cent, half dime, and dime proofs, Breen suggests in his 1977 *Proof Encyclopedia* that extant examples for each are in the range of 30 to 40 pieces. He also indicates that fewer than 30 proof quarters survive, while Larry Briggs (1991) puts the figure at 25+. Randy Wiley and Bill Bugert, in their *Liberty Seated Half Dollar* reference estimate that fewer than 25 1856 half dollars are known. Breen estimates about 40 proof silver dollars are known. This estimate is consistent with the 58 pieces seen to date (10/09) by PCGS and NGC, after one discounts resubmissions and crossovers.

Breen writes that the originally-issued 1856 silver-minor proof sets, distributed in January and February, did not contain the Flying Eagle small cent, of which he says: "Really patterns, as the design and alloy were not officially adopted until the Act of Feb. 21, 1857 became law as of the following May."

Half Cent PR62 Red and Brown. Breen 3, R.4. This variety has a doubled T in CENT. This lovely specimen is just a hair from full Red. Both sides are awash with original copper-gold luster, with the obverse showing subtle whispers of lavender and the reverse displaying soft dapples of brownish-purple in its central area. A powerful strike leaves no hints of weakness whatsoever on the design features, and no significant marks or carbon flecks are discernible. A solitary bluish-purple toning spot resides near the rim between stars 4 and 5, and strong field-motif contrast is evident on the reverse at most angles of observation. A few faint hairlines in the obverse fields that only appear under a loupe are all that stand in the way of a higher numerical grade. NGC and PCGS have to date (10/09) certified slightly more than 50 1856 proof half cents in all three color designations, a mere three of which are graded full Red.

Large Cent PR63 Brown. N-5, low R.5. This proof-only issue displays die lines down to the left below the earlobe, a light die scratch on the cheek bone, and a minute die lump on the neck between the two lowest curls. On the reverse, the E on ONE has defects at its right top and under the serif of the crossbar. Attractive medium intensity reddish-purple toning with sky-blue accents adorns each side, diminishing a bit the surface reflectivity. Fully struck, and with a wire edge evident where not concealed by the holder. No contact marks or carbon spots are visible, though a couple of minute verdigris spots occur at OF and another near the reverse rim at 6:00. Fewer than 50 proof 1856 large cents have been graded by NGC and PCGS (10/09).

Flying Eagle Cent PR65. Snow 9. A die polish line extending from the top of the I in UNITED to the rim and a bold centering dot under the top left serif of the N in CENT attribute the Snow 9 variety. The present Gem stands well above surviving examples of this die pair, of which Richard Snow (2001) writes: "... the overall quality of these pieces are not anywhere near that of the regular proof issues of the period. These usually have dull or nonexistent mirrors. Many show striking defects such as lint strike throughs and planchet flaws."

The design motifs on the current offering are exceptionally well struck, and both sides are devoid of planchet flaws, lint marks, or other strike throughs. And while the fields are not deeply mirrored, they possess enough reflectivity to noticeably highlight the devices. A medley of soft copper-gold, crimson, mint-green, and sky-blue patination adorns each face, and the few grade-consistent marks and flecks do not detract from the coin's overall appeal. Census: 30 in 65, 3 finer (10/09).

Three Cent Silver PR64. Splashes of golden-tan and powder-blue are slightly deeper in hue on the reverse of this near-Gem, and the central devices display moderate frost and are exquisitely impressed. The A in STATES is a tad soft as are the stars on the lower reverse. Numerous die polish striations run horizontally in the obverse fields, but neither side reveals mentionable abrasions, spots, or planchet flaws. Census: 3 in 64, 2 finer (10/09).

Half Dime PR64. The date is slightly right of center, the shield point is entirely left of the 1, and the skirt pendant is over the right tip of the 5. That digit is upright and slightly weaker than the others, which is typical of these proofs. The sharply struck, moderately frosted design features yield modest variance with the mirrored fields, especially on the obverse. Peripheral gold-orange patina is slightly deeper on the obverse where it is joined by reddish-purple. Faint hairlines mingle with die polish lines in the fields. Census: 5 in 64, 10 finer (10/09).

Dime PR64. Breen 3295. Doubled die obverse, with the doubling plainest at the skirt. Another diagnostic is a line that joins the loop of the R in AMERICA to the border. Breen (1988) writes: "Apparently all 1856 proof dimes are from these dies." He also calls the issue "very rare." Incredible beautiful toning embraces both sides, with soft reddish-tan patina dominating the fields and devices and cobalt-blue accents in the fields and motif interstices. Fully struck design features heighten even more the coin's outstanding eye appeal. A horizontal hair-thin mark on Liberty's chest identifies the coin. Census: 10 in 64, 6 finer (10/09).

Quarter PR61. Proof quarters of 1856 are identified by a peculiar vertical bulge in the right reverse field from AM through the wing to the arrows (Walter Breen, 1988; and Larry Briggs, 1991). The skirt outline is slightly doubled at the bottom. A narrow band of electric-blue, yellow-gold, reddish-orange, and blue-gray clings to the margins leaving the central areas brilliant. Sharply struck except for softness in a couple of the star centers. Magnification reveals wispy field marks.

Half Dollar PR65. Reverse stripe three is not clearly joined to the base of the shield and some of the lines at the top of stripe one are missing, yielding a "hollow" appearance, as described by Walter Breen (1977). Exquisite design detail endows this majestic Gem, as do splashes of golden-brown, lavender, gunmetal-blue, and violet patination concentrated at the margins, accentuating the sharp square edges and pronounced dentilation. Close inspection reveals just a few inconsequential marks that appear to barely preclude Premium Gem classification. Extremely elusive in Gem and finer. Census: 4 in 65 2 finer (10/09).

Seated Dollar PR64 ★ Cameo. NGC and PCGS have seen a mere five Cameo proof silver dollars of 1856, none of which are classified Ultra/Deep Cameos. NGC has seen fit to designate a solitary '56 proof dollar with its coveted Star--the present near-Gem in this set (10/09). The date has large numerals with a slanting or italic 5, as on business strikes. Proofs display die lines in the field above ITE of UNITED and between E and S of STATES.

Deeply mirrored fields highlight the satiny devices, confirming the Cameo contrast. A decisive strike results in completeness on the design elements, including squared-off rims and crisp dentils. Whispers of soft golden-brown and purple in the rim areas are slightly more noticeable on the obverse. Occasional, barely discernible freckles of golden-brown visit the centers, somewhat more so on the obverse. Trivial handling marks preclude Gem classification. A hair-thin mark of unknown origin is visible above Liberty's right (facing) breast.

David Bowers (1993) writes of the 1856 proof silver dollar: "I believe that most ... were issued as part of silver Proof sets, which in 1856 were just starting to have a wide following among numismatists. Some may have sold separately as well."
From The Boca Collection, Part I.

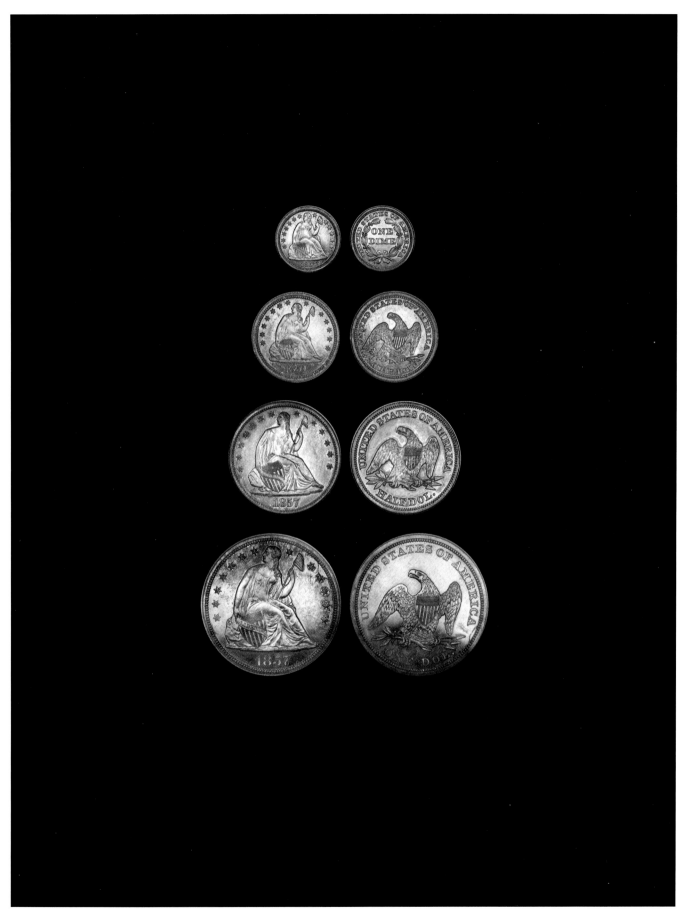

Memorable 1857 Silver-Minor Proof Set

2002   1857 Nine-Piece Proof Set NGC. Mintage figures for 1857 proof coinage, as with all proofs made prior to 1858, are unknown but certainly small for most denominations. The Flying Eagle cent is the only 1857 proof that the *Guide Book* gives a mintage for: 485 pieces. Even this estimate must be considered highly suspect, as Richard Snow (2006) indicates: "Perhaps no more than 50 were struck." NGC/PCGS population data are probably more reliable than mintage estimates. The two services have to date (11/09) certified a little more than 90 1857 proof small cents, some of which are undoubtedly resubmitted or crossed-over coins.

We can provide more definitive information on the rarity of some of the silver proof issues on which we have conducted research. For example, while Al Blythe (1992) estimates 16 to 20 1857 proof half dimes are known, we would put an estimate of perhaps 30 to 40 pieces. For the 1857 proof dime, we suggest that about 20 to 25 pieces are extant; for the proof quarter between 15 and 50 specimens; and 25 to 40 or possibly as many 45 examples of the half dollar. David Bowers' (2006) estimate of 30 to 50 extant 1857 proof dollars is probably on target.

Walter Breen (1977) writes that early silver-minor proof sets of 1857 contained the half cent and large copper cent. He says that they must have been made up in January, as that is when the copper coins were manufactured. These early sets would not have included the 1857 proof small cent.

David Bowers, in his *Flying Eagle and Indian Cents Buyer's Guide,* writes of the 1857 proof small cent that: "The known proofs of 1857 are with the (new) Style of 1857 letters." This new letter-style was initiated in a May 27, 1857 letter from contractor Anthony Paquet (appointed assistant engraver in October of that year) to Mint Director Snowden asking for approval of the new punches. It may be deduced from this that any silver-minor proof sets containing the 1857 small cent must have been minted after this date. Moreover, as Bowers, Breen, and Snow all estimate the mintage of 1857 Flying Eagle proof cent to be around 50 pieces, the number of proof sets made after May was probably around the same number.

Half Cent PR64 Brown. Cohen-1, Breen-2. Breen writes in his half cent *Encyclopedia*: "Reverse B (First Restrikes) is the die found on most proof half cents dated 1856 and 1857." It is identified by double impressions on the right side of CENT and the ribbon. The outline of T in CENT is distorted, its upright sloping down to the right, its right foot elongated. Spurs are also visible within the M and R of AMERICA, and the top of the crossbar in E is doubled. Breen assigns this proof a Rarity 4.

Bluish-purple patination covers most of Liberty's portrait ceding to yellowish-green in the fields. Sky-blue, purple, and yellow-green colors run over the reverse. The design elements are exquisitely defined, and close inspection reveals no mentionable contact marks or flecks. Census: 12 in 64 Brown for the issue, 6 finer (11/09).

Large Cent PR65 Brown. N-3. The strong, slightly curved line up to the right on the bust with a weaker vertical line down from its right end, and defects at the right top of the E in ONE and under the serif of its crossbar confirm the N-3 variety. John Grellman in his *The Die Varieties of United States Large Cents* gives this proof-only variety a low R.5 rarity rating.

Breathtaking patination consists of a melange of yellow-green, orange, aqua-green, faded red, lavender, and reddish-orange, joined by a splash of light blue on the central obverse. Reflective fields highlight the crisply defined motifs when the coin is tilted slightly under a light source. No blemishes are evident, though a moderate-size spot is visible beneath Liberty's ear. Census: 5 in 65 Brown for the issue, 6 finer (11/09).

Flying Eagle Cent PR62 Cameo. As mentioned by Bowers in the introduction above, all known 1857 small cent proofs are with the "new" Style of 1857 letters. This style differs from that of 1856 in the following ways: the bases of A and M in AMERICA are solidly connected, the center serif of E is not connected to the upper arm of that letter, and the outer edge of the diagonal in N of UNITED is perfect instead of being notched toward the bottom as in the Style of 1856.

Both sides of this PR62 Cameo specimen yield soft bluish-gold in the fields accented with slightly deeper golden-tan, which is also the color of the motifs. This subtle variance in color palette serves to further enhance the contrast between the mirrored fields and the mildly frosted, boldly impressed devices. Faint hairlines in the fields are all that stand in the way of a higher numerical grade. One of only five proofs certified as Cameo by NGC (11/09).

Three Cent Silver PR65. A medley of medium intensity bluish-purple, gold, sky-blue, and apple-green bathes the luminous surfaces of this Gem, and a powerful strike delivers crisp definition to the design elements. The shield, leaf ribbing, and arrow feathers are fully delineated. Only a couple of radial lines on, and outlines to, the prominent star are slightly less than complete. Both sides are impeccably preserved. Census: 13 in 65, 8 finer (11/09).

Half Dime PR64. Breen (1977) indicates that the only Valentine variety "ordinarily encountered" in proof is V-3, which shows the shield point over the left upright of 1 in the date, the skirt pendant over the right tip of 5, and a dent on the inner point of star 3.

Splashes of cobalt-blue, lime-green, violet, bluish-purple, and orange toning adorn each side of this gorgeous near-Gem. The design elements are exceeding well brought up, including the foot-sandal separation and the reverse leaf ribbing. Both faces have been well cared for. A light U-shaped lint mark connects the inner points of stars 2 and 4. Census: 8 in 64, 13 finer (11/09).

Dime PR64. Soft golden-orange and champagne patina dominates each side of this lovely near-Gem, displaying lavender and electric-blue accents around the obverse margin. A sharp strike characterizes the design features, and close inspection reveals just a few trivial handling marks that barely preclude Gem classification. Census: 11 in 64, 15 finer (11/09).

Quarter PR65. Splashes of cobalt-blue, lavender, and gold-orange toning occupy the lower and left obverse fields, ceding to light champagne-gold over the remaining obverse and on the reverse, which is accented with occasional dapples of reddish-gold and bluish-purple at the margins. The design elements are exquisitely defined and stand out against the reflective fields at various angles. A handful of grade-consistent reverse marks is undisturbing. Census: 5 in 65, 3 finer (11/09).

Half Dollar PR62. Golden-tan patina resides in the obverse fields flanked by deeper violet, purple, and gold-brown at the peripheries. Liberty's portrait displays a brighter silver-violet appearance. Aqua-green, sky-blue, orange-tan, and lime-green run over the reverse. A solid strike brings out sharp definition on the design elements, including Liberty's hair and foot-sandal delineation. Only the left (facing) eagle's leg and claw reveal minor softness. Faint wispy handling marks limit the numerical grade.

Seated Dollar PR63. David Bowers, in *Silver Dollars and Trade Dollars of the United States*, writes that at least two pairs of dies were used to strike proof dollars in 1857. The current offering displays a "beard" below Liberty's chin, and the shield point right of the left upright of the 1 in the date. The reverse, according to Bowers, is from the die used in 1854 and 1856 and shows die rust on the L in DOL.

Champagne patina dominates both sides of this Select specimen, accented with whispers of soft sky-blue and tan-purple. A well executed strike emboldens the design features that exhibit a degree of contrast with the mirrored fields, especially on the reverse. Close inspection reveals no mentionable abrasions, just a few inoffensive hairlines that mingle with die polish lines in the fields.
From The Boca Collection, Part I. (Total: 9 coins)

Seven-Piece 1858 Proof Set
All Coins Select or Better

2003   Seven-Piece 1858 Proof Set. Mint director J.R. Snowden began the wholesale advertising of proof sets of the current year's coinage for sale to the general public in 1858. Prior to this time, the Mint had for many years struck proof (or "specimen") coins for special occasions, foreign dignitaries, or various collectors having close connections with some Mint personnel.

The striking of proof sets for public sale in 1858 corresponds with the first major boom in coin collecting in America. Collectors from all walks of life began seeking regular-issue U.S. coinage, and the nation saw the incipient development of professional numismatic societies. The Philadelphia Numismatic and Antiquarian Society was established in January 1858, for example, followed a couple of months later by the founding of the American Numismatic Society. And 1858 was the year that Edward Cogan established the first professional coin dealership in America.

While there are some indications that proof coins in earlier years were sold for face value, Mint officials eventually began selling the specially prepared proofs at a premium. In their *Proof Sets and Mint Sets* treatise, Ron Guth and Bill Gale write:

"... for a small premium, collectors could purchase regular Proof Sets (one example of each of the base metal and Silver coins), Gold Proof Sets (one example each of the Gold coins), or complete Proof Sets (a combination of the Regular and Gold Proof Sets)."

Mintage records for 1858 proof coinage were apparently not kept or have been lost or destroyed. This has led to a debate as to how many proof coins were in fact made. With respect to silver dollars, Walter Breen, in his *Proof Encyclopedia*, says: "Long estimated to have been about 80 struck, this estimate originating apparently with the Chapman brothers of Philadelphia, who had it *supposedly* from mint sources (Patterson, DuBois?)."

Weimar White's research on the mintages for the proof half dimes, dimes, quarters, half dollars, and silver dollars of 1858 published in Issue #50 of the March 1991 *Gobrecht Journal*, however, provides evidence to the contrary that only 80 specimens were struck. He demonstrates that between 282 and 382 proof 1858 pieces were probably coined for these denominations.

Cent (Large Letters) PR65 PCGS. Rich orange color overall with glimpses of green and gold. A strongly detailed specimen of the Large Letters type, projected by Snow to be twice as rare in proof as the Small Letters variety.

Three Cent Silver PR64 NGC. Rich golden-tan color embraces much of each side. The obverse has peripheral cerulean shadings, while the reverse toning is more even.

Half Dime PR64 NGC. Liquid gold and rose-violet shadings enrich the shining surfaces, with the latter hue most prominent at the left obverse and the former color dominant elsewhere. A near-Gem proof with excellent eye appeal.

Dime PR65 NGC. Bold gold-orange luster forms a seeming undercoat on the obverse, with numerous dots of blue and violet patina around the rims and coalescing in patches at the right. On the reverse, the gold-orange toning stands on its own, lending that side understated but elegant eye appeal. A charming Gem.

Quarter PR64 PCGS. A richly toned and rewarding near-Gem specimen. Both sides display varying levels of blue-violet and golden toning, with the former color dominant on the obverse and the latter prevailing on the reverse. The fields around the eagle offer particularly strong mirrors through the patina.

Half Dollar PR64 NGC. Colorful patina offers immense beauty on this exquisite near-Gem. It is considerably contrasted for a non-Cameo piece, though this has more to do with the sense of ivory frost on the devices than the mirrors. Still, the coin's inherent reflectivity brings both the central golden toning and the cobalt-blue peripheral tints to life.

Seated Dollar PR63 NGC. A charming Select proof, richly toned yet charmingly reflective. Deep blue-green and antique-gold shadings drape each side, and the crisply detailed devices echo past frostiness. Small, scattered hairlines and a few contact marks in the reverse fields account for the grade. Census: 18 in 63, 21 finer (11/09).
From The Boca Collection, Part I. (Total: 7 coins)

Seven-Piece 1859 Silver-Minor Proof Set

2004   1859 Seven-Piece Proof Set NGC. Mint Director Snowden assumed that the plethora of new collectors in America would result in a ready market for proof sets. Thus 1859 was the first year of serious proof coinage, which showed significant increases over previous years. The 2010 *Guide Book* lists a proof mintage of 800 pieces each for the 1859 cent through silver dollar denominations. This compares with 300 coins each for the 1858 cent, half dime, quarter, and silver dollar, and 300+ pieces each for the 1858 dime and half dollar. The *Guide Book* gives a mintage of 80 coins for each of the six 1859 proof gold denominations. The mintage of proof gold prior to 1859 is unknown.

The demand for proof coins in 1859 did not match the relatively large mintages. A recent article posted on the Web by *American Gold Exchange* says of the proof gold coins: "Most of the 80 proof sets were melted, as only a dozen or so actually sold." As might be expected from these figures, 1859 proof gold coins are rare. Silver-minor proof coinages, despite the relatively high mintages, apparently fared little better and are quite scarce in their own right.

Cent PR64. The 1859 copper-nickel Indian Head cent with a laurel wreath reverse is a one-year type. Proof examples especially are under high demand by type collectors. Highly attractive golden-tan coloration adorns this near-Gem specimen, and a well executed strike delivers virtually complete detail to the design elements. Rotating the coin ever so slightly beneath a light source results in stunning contrast between the fields and devices. Scattered reverse flecks preclude Gem designation. Census: 78 in 64, 53 finer (10/09).

Three Cent Silver PR65. This was the first year of the Type Three three cent silver design type (1859-1873). It features two outlines on the obverse star instead of the three of the previous design type. A medley of electric-blue, lavender, and orange-gold toning bathes the obverse of this exquisitely struck Gem, while yellow-gold patination dominates the reverse. Luminous surfaces are flawless and loaded with charming eye appeal. Census: 21 in 65, 11 finer (10/09).

Half Dime PR63. The 1 and 9 of this Select specimen show strong repunching at their bases, the 8 and 5 only slight repunching at bases. Also, the pendant is centered between the 5 and 9, and the shield points to the flag of the 5. This variety is likely V-3 as described by Al Blythe in *The Complete Guide to Liberty Seated Half Dimes*. Blythe writes of the V-3: "Repolishing of the die caused only the 1 and 9's bases to show, with even these eventually disappearing."

Delicate apple-green and violet patina covers both obverse and reverse, and is slightly deeper on the former. The design elements exhibit crisp definition, including Liberty's head and foot, the shield and stars, and the leaf ribbing. The surface reflectivity is somewhat subdued on both sides.

Dime PR67 ★ Cameo. NGC has assigned the Star designation to only four 1859 Cameo proof dimes—two Superb Gems, including the one in this set—and two Premium Gems. Exceptionally mirrored fields highlight the frosty devices, and gorgeous cobalt-blue, lavender, and orange-tan patination in the fields further accentuate the silver-white central motif on the obverse, while dappled violet and sky-blue colors run over the reverse. Immaculately preserved surfaces reveal some small die-polish areas on the left (facing) arm. This coin has phenomenal overall eye appeal.

Quarter PR64. Breen-4018. Type One obverse and reverse, which Walter Breen in his *Complete Encyclopedia* describes as very rare. The variety is attributed by a single hair ribbon, nearly straight fingers on pole, no vertical shield lines above the E in LIBERTY, a hollow or concave eagle's eye, and closed claws.

Warm aqua-green and bluish-purple toning decorates the obverse while soft cobalt-blue and beige visit the reverse. The rims are squared-off and feature bold dentilation; likewise, the remaining design motifs are fully delineated. Impeccably preserved surfaces reveal a faint unobtrusive linear field mark above the left (facing) wing.

Half Dollar PR63 Cameo. Breen-4888. Type One Reverse. The tops of LF in HALF are close and the arrowheads are large. Breen contends many proofs were melted as unsold.

Cameo contrast is evident at all angles of observation and a powerful strike imparts razor-sharp definition to all of the design elements. Soft violet patina and reddish-brown freckles concentrate in the right obverse field while deeper violet occurs around the lower and right reverse margin. Wispy handling marks in the obverse fields limit the grade. Census: 3 in 64 Cameo, 12 finer (10/09).

Seated Dollar PR64. Discussing the 800-piece 1859 proof silver dollar in his *Silver Dollars and Trade Dollars of the United States*, David Bowers writes:

"... today the issue is quite rare, and it is likely that 450 or fewer were actually distributed. Even that figure might be on the high side. There were hardly 450 numismatists in 1859 interested in buying Proof dollars from the Mint. However, enough survive today to indicate that 450 is a reasonable estimate of distribution. "

Along a similar vein, Breen, in his *Complete Encyclopedia*, opines that many 1859 silver dollars were melted as unsold.

The broad rims and sharp dentils on this near-Gem complement the exquisitely struck design features, and reddish-gold and sky-blue peripheral toning is more extensive and displays deeper hues on the obverse. Fine hairlines in the obverse fields barely deny the attainment of Gem classification. The base of the 1 in the date is repunched. Census: 41 in 64, 37 finer (10/09).

From The Boca Collection, Part I. (Total: 7 coins)

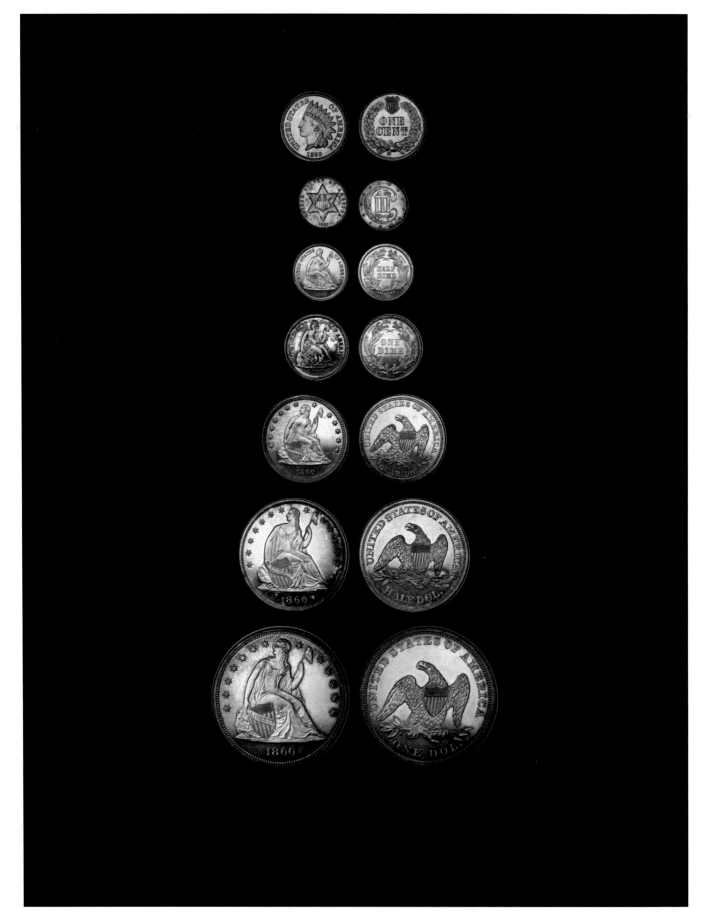

Seven-Piece 1860 Proof Set
Showcasing Stunning PR68 Cameo Dime

2005   Seven-Piece 1860 Proof Set NGC. The Mint increased the production of proof coinage in 1860 over the previous year, at least for the most part. The mintage of cents through half dollars rose from 800 pieces in 1859 to 1,000 coins in 1860. Silver dollar production in 1860, however, was bumped to 1,330 pieces from the previous year's figure of 800 coins. Mintages of gold dollars, quarter eagles, and three dollar pieces increased slightly from 1859, while those of half eagles, eagles, and double eagles declined. Sales of proof coins were apparently lackluster in 1860, and roughly half of the silver-minor coins were melted as unsold.

In the silver-minor proof coinage, several notable design changes took place between 1859 and 1860. The copper-nickel Indian cent was changed from a laurel wreath reverse to an oak wreath with shield reverse. The obverse of both the half dime and dime changed from peripheral stars to the legend UNITED STATES OF AMERICA.

Cent PR65. This Gem boasts copper-gold fire with duskier peach-orange shadings at parts of the margins. Boldly impressed for the copper-nickel design type and an attractive specimen of this initial Oak Wreath Reverse proof issue. Census: 15 in 65, 13 finer (11/09).

Three Cent Silver PR63. A luminous Select proof with toning that ranges from gray-gold to blue-green, with the former color at generally light centers that deepen to the latter shade close to the rims. Modestly hairlined beneath the extensive patina.

Half Dime—Reverse Rim Damage—Proof. Looking only at the fields and devices, this is a pleasing specimen with a subtle wash of golden toning over otherwise bright silver-white surfaces. Mildly frosted devices supply a degree of contrast. The upper-right reverse rim, however, shows several cuts which preclude an actual numeric grade.

Dime PR68 Cameo. As one of five PR68 Cameo coins graded by NGC with none finer (11/09), this dime is the crown jewel of the set. Sea-green, blue, and gold patina drapes most of the obverse and the outer reverse, but the specimen's inherent contrast shines through. Both sides are essentially free of hairlines or contact, though the toning at the upper obverse suggests a fingerprint pattern. Regardless, this is a piece of unquestionable importance.

Quarter PR65 Cameo. Though not at the same technical level as the dime, this quarter has plenty of eye appeal to call its own. Light pink-gold color of varying opacity visits parts of the margins on each side, but the mirrors remain strong and offer considerable contrast with the frost over Liberty and the eagle. A few small flaws near the softly struck right obverse stars are of little significance.

Half Dollar PR65 Cameo. Outstanding contrast and distinctive patina grant this Gem Cameo specimen winning eye appeal. The left obverse and upper reverse are pale silver-white, but the color quickly shifts to champagne and orange with ruby and sapphire elements at the distant rims. The obverse also displays a few spots of milky toning.

Seated Dollar PR62. Finishing the set is this Seated dollar, lightly hairlined throughout the fields but more attractive than the grade might suggest, thanks to modest but decidedly appealing patina. Light silver-gray centers give way to subtle blue-green and tan peripheral tints. *From The Boca Collection, Part I.* (Total: 7 coins)

A 15% BUYER'S PREMIUM ($14 MIN.) APPLIES TO ALL LOTS.

Magnificent 1861 Seven-Piece Proof Set

2006   1861 Seven-Piece Proof Set NGC. In 1861, President Lincoln appointed James Pollock director of the United States Mint in Philadelphia. Prior to this appointment, Pollock was chairman of the Pennsylvania delegation to the Washington Peace Convention, which unfortunately failed to prevent the Civil War. He served as mint director from 1861 to 1866 and then was reappointed by President Grant in 1869. From 1873 to 1879, he served as superintendent of the Mint when that agency became part of the U.S. Department of the Treasury.

Pollock's leadership at the Mint led to the adoption of the motto IN GOD WE TRUST on U. S. coins, which coincided with increased religious sentiment during the Civil War. The initial impetus for the motto apparently emanates from a November 1861 letter from Reverend M.R. Watkinson, Minister of the gospel from Ridleyville, Pennsylvania to Secretary of the Treasury Salmon P. Chase urging the recognition of the Deity on United States coins. Regardless of who should receive credit for the inscription of the motto, we know that it first appeared on the two cent piece in 1864.

All 1861 silver-minor proof coins from cents to half dollars saw the same 1,000-piece mintage as in 1860. Silver dollar proof production declined from 1,330 pieces in 1860 to 1,000 coins in 1861.

Walter Breen writes in his 1977 proof *Encyclopedia* that all 1,000 silver-minor proof sets were struck April 15. He also contends that: "Probably only three to four hundred in all sold as sets, others as individual coins, the remainder (at least 600 sets, per R.W. Julian) melted in 1862."

Cent PR65. Most of the original 1,000-piece 1861 proof cent mintage was apparently unsold and may have been melted or simply released into circulation. Indeed, Richard Snow, in his 2009 *Guide Book of Flying Eagle and Indian Head Cents*, says: "This is the key date in the Proof series, partly due to low mintage, but also because of poor quality of the dies and poor striking quality." Moreover, it is in high demand because of the relatively low business strike mintage (10.1 million, the lowest of the Type Two Indian Head series).

This Gem specimen reveals no visible planchet flaws or issues resulting from worn dies. The design elements exhibit a sharp strike, including crispness on all four diamonds and most of the reverse wreath. The feather tips, however, are just a tad soft. Golden-tan surfaces are devoid of marks or flecks, and what appears to be a small strikethrough is noted at 7:00 on the obverse rim. Census: 19 in 65, 6 finer (11/09).

Three Cent Silver PR66. Breen (1977) writing of the 1861 proof trime says that: "... survivors are only a minority of the original mintage (1,000 pieces). Fewer known than of 1862 and later years despite the mintage."

This Premium Gem is exquisitely impressed, including fullness on the radials and outlines of the prominent star. Blushes of gunmetal-blue, lavender, yellow-gold, and powder-blue cover the obverse, while the same color palette gravitates to the reverse border, leaving the center color free. Impeccably preserved and revealing great eye appeal. Census: 8 in 66, 4 finer (11/09).

Half Dime PR64. Variegated blue, gold, orange, and bluish-gray take on slightly deeper hues on the reverse of this near-Gem. A well directed strike leaves strong definition on the devices that are accentuated on the obverse by the semireflective fields. Reverse reflectivity is subdued by the depth of the toning. There are no contact marks worthy of note.

Dime PR64. Breen (1977) implies two varieties of 1861 proof dimes. The example in this set lacks a rust pit on the I of UNITED but displays this feature on the right upright of the M in DIME.

Soft cobalt-blue and lavender patination covers the obverse of this near-Gem, while the same colors are joined by purple and deep bluish-purple on the reverse center. The design elements show excellent detail, save for softness in the upper left wreath. The obverse displays more field-motif contrast. Light obverse marks deny Gem status.

Quarter PR65. Larry Briggs opines in his *Encyclopedia of Liberty Seated Quarters* that 600 or more of the proof quarters struck in 1861 were melted.

Russet, lilac, and golden-tan freckles cascade over the delicately colored cobalt-blue obverse while deeper sky-blue and orange-gold reside on the reverse of this attractive Gem. Sharply struck design motifs and well cared for surfaces round out the coin's pleasing eye appeal. A solitary small mark on Liberty's left (facing) arm is mentioned solely for identifying the coin. Census: 13 in 65, 10 finer (11/09).

Half Dollar PR64. Bright aqua-blue clings to the margins of both sides and outlines Liberty's portrait and the stars. Champagne-silver dominates the central areas on both obverse and reverse along with lavender accents, and an exacting strike imparts strong definition to the design elements. Wispy handling marks preclude the attainment of Gem designation.

Seated Dollar PR65. David Bowers, in his 1993 *Silver Dollars* treatise, says of the 1,000 proof dollars minted in 1861: "... it is believed that only about 350 were ever sold." He goes on to write: "Today, 1861 Proof dollars are very elusive. Not only was the distribution low ... but those sold seem to have had an unusually high attrition rate."

Delicate sky-blue, golden-brown, lavender, and grayish-tan visit the obverse of this gorgeous Gem, while soft silver-gray dominates the reverse. A sharp strike uniformly graces the design elements, and impeccable preservation characterizes both sides. These attributes combine to generate magnificent eye appeal.
From The Boca Collection, Part I. (Total: 7 coins)

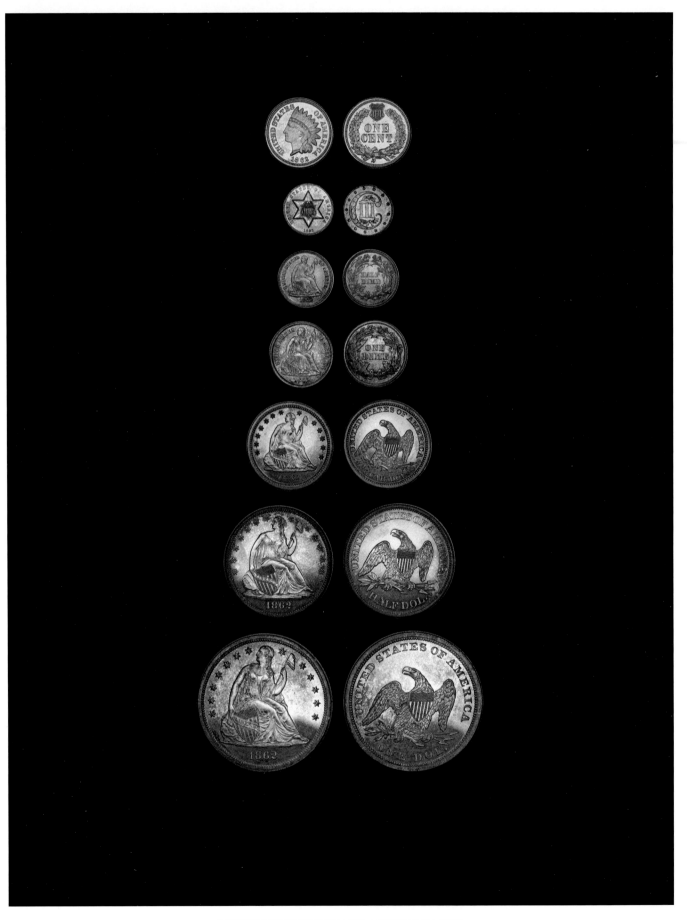

A 15% BUYER'S PREMIUM ($14 MIN.) APPLIES TO ALL LOTS.

Charming 1862 Silver-Minor Proof Set

2007   **1862 Seven-Piece Proof Set NGC.** After somewhat lackluster performance in sales for the past four years, Mint officials decided to scale back the annual output of proof coinage. The silver-minor coins were reduced from 1,000 to 550 pieces. Proof gold mintage dropped to 35 coins for all denominations in 1862, a number more commensurate with demand than with speculation. Mintages for most silver-minor pieces continued to hover in the 400 to 600 range until 1870 when they sharply increased. Proof gold mintage remained in the area of 20 to 50 pieces for the next twenty years when they again jumped from increased demand.

The year 1862 resulted in changes other than reduced proof-coin mintage. In a December 3, 2008 *Numismatic News* article, Robert Julian writes:

"At the beginning of 1862, Mint Director James Pollock changed the rules by requiring that full sets of coins be purchased; those specializing in proof quarter eagles, for example, now had to purchase the full gold proof set. Cent pieces could not be obtained separately, being included in the 'silver' proof set."

The lower mintages of proof coins in 1862 were apparently much more in line with demand than in the previous four years. According to Walter Breen writing in his *Proof Encyclopedia*, 430 of the 550 silver-minor proof sets were sold, with the rest melted. He also says: "Other individual coins may have been sold. Most of the sets now extant were assembled in recent decades. This could be done very cheaply during the 1940s and early 1950s."

One Cent PR65. The 1862 is perhaps the most common date in the Indian Head copper-nickel proof series. Richard Snow (2009) suggests that unsold examples were saved by the mint and resold to collectors at some later date, possibly after the Civil War. Certified population figures show that most survivors are around the near-Gem level of preservation.

Copper-gold surfaces on the current Gem are imbued with occasional whispers of light tan and a decisive strike leaves crisp definition on the design elements, including the feather tips, the four diamonds, and the leaf ribbing. Close examination reveals no noteworthy blemishes. Census: 28 in 65, 6 finer (11/09).

Three Cent Silver PR64. Beautiful toning jumps out at the observer of this near-Gem. The obverse reveals variegated low to medium intensity cobalt blue, lavender, gold-orange, and bluish-purple coloration, while the reverse displays soft hues of yellow-green, violet, lime-green, gold-orange, and sky-blue. An exacting strike further enhances the coin's eye appeal, particularly on the obverse star and its outlines, arrow feathers, and leaf sprigs. Only the round elements in the upper left of the reverse C are weak. A few trivial reverse handling marks may help to preclude Gem designation.

Half Dime PR63. Breen (1977) writes of the 1862 proof half dime "... at least four die varieties." The coin in the present set appears to be V-3, the diagnostics of which are: the shield point well to the left of the 1 in the date, the skirt pendant minutely right of center above 6, upper part of second S in STATES slightly filled in, and the right end of the ribbon clear of the wreath.

A melange of aqua-green, gold-orange, sky-blue, light green, and lavender drapes both sides of this Select example, each of which exhibits sharply struck design elements. A few minuscule marks limit the grade.

Dime PR64. Breen (1977) implies there are two varieties of 1862 proof dimes, a "light" date and a "heavy" date. He gives few diagnostics except to say for the heavy date: "Shield point far to left of 1, pendant over inner left curve of 6." The current dime appears to match the latter variety.

Orange, yellow-gold, violet, and lime-green patination visits the obverse surfaces of this near-Gem, ceding to bluish-green at the reverse margin and orange-gold in the center. Sharply struck and devoid of mentionable marks. Census: 42 in 65, 16 finer (11/09).

Quarter PR64 Cameo. Peripheral gunmetal-blue and lavender frame the champagne centers of this near-Gem, joined by golden-orange on the reverse border. Mirrored fields highlight the mildly frosted design elements which have benefited from a solid strike. A few wispy field marks preclude Gem status. Census: 38 in 65, 20 finer (11/09).

Half Dollar PR65 Cameo. Breen (1977) lists two 1862 proof half dollar varieties, per Beistle. The specimen in this set shows a spine from the upper left serif of F, classifying it as Beistle 1-A. Breen considers this to be the rarer variety.

Electric-blue, purple, and golden-orange gravitate to the margins of this Gem, framing soft champagne-gold and silver in the centers. Exquisitely struck design motifs stand amidst the mirrored fields. Well preserved throughout. Census: 24 in 65, 10 finer (11/09).

Seated Dollar PR64. David Bowers writes in his 1993 *Silver Dollars* reference: "Proof dollars of 1862 are especially desired today due to the enticingly low business strike mintage of just 11,540 coins."

Splashes of cobalt-blue and lavender grace the margins of this near-Gem, transitioning to dapples of golden-brown residing in the centers. The design elements exhibit superb detail. Faint hairlines that only appear under high magnification prevent the attainment of full Gem classification.

From The Boca Collection, Part I. (Total: 7 coins)

Captivating 1863 Silver-Minor Proof Set

2008   1863 Seven-Piece Proof Set NGC. Mintages for most U.S. proof coins continued to drop in 1863, a not unexpected occurrence for these Civil War-era issues. The production for each silver-minor proof denomination (cent, three cent silver, half dime, dime, quarter, half dollar, and dollar) declined from 550 pieces in 1862 to 460 coins in 1863. With the exception of slight increases in one and three dollar proof gold coinage, each of the remaining proof gold denominations (quarter eagle, half eagle, eagle, and double eagle) declined from 35 specimens in 1862 to 30 pieces in 1863.

Mint records indicate that 1863 silver-minor proof sets were delivered on the following dates: 100 sets on March 5, 160 on March 8, and 200 on May 26. Walter Breen, in his 1977 *Proof Encyclopedia*, opines that most surviving sets appear to have been assembled.

David Bowers, in his *Silver Dollars & Trade Dollars of the United States*, points out the implications to coin collectors in 1863 of the depreciation of legal tender "greenback" paper notes:

"During this time the United States government would not accept its own paper money for the purchase of Proof coins and sets, and collectors were forced to pay in coin."

Cent PR64. Breen (1977) suggests that the 1863 proof cent is somewhat more plentiful than the 1862. David Bowers' 1996 *Guide to Flying Eagle and Indian Cents*, on the other hand, considers the 1863 is "to be *much rarer* than 1862 and to be a sleeper," a feeling shared by Richard Snow in his 2009 *A Guide Book of Flying Eagle and Indian Cents*.

Luminous copper-gold surfaces of this near-Gem exhibit sharp definition on the design elements, including the feather tips, diamonds, shield lines, and leaf ribbing. A few minute flecks are scattered about, especially on the obverse, but these present little distraction.

Three Cent Silver PR67. Deep mirrored fields highlight the frosty obverse design features, yielding stunning Cameo contrast; field-motif variance on the reverse is less strong, precluding an overall Cameo designation. Despite this, dazzling eye appeal is apparent throughout this Superb Gem. Impeccably preserved surfaces exhibit razor-sharp detail and present peripheral electric-blue, lavender, and gold-orange patination on the obverse and a mixture of soft sky-blue and beige-gold coloration on the reverse. Census: 6 in 67, 1 finer (10/09).

Half Dime PR65. Both business strikes and proofs come only with repunched 18 of the date. Al Blythe, in his *The Complete Guide to Liberty Seated Half Dimes*, says: "There is no repunching on the restrike which was made about 1870."

Vivid gunmetal-blue, purple, and golden-orange patination concentrates around the borders of this highly attractive Gem, and is slightly more extensive on the obverse. Sharply impressed design elements complement the wonderful toning and establish a good degree of contrast with the reflective fields. Close inspection with a loupe reveals the surfaces to be well cared for. Census: 20 in 65, 17 finer (10/09).

Dime PR65 Cameo. Dimes of this year have the lowest proof mintage of all With Legend dimes and are under date pressure owing to the small mintage of circulation strikes (14,000 pieces).

Splashes of electric-blue, lavender, and golden-tan around the borders are more widespread on the reverse. A powerful strike leaves strong definition on the design features save for minor softness on the upper left reverse wreath. Strongly cameoed, virtually flawless surfaces greet the observer of this delightful Gem. Census: 10 in 65, 7 finer (10/09).

Quarter PR66 ★ Cameo. Proof quarters of 1863 come in three minor varieties. This variety shows the date high and slanting up, the shield point right of the right upright of the 1 in the date, and two reverse arrows joined.

Peripheral electric-blue, lavender, and gold-orange patina takes on a more unbroken pattern on the left obverse margin. The Liberty motif is stone-white while the eagle is more grayish-white with whispers of gold-orange. The design features are crisply struck and appear to be suspended above the deep mirrored fields. Both sides are beautifully preserved. This specimen is the *only* 1863 proof quarter designated with NGC's coveted Star!

Half Dollar PR62. Luminous surfaces are enveloped in gorgeous toning consisting of medium intensity bluish-green and sky-blue around the borders that blend into subtle lavender and yellow-gold. The central motifs yield a silvery appearance splashed with whispers of lavender and orange-gold on Liberty and soft yellow-gold on the eagle. An exacting strike emboldens the design elements, including fullness on the rims and dentilation. Some unobtrusive hairlines in the fields prevent a higher grade. Nevertheless, both sides exhibit captivating eye appeal for the numerical designation.

Seated Dollar PR64. Breen-5469. The date is slightly low and a bit right of center. The shield point is left of the tip of the 1 in the date, the left base of 1 is over a space between border denticles, and an unpolished area joins the upper and center leaves.

Relatively deep bluish-purple toning bathes both sides of this near-Gem, each of which displays gold-beige accents. Excellent definition is noted on the design features, including Liberty's hair and gown lines, star centers, eagle's plumage, and dentilation. The fields still exhibit a degree of reflectivity despite the depth of the toning and yield modest contrast with the devices when the coin is tilted under a light source. Census: 40 in 64, 24 finer (10/09).
From The Boca Collection, Part I. (Total: 7 coins)

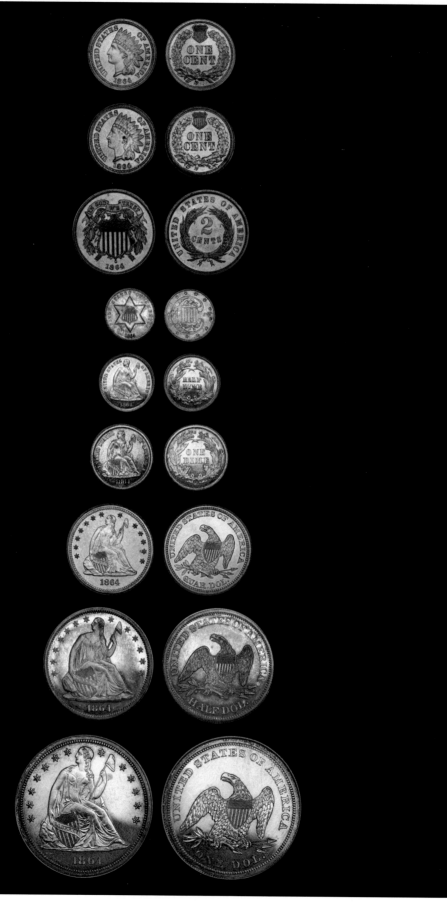

A 15% BUYER'S PREMIUM ($14 MIN.) APPLIES TO ALL LOTS.

Nine-Piece 1864 Proof Set Containing
Copper-Nickel and Bronze Cents

2009   1864 Nine-Piece Proof Set NGC. The year 1864 is significant for proof coinage, specifically for the silver-minor pieces. Three types of one cent coins were made: 370 copper-nickel cents, oak wreath with shield reverse; 150 or more bronze coins with No L on the ribbon; and 20 or so bronze specimens with L. The two cent piece made its debut in July 1864. The 2010 *Guide Book* indicates a mintage of 100+ proof specimens for this new denomination, all with the Large Motto. Walter Breen (1989), however, also lists the Small Motto variety in proof, opining:

> "Mintage unknown. Thought to have formed an extremely small percentage of the 100 proofs issued in July 1864 (that is, the above-mentioned Large Motto production), but more likely to have been made in infinitesimal quantity (of the order of magnitude of a dozen or fifteen pieces?) late in April, outside the normal issue of proof sets."

Kevin Flynn, in a March 12, 1996 *Numismatic News* article, agrees with Breen's estimate of 12 to 15 Small Date proofs, but contends that they are patterns, not regular issues.

Mint records indicate that a total of 470 silver-minor proof sets were minted in 1864. Breen suggests that the 370 sets made in February and March of this year contained copper-nickel cents, and the 100 sets coined in July included the bronze cents and two cent pieces.

Copper-Nickel Cent PR65 Cameo. An impressively contrasted Gem specimen, with the cameo effect emboldened by the fantastic reflectivity of the pale copper-orange fields. The richly frosted devices show a few flyspecks, most noticeably at the bases of the feathers in the headdress.

Bronze, No L Cent PR63 Red and Brown. Strongly reflective and boldly impressed with lilac and blue overtones gracing copper-gold surfaces. Several carbon spots are visible, including one over Liberty's ear and another on the reverse rim to the right of the arrowheads.

Large Motto Two Cent PR65 Red and Brown. The more available Large Motto variant of this first-year specimen issue. The bold copper-orange and magenta-lavender hues of the obverse are more muted on the reverse. This Gem is attractive both at first glance and on closer inspection.

Three Cent Silver PR64. Dappled blue, mustard-gold, and rose toning drapes gleaming surfaces that are otherwise pale silver-gray. A few light hairlines are hidden beneath the patina.

Half Dime PR65 Cameo. A gorgeous Gem with silver-white frost-and-mirrors centers and a hint of gold-orange peripheral toning. A few small planchet flaws are visible in the obverse fields.

Dime PR63 Cameo. Great reflectivity and impressive contrast. Dappled violet, blue, and gold patina covers much of the obverse fields, though these colors are present only at the rims on the reverse. Scattered hairlines and a few points of contact account for the grade.

Quarter PR62. Both sides show a light gold and apricot cast. Contrast is appreciable, though not to Cameo levels. The fields exhibit scattered hairlines, and several contact marks are noted to the right of Liberty's head.

Half Dollar PR66 ★. This stunningly toned Premium Gem proof is a highlight of the set. Blue and green outer bands fade into violet and finally peach at the centers. Boldly impressed and gorgeous.

Seated Dollar PR64. Lavender-blue and gold rim shadings give way to shining silver-gray at the centers. A splash of color is also visible near the hand supporting the pole. Mildly contrasted with only a handful of small faults precluding an even finer designation.
From The Boca Collection, Part I. (Total: 9 coins)

A 15% BUYER'S PREMIUM ($14 MIN.) APPLIES TO ALL LOTS.

Attractive 1865 Proof Set, PR63 to PR66

2010   1865 Nine-Piece Proof Set NGC. Production for most silver-minor proof sets increased slightly in 1865 from the previous year. The 2010 *Guide Book* gives a mintage of 500+ coins for each denomination.

The three cent nickel was introduced to the line of United States coinage in 1865. Unlike the *Guide Book* mintage figure of 500+ coins for this new denomination, Walter Breen, in his *Proof Encyclopedia*, puts the mintage at 400+ pieces. His rationale for this is that the three cent nickel was authorized by an Act of Congress, March 3, 1865 and was therefore not included in the February 25 delivery of 100 proof sets. He notes that the denomination was included in the March 10, 16, 20, and 24 deliveries, each of which included 100 sets. Breen goes on to say of the three cent nickel that: "Extras presumably might have been struck to memorialize the new denomination."

Cent PR63 Brown. All 1865 proof cents come with a Plain 5 that has a simple slight curvature at the top. This is one of the more difficult dates in the early Indian Head proof cent series. In this regard, Richard Snow says in his *Flying Eagle and Indian Head Cents*: "Its rarity is equal to that of the 1864 No L, but is typically priced lower because it is not a one-year type." Full Red examples are extremely difficult to locate, especially without spots or other problems. Indeed, David Bowers writes in *A Buyer's and Enthusiast's Guide to Flying Eagle and Indian Cents*: "Most are toned brown or brown with traces of red."

Considerable copper-gold luster shows beneath freckled sky-blue patination accented with light green. The design elements are well impressed, including most of the feather tips and all four diamonds. Close inspection reveals no mentionable contact marks, and both sides are remarkably devoid of carbon flecks. All in all, this is a truly appealing piece for the grade and color designation. Census: 6 in 63 Brown, 1 finer (10/09).

Two Cent Piece PR66 Red and Brown. Reflective fields accentuate the design elements when the coin is rotated ever so slightly beneath a light source, especially on the obverse. Whispers of blue-green and red, slightly more evident on the reverse, visit the golden-orange surfaces, and a decisive strike is manifested in virtually complete delineation on the devices. Both sides of this lovely two cent piece are nicely preserved, revealing no contacts or spots. Census: 9 in 66 Red and Brown, 2 finer (10/09).

Three Cent Silver PR65. Beautifully toned, with peripheral gunmetal-blue and purple that is more extensive on the obverse. This coloration transitions to gold-beige in the central areas. The design features are exquisitely struck, and the central devices appear to reach out from the mirrored fields to the observer. These attributes synergistically combine with the impeccably preserved surfaces to project breathtaking eye appeal. Census: 27 in 65, 25 finer (10/09).

Three Cent Nickel PR65. Breen's *Proof Encyclopedia* recognizes three varieties of the 1865 proof three cent nickel. The coin in the present set is B. 2-B, showing a double date that was first punched too far left, then effaced except for the upper left parts of 65 and corrected. This is the variety most often seen. Breen writes that the '65 three cent is "Popular because first year of issue and because actually rare."

Whispers of nearly imperceptible powder-blue and gold-beige colors concentrate on the reflective fields of this Gem, leaving the frosty motifs in light gray. The design elements are generally well struck save for the often-seen weakness in the lines in the center of the first upright of the III denomination. A few tiny flecks are undisturbing. Census: 58 in 63, 15 finer (10/09).

Half Dime PR64 Cameo. The upper right part of the base of the 1 in the date is doubled, the skirt pendant is about over the knob in the 6, double outlines show to the right sides of HA and DI in HALF DIME, and both ribbon ends are clear of the wreath.

Splashes of electric-blue, gold-orange, and reddish-purple make occasional visits to the border, leaving the obverse center color free and a touch of gold in the reverse central area. Both sides display pleasing field-motif contrast regardless of the angle of observation, and high magnification brings out a few faint hairlines interspersed with die polish lines in the fields. Great overall eye appeal.

Dime PR64. The silver-white portrait of Liberty cedes to soft orange patina in the adjacent fields before taking on purple and gunmetal-blue at the borders. The same color scheme occurs on the reverse except that the orange toning covers the center. A powerful strike lends bold detail to the design motifs, including the reverse wreath elements that often reveal localized weakness. This well preserved near-Gem possesses definite Cameo characteristics. Census: 37 in 64, 26 finer (10/09).

Quarter PR65 Cameo. The toning on this Gem is simply astounding, consisting of a delicate blend of blue-green, electric-blue, lavender, and orange, which all assume somewhat deeper shades on the reverse. Strong field-design variance confirms the Cameo designation. Both sides exhibit razor-sharp devices, complemented with broad square rims and full dentilation. A couple of unobtrusive ticks subtract absolutely nothing from the coin's outstanding eye appeal.

Half Dollar PR63. Speckled russet, purple, and electric-blue gravitate to the margins of this Select proof, ceding to a veneer of soft golden-tan in the obverse center and grayish-tan in the reverse center. An exacting strike imparts crisp definition to the moderately frosted design features that stand out against the mirrored fields, especially on the obverse. Some inoffensive handling marks in the fields are visible with high magnification.

Seated Dollar PR64. Blushes of sky-blue, yellow-gold, lilac, rose, and burnt-orange patina adhere to the obverse fields, transitioning to soft golden-gray on the Liberty motif. Medium intensity gold-orange dominates the reverse, accented with splashes of bluish-purple, lilac, and sky-blue. A solid strike brings out complete definition on the design elements. Striae are evident in the fields under a loupe, particularly on the reverse. A few light hairlines in the fields are undistracting.
From The Boca Collection, Part I. (Total: 9 coins)

A 15% BUYER'S PREMIUM ($14 MIN.) APPLIES TO ALL LOTS.

1866 10-Piece Proof Set Featuring
PR66 Cameo Seated Dollar

2011   10-Piece 1866 Proof Set. As with 1865, the proof set of 1866 includes the beginning of a denomination that heralds the end of another. With the introduction of the five cent nickel in 1866, the silver half dime, like the three cent silver, faced competition from a base-metal version. The two smallest silver denominations would fall together, massacred in the "Crime of '73," but no other mainstream silver denomination would lose its precious-metal content until 1965.

The other major change in the minor-silver proof set affects the quarter, half dollar, and Seated dollar. The motto IN GOD WE TRUST, first introduced on the two cent piece in 1864, was mandated on the larger-diameter silver and gold denominations as part of the Act of March 3, 1865, which is better known for authorizing the three cent nickel denomination. The changeover occurred in 1866, the next year. While the five cent nickel was not included in the Act, since it did not yet exist, the Shield design bore the motto from the start.

Walter Breen's *Proof Encyclopedia* notes delivery of 725 silver-minor proof sets in 1866, but he also asserts that all but 125 of those sets were delivered prior to the authorization of the five cent nickel. As acknowledged by Breen, the restrike caveat applies: the 2010 edition of the *Guide Book* claims a mintage of 600+, and certified population data for the 1866 issue are similar to other, slightly later issues. Still, the 1866 remains one of the most expensive proof Shield nickels.

Cent—Altered Color—Proof NGC. Sharply struck with readily appreciable mirrors. At first glance, this coin appears Red and Brown, more the former with copper-orange surfaces showing just a few hints of mahogany and mint-green, but closer inspection raises questions about the color's originality.

Two Cent PR64 Red ANACS. Crisply detailed with strong mirrors. Light copper color on the obverse gives way to deep orange over much of the reverse. Sharply struck with a few flecks on the obverse.

Three Cent Silver PR63 Cameo NGC. Light silver-gray with echoes of golden color over the obverse fields and at parts of the reverse margins. Modestly hairlined but pleasingly contrasted.

Three Cent Nickel PR66 Cameo NGC. Excellent contrast with just a hint of toning, white-on-white. Flashy mirrors are carefully preserved. All things considered, an extraordinary specimen. Census: 10 in 66 Cameo, 1 finer (11/09).

Five Cent Nickel PR65 NGC. The first-year issue in the set and a definite prize. While the obverse shows considerable contrast between the canary-yellow mirrors and the nickel-gray frost on the devices, the toning on the reverse is more comprehensive and also contains light blue elements.

Half Dime PR63 NGC. Bold gold, orange, green, and silver-white elements appear over different parts of this Select proof. Impressively detailed with mild contrast and scattered hairlines beneath the toning.

Dime PR65 NGC. A richly toned Gem proof with cerulean and azure peripheral tints yielding to rose and sunset-orange at the centers. The latter color covers significantly more area on the obverse. Light green tints also visit the rims.

Quarter (With Motto) PR64 Cameo NGC. A captivating coin with considerable contrast, edged in blue-violet and champagne with a quick fade to silver-white. Excellent frost-and-mirrors with only a few hairlines of any significance.

Half Dollar (With Motto) PR63 Cameo NGC. Impressively contrasted through considerable patina, light gold-gray at the centers that shifts to orange and lavender close to the rims. Faintly hairlined with a fingerprint visible in the right obverse field.

Seated Dollar (With Motto) PR66 Cameo NGC. This Premium Gem is the jewel of the set, thickly frosted on the devices with outstanding core white-on-white contrast. At the margins, amber, sunset-orange, and ocean-blue toning takes hold. Breathtaking eye appeal. Census: 4 in 66 Cameo, 4 finer (11/09).
From The Boca Collection, Part I. (Total: 10 coins)

Nine-Piece 1867 Proof Set
Cent to Half Dime, Quarter to Dollar

2012 Nine-Piece 1867 Proof Set NGC. As was the case with most years during and immediately after the Civil War, the minor and silver proof sets mirror each others' mintages, in this case with official production of 625 pieces per denomination. Also in keeping with the trend, the actual output of proof minor sets was higher than the official number, though to what extent is not completely known.

The five cent nickel denomination, first struck for circulation (and official proof sets) in 1866, had its first redesign the next year, when the rays between the reverse stars were removed. No Rays pieces vastly outnumber With Rays coins in both the proof and the business strike populations. The change must have come early in the year.

Circumstantial evidence comes from Walter Breen: in his *Proof Encyclopedia,* Breen claimed that most of the silver proof sets of 1867 were delivered in February and March, with a final delivery of 100 sets in June. Breen also notes that the 1867 proof set in the Smithsonian holdings "contains only the nickel without rays, though it was obtained from the Coiner March 7." Similarly, the proof set offered here, like the vast majority of sets from the year, contains a No Rays five cent coin.

Note: This set contains nine pieces. The dime is absent.

Cent PR65 Red and Brown Cameo. The copper-gold obverse offers distinct contrast despite the dots of mint-green and brown visiting that side. The reverse, while a deeper copper-orange color overall, offers a cameo effect of similar strength. Carefully preserved and attractive.

Two Cent PR64 Red and Brown. Similar copper-gold color to the cent, also with patches of the deeper orange that fade into mahogany on this example. Modestly contrasted with appreciable strength of mirrors.

Three Cent Silver PR63. The Select grade does not reflect the eye appeal of this lovely trime. Though PR63 might be accurate in a technical sense, owing to a scattering of hairlines and contact, the surfaces are awash in utterly charming blue-green and olive-gold patina.

Three Cent Nickel PR66 Cameo. Unusually bold and eye-catching contrast defines the eye appeal of this Premium Gem. Thickly frosted devices are well struck and snowy, though a halo of peripheral green-gold on each side precludes an absolute black-and-white effect.

Five Cent Nickel, No Rays PR63. The obverse is primarily nickel-white with an echo of golden patina along IN GOD WE TRUST and the lower rim. The reverse is closer to pearl-gray with green-gold overtones.

Half Dime PR64 Cameo. Liquid green-gold peripheral elements give way to gorgeous silver-white color at the centers. Strongly contrasted with the frost over Liberty particularly noteworthy.

Dime not present.

Quarter PR64 Cameo. A boldly contrasted piece like the half dime, minimally toned save for a suggestion of the same green-gold in the fields. Well-defined in the centers but slightly soft on the stars at right.

Half Dollar PR63. Though not labeled as Cameo, this coin could make a case for the designation, though the obverse is stronger in that respect than the reverse. Both sides show dappled violet, blue, and green-gold peripheral color; while this gives way to an almost black-and-white center on the obverse, the reverse has toning over the eagle as well.

Seated Dollar PR65 Cameo. Elegant champagne patina over most of each side, with a window of powder-blue below the eagle's beak and down across the wing to the space beneath the olive branch. Intensely mirrored with no-questions contrast and excellent preservation for this Motto Seated dollar issue. Census: 11 in 65 Cameo, 12 finer.
From The Boca Collection, Part I. (Total: 9 coins)

Memorable 10-Piece 1868 Proof Set

2013   10-Piece 1868 Proof Set. Specie payments, first suspended in 1862, remained under suspension in 1868, while paper fractional notes continued to take the place of smaller silver denominations. Contemporary collectors continued to order proof coins during this period, especially in light of the specie suspension that eliminated the option of acquiring business strikes.

Silver proofs were coined to the extent of 600 pieces during the year, with a few hundred additional minor proof sets available to collectors. Modern estimates of the total proof mintage of minor coins (cent, two cent, three cent nickel, and nickel five cent) usually fall in the range of 750 to 1,000 pieces, probably closer to the latter. In addition to the regular production proof sets, at least five complete proof sets from the cent to the double eagle were coined in aluminum.

Present-day estimates suggest that approximately half of the proofs minted are still in existence, or about 300 of each silver denomination, and 400 to 500 of each minor coin denomination. Today, survivors across all denominations are apt to be in higher grades than those of a decade earlier, the result of better preservation by collectors and dealers. The quality of strike is usually adequate, although a few coins show slight weakness. Cameo contrast is infrequently seen on any of the proof coins of 1868, although it is more prevalent than on most earlier dates.

Proof varieties included a minority of Indian cents with the reverse rotated about 170 degrees, at least two doubled date two cent varieties, a majority of Shield nickels with the 68 doubled to the south, and some Seated dimes with a blundered date.

Cent PR65 Red and Brown PCGS. Rotated reverse. Blue-green overtones grace fiery ruby-orange fields. Crisply detailed and well-preserved with winning visual appeal.

Two Cent PR64 Red and Brown NGC. The obverse is primarily copper-gold with a few small brown spots, but the reverse shows deeper orange and green hues. Modestly hairlined for the grade assigned.

Three Cent Silver PR64 NGC. Shining surfaces are awash in blue-green and champagne patina. A sharply struck beauty from a post-Civil War issue associated with a heavily melted and low-mintage business strike edition.

Three Cent Nickel PR65 NGC. Lightly gold-toned overall with a touch of mint-green on the reverse. A gleaming Gem proof with top-flight eye appeal for the grade.

Five Cent Nickel PR65 PCGS. Bold lemongrass outer toning gives way to powder-blue and finally to lavender-pink at the centers. Both sides are impressively mirrored beneath the toning. Housed in a green label holder.

Half Dime PR64 NGC. Like many of its fellows, this half dime offers lovely green-gold toning, this time encompassing most of each side. Mildly contrasted with just a few small hairlines found in the fields.

Dime PR64 Cameo NGC. Richly frosted central devices have largely resisted the ocean-blue and golden-tan toning found at the peripheral fields. Profoundly reflective beneath the patina and virtually irresistible.

Quarter PR62 PCGS. Though the fields show substantial evidence of hairlines and contact, the real story of this specimen is its toning. While the reverse shows only gold-gray color, the reverse has a silver-gray center surrounded by arcs of gold-orange and deep blue.

Half Dollar—Artificial Toning—Proof NGC. Sharply struck with intense mirrors visible at the central reverse. On the rest of the coin, thick polychrome patina floats on the surfaces.

Seated Dollar PR62 NGC. A moderately hairlined specimen with understated but elegant patina. Orange-tinged gold-gray peripheral tints visit each side, but while the same color extends across the entire reverse, the obverse shows pale ice-blue toning at its center. Stronger eye appeal than the grade might suggest.
From The Boca Collection, Part I. (Total: 10 coins)

Impressive 10-Piece 1869 Proof Set
Six Cameo Coins

2014   10-Piece 1869 Proof Set NGC. Mint records for silver proofs total 600 coins in seven individual deliveries dated from February 1 to October 8, 1869. The first quarter of the year saw 400 proof sets produced, with 50 more in the second quarter, 50 in the third quarter, and 100 in the fourth quarter. The number of minor proof coins struck in 1869 is similar to that of 1868, about 800 to 1,000 coins in all.

A few proof three cent silver pieces exist from an overdated obverse die, 1869 over 8. That is the only significant variety among the minor and silver denomination proofs for the year, although some half dimes are known with a minor repunched date.

Like most years from this time period, about half of the original mintage survives today. Current NGC and PCGS population data shows a certified population of more than half the mintage for each silver denomination, including 454 proof 1869 silver dollars. The number of resubmissions in those total figures remains unknown. Nearly all survivors across all denominations are sharply struck with deeply mirrored fields. Coins with full cameo contrast are rare but more available than from earlier years.

Cent PR65 Red and Brown. Blushes of lavender and rose visit otherwise pale copper-orange surfaces. This sharply struck and charming Gem shows a tiny contact mark between the date and the U in UNITED.

Two Cent PR65 Red and Brown. Distinctly more Red than Brown with copper-orange color dominant, though the obverse margins show their share of tan and mahogany. A crisply detailed specimen with minimal carbon.

Three Cent Silver PR65 Cameo. The amber, green, and blue patina that occupies much of the margins gives way to silver-green at the centers, where the frosted devices set up attractive contrast. A well defined and lovely Cameo Gem.

Three Cent Nickel PR65 Cameo. More heavily frosted devices than often seen on this denomination, with the portrait particularly attractive in this respect. Small glimpses of green-gold toning visit otherwise nickel-white fields. A few shallow depressions are visible on the III within the wreath.

Five Cent Nickel PR65 Cameo. A gleaming Gem with essentially brilliant fields and delightful snow-white devices. If the frost were a trifle thicker on the obverse, this could make a claim to Ultra Cameo status.

Half Dime PR67. This Superb Gem displays considerable contrast for a coin not designated as Cameo, though the color progression on the obverse, from light green on the outside through to blue and a violet center, dampens the effect on that side. Similarly, if more lightly toned on the reverse and exquisitely preserved in every respect.

Dime PR63 Cameo. Outstanding contrast with broad areas of gold and orange patina over otherwise silver-white surfaces. Additional blue elements are present at the rims. Sharply struck devices offer rich frost.

Quarter PR65 Cameo. Bold gold-orange obverse toning eases slightly toward champagne on the reverse. Impressively detailed with wonderful snow-white devices. A carefully preserved Cameo Gem.

Half Dollar PR64 Cameo. Dots of gold, blue, and green patina decorate the rims of this Choice Cameo coin, while the minimally toned centers are reflective in the fields and frosty on the devices. Boldly impressed and highly appealing for the grade.

Seated Dollar PR64. Green-gold and blue patina embraces each side of this Seated dollar, with additional champagne elements present on the reverse. On the obverse, Liberty's portrait is thickly frosted, an effect that persists even through the patina.
From The Boca Collection, Part I. (Total: 10 coins)

Important 10-Piece 1870 Proof Set Featuring
Singular PR67 Cameo Quarter

2015   10-Piece 1870 Proof Set. The Philadelphia Mint produced 1,000 proofs of each silver denomination in 1870, and most were distributed in silver and minor proof sets of the year, although an unknown quantity may have been melted at a later date. In fact, the surviving population of all silver denominations is comparable to the issues of the late 1860s and the following few years, most which have considerably lower proof mintages.

It seems logical that the number of proofs coined in 1870 was much greater than the number of sets actually sold, with the balance melted over the next few years. Alternatively, delivery of small quantities of proof coins throughout the year would indicate a continuous demand for those coins.

An additional quantity of minor proof sets may have been coined, although the likely excess of silver coins may mean that no additional minor coins were needed. All attempts to correlate current population data and original mintage estimates have been unsuccessful. Aside from a few minor date recuttings, there are no significant proof varieties for 1870. However, early and late states of the same die marriage are noted on some issues.

Cent PR64 Red and Brown NGC. Both sides show copper-gold fire and cooler lavender-blue color, but in different mixtures. The obverse has a broad copper-gold center edged in the lavender-blue, but on the reverse, an interior wedge of the latter color floats in a sea of the former.

Two Cent PR64 Brown PCGS. Deep old-copper color with rose-plum overtones. A sharply struck near-Gem with generally smooth surfaces, though scattered hairlines and faint contact preclude a finer designation.

Three Cent Silver PR66 Cameo NGC. Violet and gold peripheral tints give way to virtually untoned centers where frosted devices contrast with the gleaming fields. A sharp Premium Gem that shows a small planchet flaw just to the right of the lowest arm of the star.

Three Cent Nickel PR64 NGC. Moderately reflective nickel-white surfaces offer faint contrast with satiny, softly struck devices. Liberty's portrait shows a diagonal graze, and the fields show a handful of hairlines.

Five Cent Nickel PR65 Cameo NGC. Aside from faint golden tints, the only patina on this Cameo Gem is a small, cloudy spot between the two rightmost bars in the shield. Sharply struck and pleasingly preserved.

Half Dime PR63 NGC. Minor hairlines through the obverse fields define the technical grade, but reflectivity and peripheral gold-orange toning are key to the eye appeal. Well-defined devices are mildly frosted.

Dime PR65 Cameo NGC. The obverse coloration is similar to the half dime's but with the addition of blue. The reverse is silver-white almost completely. Both sides offer thickly frosted devices and excellent contrast.

Quarter PR67 Cameo NGC. Truly a coin to celebrate; it is the single-finest Cameo specimen found in the NGC *Census Report* (11/09). The immensely reflective obverse has subtle mauve and gold peripheral tints, with the former color deepening to violet-blue on the reverse. Outstanding contrast and preservation lead to incredible visual appeal.

Half Dollar PR64 NGC. Dusky blue-violet and pearl-gray shadings dominate the obverse, while the reverse shows green-gold, silver-gray, and sage toning. Both the frost on Liberty and the reverse's considerable contrast hint at a coin that once would have qualified as Cameo.

Seated Dollar PR63 NGC. Charming turquoise and champagne patina embraces the shining surfaces of this Select proof. Though lightly hairlined, this sharp specimen remains immensely appealing.
From The Boca Collection, Part I. (Total: 10 coins)

A 15% BUYER'S PREMIUM ($14 MIN.) APPLIES TO ALL LOTS.

Strong 1871 Proof Set Featuring
Superb Gem Dime

2016   1871 Nine-Piece Proof Set NGC. Many of the proof coins of all denominations issued in 1871 were from regular business strike dies that were polished prior to proof production. Such coins exhibit moderately mirrored fields rather than the deeply mirrored fields of earlier years. Cameo contrast can be found, but deep or ultra cameo contrast is rarely seen. In most denominations, the 1871 proofs are scarcer than those of earlier years, and are usually found in lower grades.

Some of the Seated dollars are known from a doubled reverse die. Breen described a sharply doubled date Shield nickel variety in his *Proof Encyclopedia,* although Bowers made no mention of it in his Shield and Liberty nickel reference.

The recorded mintage of proof silver coinage was 960 pieces, made in 11 individual groups from January through November 1871. As in 1870, there may have been additional minor proof coins minted, although the 960-coin silver mintage was probably more than enough to supply orders, with the balance of the silver melted, and the minor coins sold in sets.

Cent PR64 Red and Brown. The prevailing magenta and copper-orange colors shade into violet and mahogany. Crisply struck and attractive with only a few stray hairlines visible in the fields.

Three Cent Nickel PR65. A beguiling Gem proof that is primarily pale nickel-gray but with hints of gold on the obverse and a few faint streaks of sage on the reverse. The detail on Liberty's hair is admirable, if a trifle soft as always close to the ear.

Three Cent Silver PR65. Orange, peach, and violet overtones at the margins with lighter silver-gray and gold shadings closer to the centers. Light frost on the obverse star gives that side a degree of contrast. The fields offer watery reflectivity, and the devices are crisply defined.

Five Cent Nickel PR64 Cameo. Faint pink and gold accents visit lightly toned-over obverse surfaces that are pale nickel-gray. The reverse shows stronger rose-orange and blue elements. Attractively contrasted, though a few small contact marks hide among the scattered planchet flaws in the fields.

Half Dime PR65 Cameo. Though the silver-gray toning over most of the obverse is thick (and the blue, violet, rose, and gold elements at the rims are thicker still), this Gem's essential contrast shines through, thanks to the rich frost over the figure of Liberty. On the gold-tinged reverse, the cameo effect is more overt.

Dime PR67. An utterly enchanting Superb Gem, purple and blue in the centers with pale green peripheral elements. Exquisitely preserved beneath the patina and an all-around noteworthy specimen. Census: 3 in 67, 1 finer (10/09).

Quarter PR66 Cameo. The centers are essentially untoned and profoundly contrasted, while the margins show varying patina, gold and blue on the obverse and orange on the reverse. Strongly mirrored and thoroughly appealing. Census: 3 in 66 Cameo, 1 finer (10/09).

Half Dollar PR64. The luminous gold-gray color of the centers fades through dusky orange closer to the rims, with an additional layer of blue on the obverse. Hairlines are present in the fields, most noticeably to the left of Liberty.

Seated Dollar PR63. Boldly defined with minimally toned centers and blue and orange peripheral shadings. Though the right obverse field is significantly hairlined, the reverse is comparatively clean.
From The Boca Collection, Part I. (Total: 9 coins)

Desirable 1872 10-Piece Proof Set

2017   1872 10-Piece Proof Set NGC. Specie payments were still under suspension in 1872, and some young Americans had never seen or handled small change, being accustomed to the fractional paper currency. Although business strike mintages increased dramatically in nearly every denomination, the individual coins remain rare, especially in higher grades. In many cases, the proof coins ordered by collectors may be the only examples they ever encountered.

As they have for over a century, proof coins often serve collectors who seek the date, dramatically increasing the demand for every denomination. Breen discussed the matter in his *Proof Encyclopedia* for the 1872 silver three cent piece: "only 1000 business strikes were minted and I have seen exactly two of them in the past 25 years, one in the Ruby collection, but the proofs turn up with reasonable frequency - sometimes impaired."

Many proof coins of 1872 are somewhat lacking in overall quality, sometimes with poor strikes and sometimes with unattractive proof surfaces. That is especially true for the nickel alloy coins, where the composition presented its own set of challenges related to difficulty in striking.

Unusual proof varieties include a doubled obverse Shield nickel, a blundered date dime, and a doubled reverse die Seated dollar.

Cent PR65 Red and Brown. Both sides exhibit sharp details including full feathers and diamonds on the obverse, and bold leaves and shield on the reverse. Little mirrored surface remains on this Gem proof, with reflective obverse and reverse fields surrounding lustrous devices. Light bluish-brown toning accompanies the pale orange surfaces of this lovely cent. NGC Census: 42 in PR65 Red and Brown; 8 finer (10/09). NGC has also certified 19 Gem or finer pieces with higher level designations.

Two Cent PR65 Red and Brown. A wonderful Gem, this elusive two cent piece has bold and complete design definition on both sides. Both sides have full reflectivity with mirrored fields and lustrous devices. A minor spot is evident on the obverse below the left end of the ribbon. The obverse has light blue and violet toning while the reverse is fully brilliant mint orange.

Three Cent Silver PR64. Remarkably well struck, this piece has crisp obverse and reverse details including a full star on the obverse. Deeply mirrored fields and lustrous devices create cameo contrast that is visible beneath the toning, although insufficient to receive the Cameo designation. Attractive light gold, magenta, and emerald-green toning is seen on the obverse, with the addition of cobalt-blue on the reverse.

Three Cent Nickel PR65. This pleasing three cent nickel lacks some central obverse definition with reverse weakness at the center of the first element and the top of the third element in the denomination. The fields and devices have satiny luster with mild reflectivity, although the fields are only slightly mirrored. Both sides are fully brilliant nickel-gray without toning.

Five Cent Nickel PR66. FS-101. Doubled obverse die with most of the shield and leaf details showing clear doubling. NGC did not provide the attribution for this piece, although it is a variety the firm recognizes. Slight doubling is also visible on the motto, but no doubling is evident on the date. Both sides have bold and crisp details. Pristine and reflective surfaces are lightly mirrored. Traces of champagne and blue toning add to its eye appeal. NGC has certified exactly three attributed examples of the proof doubled die, along with 319 other proof submissions. NGC Census: 45 in PR66; 5 finer (10/09).

Half Dime PR65. The strike is excellent with full head details on the obverse and full wreath details on the reverse. The fields are fully mirrored with excellent contrast built around lustrous devices. The cameo appearance is clearly visible through the toning. The obverse has vivid gold, rose, mauve, and blue toning. The reverse has rich blue, emerald, and gold toning. NGC Census: 27 in PR65; 14 finer (10/09). NGC has also graded 20 pieces in PR65 Cameo or finer.

Dime PR65. The left branch of the wreath shows weakness, but all other intricate die details are fully visible. This deeply mirrored Gem proof has excellent contrast on both sides. The obverse is turquoise and pale blue, and the reverse is deep blue, purple, and pale green. NGC Census: 22 in PR65; 10 finer (10/09). NGC has also graded 16 pieces in PR65 Cameo or finer.

Quarter PR64. The obverse and reverse exhibit full, sharp design definition. The heavy toning on this piece tends to subdue the proof mirrors. A few faint hairlines and contract marks limit the grade. Pale blue and light green toning is evident on the obverse, with deep blue-green and gray-violet on the reverse.

Half Dollar PR64 Cameo. Each and every individual design element on both sides is sharp and complete. This remarkable half dollar has exceptional aesthetic desirability, with bold cameo contrast. The surfaces are outstanding for the numerical grade. The obverse has vivid emerald and gold toning, and the reverse has light gold at the center, with peripheral violet and bright blue. NGC Census: 3; 12 finer (10/09).

Seated Dollar PR64. All letters in the motto are sharply doubled. This strike is exceptional, with full head, gown, and star details on the obverse, and bold wreath and eagle details on the reverse. Fully mirrored fields frame the frosty devices of this lovely Choice proof Seated dollar. The toning tends to mask the contrast slightly, but it still should be given a Cameo designation. Pale magenta, olive-gold, and light blue toning on the obverse contrasts with deeper blue and green toning on the reverse.
From The Boca Collection, Part I. (Total: 10 coins)

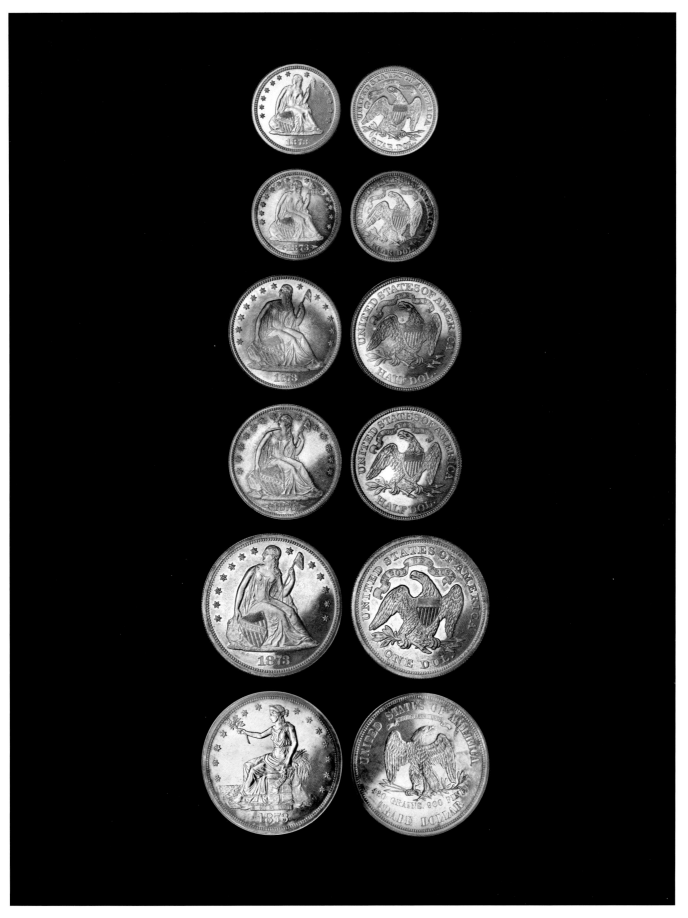

Tremendous 1873 Proof Set
NGC Certified 14-Piece Set

2018 **1873 14-Piece Proof Set NGC.** Several events contributed to the numismatic importance of the year 1873. Early in the year, public criticism of the new 1873 coins led to slight adjustment of the date logotypes. The first coins of most denominations had unusually large knobs on the 3, making that digit look too similar to an 8. Many thought the coins were incorrectly dated 1878. New date logotypes were created for each denomination, with more space between the upper and lower knobs of the 3. That process created varieties that eventually became known as the Closed 3 (or Close 3) and Open 3 coins. Nearly all proof coins of all denominations are the Closed 3 coins, struck early in the year. Exceptions are the With Arrows coins and the Trade dollar that have the Open 3 date style.

Congressional legislation called the "Crime of '73" by Western mine owners firmly tied the nation to the gold standard. It also eliminated the two cent piece, silver three cent piece, and the half dime, changing the makeup of proof sets for the rest of the century. The same legislation converted U.S. coinage weights to the metric system, slightly increasing the weight of the dime, quarter, and half dollar. To distinguish between 1873-dated coins of the old and new weight standards, Mint officials added small arrowheads to the left and right of the date on the new coins, much as they had done twenty years earlier. The date correction from the Closed 3 to Open 3 coins happened well enough before the new issue of With Arrows coins that the latter all have Open 3 date styles.

The Seated Liberty dollar was discontinued in 1873, and in its place was the new Trade dollar, specifically designed to compete with other similar coins in Oriental commerce. All of these events led to an assortment of coins that could be studied for a lifetime. In fact, one collector, Harry X Boosel, did just that, eventually publishing a book on the coins of 1873.

Mintage figures in 1873 include 600 of the No Arrows silver proofs, and 800 of the With Arrows coins. The number of minor proof coins, if any, in addition to those supplied with complete proof sets remains unknown. With all of the varieties included, a complete 1873 proof set consists of five minor coins, 10 silver coins, and seven gold coins. The present offering is a 14-piece set that includes all of the silver coins and four minor coins, lacking the 1873 Open 3 two cent piece.

Cent PR64 Red and Brown Cameo. S-PR1. The only die pair for proof 1873 Indian cents has heavily polished dies, with faint polishing lines visible in the fields. The base of the first feather and the eye socket are both polished into the field as described by Rick Snow in *The Flying Eagle & Indian Cent Attribution Guide*. The Close 3 is extremely tight with little space between the knobs and crossbar.

Both sides have pale orange proof surfaces with hints of peripheral lilac. Trivial spots and streaks are of no concern on this lovely piece. Design elements are fully defined, and contrast nicely with the fields. NGC Census: 3 in PR64 Red and Brown Cameo; none finer (10/09). They have also certified two as Red Cameo, one PR64 and the other PR65. No Ultra Cameo examples have been certified.

Two Cent PR65 Red and Brown. Closed 3. Both dies are well made with no unusual characteristics. The 1873 issue of two cent coins is a proof-only issue, with no known circulation strikes. Varieties are known with a Closed 3 and an Open 3, the latter missing from the current set.

This boldly detailed two cent piece has gorgeous Indian-red surfaces with hints of emerald and mauve toning on the obverse. The reverse has splashes of steel-blue toning, and the combination prevents a full Red color designation. The fields are moderately mirrored with modest cameo contrast. A few tiny spots and imperfections are evident, including a long, wavy lint mark through the first S in STATES. NGC Census: 55 in PR65 Red and Brown; 36 finer (10/09).

Three Cent Silver PR64. Well-made dies, the obverse with noticeable space between the top and bottom knobs of the 3, primarily due to a broken punch that lacks a crossbar on that digit. The top and bottom sections of the 3 join to form a short point.

The obverse is primarily pale cinnamon with a delightful iridescent frame near the border. The reverse exhibits a lovely blend of salmon, magenta, and cobalt toning over light silver-gray surfaces. Both sides have deeply mirrored fields around lustrous devices, although insufficient for a Cameo designation. The obverse has a few tiny contact marks and faint hairlines that limit the grade, while the reverse is substantially finer.

Three Cent Nickel PR65. The 3 is similar to that described above for the three cent silver piece, lacking a definite crossbar. A sharply defined light nickel-gray proof with modestly mirrored fields and satiny devices. A faint splash of light yellow-orange toning appears on the reverse of this otherwise untoned example. Trivial spots and blemishes are consistent with the grade. NGC has certified 27 finer non-Cameo proofs and 20 finer Cameo proofs (10/09).

Five Cent Nickel PR65. The 1 is repunched below and the 3 lacks a crossbar, much like both three cent pieces. The date logotype appears to be identical to the three cent nickel piece. The strike of this light gray proof is bold and well defined, with full detail throughout. Moderately mirrored fields surround the faintly contrasting devices, with delicate champagne toning on the dusky reverse. NGC has certified 51 finer examples (10/09), including non-Cameo and Cameo proofs.

Half Dime PR66 Cameo. Although this is a Closed 3 variety, as are all proof 1873 half dimes, a first glance gives the appearance of an Open 3 with widely spaced upper and lower knobs. Heavy diagonal polishing lines are especially visible on the obverse of this amazing Premium Gem. The fields are deeply mirrored and the devices are highly lustrous, the entire presentation brilliant and untoned with bright silver surfaces. NGC Census: 5 in PR66 Cameo; 4 finer (10/09). NGC has also certified one PR66 Ultra Cameo and one PR67 Ultra Cameo.

Dime No Arrows PR64. Fortin-101. The only currently identified proof variety for the 1873 No Arrows dimes, although Kamal Ahwash recorded a second (and currently unseen) obverse die for these proofs. This lovely dime has a bold strike and light silver surfaces with peripheral gold and iridescent toning on each side. Some irregular planchet imperfections are mostly visible on the obverse, consistent with the final grade determination. NGC Census: 45 in PR64; 37 finer (10/09).

Dime With Arrows PR64. Fortin-102. The only proof variety known for the 1873 With Arrows dimes, identified by tiny die defects of Liberty's left (facing) leg. This same obverse die was also used for some business strikes. Most of the obverse and reverse surfaces have yellow-brown toning with a frame of crimson and bright blue along parts of the borders. Light cameo contrast is evident, although insufficient to receive a Cameo designation. The strike is crisp and the eye appeal is excellent. NGC Census: 31 in PR64; 25 finer (10/09).

Quarter No Arrows PR63. Briggs 1-A. The only No Arrows proof variety recorded in the Briggs reference. Both 1873 quarters in this set are from the same reverse die, first used in 1872, and identified by a small raised die scratch across the left shield border. This sharply struck proof has fully mirrored fields and entirely untoned silver surfaces. A few blemishes, contact marks, and hairlines limit the grade.

Quarter With Arrows PR64 Cameo. Briggs 5-D. The only With Arrows proof variety recorded in the Briggs reference. This boldly defined and highly appealing quarter has natural "album toning" with light silver centers, surrounded by intense gold, magenta, and sky-blue toning on each side. The fields are fully and deeply mirrored, and the contrast is exceptional. NGC Census: 6 in PR64 Cameo; 4 finer (10/09).

Half Dollar No Arrows PR67 ★. Closed 3. There are no major die characteristics, so this half dollar has no Wiley-Bugert variety attribution. All minute reverse die markers are identical on the reverse of this half dollar and the reverse of the 1873 With Arrows half dollar in this set. An exceptional piece, this Superb Gem carries the NGC Star designation, and it is easily the star of the set. Only five 1873 No Arrows half dollars have received the coveted additional NGC designation for exceptional quality, the other four being Cameo proofs. This piece would probably have also received the Cameo designation, except the amazing toning prevents the contrast from being obvious. All design details are exceptionally sharp with the exception of the left end of the ribbon and motto. The centers on each side are pale mauve, giving way to electric-blue and lemon-yellow. NGC Census: 1 in PR67 ★; 0 finer (10/09).

Half Dollar With Arrows PR63. All 1873 With Arrows half dollars have an Open 3 in the date, as do all other With Arrows coins. This example is sharply struck with considerable contrast, although there is no designation assigned for that contrast. Faint hairlines and contact marks limit the grade. The centers exhibit delicate gold toning, with a frame of magenta and light blue on the obverse. The reverse is similar, with a thicker frame of greenish-blue toning. NGC Census: 29 in PR63; 64 finer (10/09).

Seated Dollar PR63. All letters of IN GOD WE TRUST and the ribbon that carries the motto are doubled, more prominent to the left. This same reverse die was used earlier in 1871 and 1872, and also appears on some silver dollar patterns. A second reverse die was also used for the 1873 Seated silver dollar proofs, combined with a single obverse die. The relative scarcity of the two proof varieties is unknown. Both sides have the usual trivial blemishes that prevent a higher grade. However, the aesthetic presentation is exceptional with rich turquoise and reddish-gold toning blended together on both sides. Every aspect of the strike is crisp, with bold design definition.

Trade Dollar PR64. Proofs of this issue are popular as they represent the first year of issue for the Trade dollar. This proof is an early die state of the so-called "Patched Reverse" variety recorded in Dave Bowers' *Silver Dollars & Trade Dollars of the United States*. The common obverse die has a heavy, straight die scratch from the bottom left bale of cotton into the sea, traversing slightly up to the left. Much of the obverse is brilliant and untoned, with a frame of gold, magenta, and bright blue toning. The reverse has delicate yellow-brown toning at the center, with vibrant blue and violet toning near the border. A few minor contact marks, hairlines, and other minuscule blemishes keep this piece below the Gem category. NGC Census: 40 in PR64; 17 finer (10/09). In addition, NGC has certified four finer Cameo proofs.
From The Boca Collection, Part I. (Total: 14 coins)

A 15% BUYER'S PREMIUM ($14 MIN.) APPLIES TO ALL LOTS.

Pleasing Seven-Piece 1874 Proof Set

2019   1874 Seven-Piece Proof Set NGC. Most 1874 proof coins were struck early in the year. Of the 700 Trade dollars struck, 500 proofs were produced in the first four months, another 100 were minted in June, and the last 100 were split evenly between September and December. It is likely that 500 proof sets produced in the first few months were sold to collectors, with additional pieces minted on an as-needed basis. The 1874 proof set, at just seven pieces, is considerably smaller than that of 1873, with denominations such as the two cent piece, three cent silver, half dime, and Seated dollar left by the wayside.

Proof mintages of the smaller denominations included 700 dimes, 850 quarters, and 750 half dollars. An unknown additional quantity of minor proofs (cent, three cent nickel, and nickel five cent) was produced for three coin sets; this figure is given as 700+ pieces traditionally, to allow for the possibility of single coins or non-silver proof sets.

The temporary With Arrows design of 1873 continued throughout 1874 on the Seated Liberty silver coins, creating a two-year type coin. The 1874 With Arrows proof silver coins are relatively common and usually available at some moderate price level. Demand for these proof coins comes from a broad numismatic base that includes date collectors, proof set collectors, and type collectors.

Cent PR65 Red and Brown. With its warm copper-orange and reddish-peach patina, this sharply struck cent is decidedly more Red than Brown. Excellent surface preservation with only a handful of minor flaws visible under magnification, none of them materially affecting the eye appeal.

Three Cent Nickel PR66 Cameo. Each side has gleaming nickel-white surfaces with only a suggestion of champagne or coral-pink. Strongly struck with far richer frost on the portrait of Liberty than usually seen. An excellent Premium Gem. Census: 23 in 66 Cameo, 5 finer (10/09).

Five Cent Nickel PR65. The obverse is strikingly contrasted beneath a thin layer of nickel-gray toning, but the reverse contrast falls short of Cameo standards. Nonetheless, this is a thoroughly appealing Gem that offers strong eye appeal for the grade. Definition is bold overall, though the lower right stars in the circle on the reverse are a trifle soft.

Dime PR64. The light gold-orange toning that graces a good deal of the obverse deepens considerably on the reverse. Boldly defined with potent mirrors that pierce the patina, though minor, scattered hairlines on each side preclude a finer designation.

Quarter PR63. Pale gold and silver-white color prevails in the centers, but the margins have sky-blue, orange, rose-violet, and umber shadings, with the deepest colors visible on the reverse. Sharply struck with considerable contrast on the reverse.

Half PR64. The most beautifully toned specimen in the set, this Choice proof has dazzling electric-blue borders on the obverse that have a short fade into violet before giving way to luminous gold-gray color at the centers. The latter two colors figure prominently on the reverse. Though not designated as a Cameo, each side has appreciable contrast.

Trade Dollar PR64. Liquid blue, green, and gold peripheral colors yield to light silver-gray at the centers of this near-Gem. This exquisitely detailed example shows only a handful of modest flaws to the unaided eye, though these few hairlines are sufficient to account for the grade.
From The Boca Collection, Part I. (Total: 7 coins)

A 15% BUYER'S PREMIUM ($14 MIN.) APPLIES TO ALL LOTS.

Appealing Eight-Piece 1875 Proof Set
With PR66 ★ Cameo Three Cent Nickel

2020   1875 Eight-Piece Proof Set NGC. The twenty cent piece was introduced to the nation in 1875. The obverse was virtually identical to the Seated Liberty quarters and both business strikes and proofs were minted, with additional examples struck in San Francisco and Carson City. The denomination was a major failure, lasting only one more year for business strikes and another two years after that for proofs. The success of such a denomination would have required a different design, or a distinctly different size. Even then, as we saw more than a century later with the Anthony and Sacagawea dollars, the size, design, or even the color was insufficient to create a successful circulating coinage. The proof mintage of twenty cent pieces amount to 2,790 coins, a large figure that suggests the mint planned on individual coin sales.

Business strike Trade dollars were coined to a limited extent, and many collectors acquired proofs since they were easier to locate. Most other denominations had larger business strike mintages with less demand for the proofs. There were 630 proof quarters minted, along with 700 dimes, 650 half dollars, and 700 Trade dollars. As before, the number of minor proof coins produced is not precisely known.

Cent PR63 Red and Brown. The lemon-gold and copper-orange surfaces are decidedly more Red than Brown, though a degree of turning is present. Strongly struck with a few pinpoint contact marks and light hairlines scattered in the fields.

Three Cent Nickel PR66 ★ Cameo. A stunningly contrasted example of an issue rarely found that way; NGC has graded just eight Cameo examples versus 212 non-Cameo coins, and this PR66 specimen is tied for numerically finest (10/09). Each side is essentially untoned save for a hint of gold on the reverse. Both sides show glassy mirrors, the obverse especially so, and richly frosted devices.

Five Cent Nickel PR65. Pale sky-blue and gold tints have settled over much of this gleaming Gem proof. The strike is strong throughout, and the eye appeal is a great match for the PR65 level of preservation.

Dime PR66 Cameo. Intensely frosted devices give way to silver-gray fields in the centers and deep blue, violet, and orange shadings close to the rims. A fantastically mirrored specimen with undeniable contrast and eye appeal. Census: 13 in 66 Cameo, 4 finer (10/09).

Twenty Cent PR64. Rich blue-green and violet-rose shadings converge on this strongly struck Choice proof from the first year of the twenty cent denomination. Pleasingly mirrored, though several grade-defining contact marks are noted just to the right of Liberty's head.

Quarter PR64 Cameo. This coin's contrast persists through considerable patina, light smoky-gray over the centers with reddish-orange and sage peripheral toning. A single set of hairlines is visible to the unaided eye in the right obverse field.

Half Dollar PR61. Though a number of short hairlines and contact marks are visible on each side, this gleaming silver-gray piece with gold-kissed rims offers strong visual appeal for the PR61 designation. A faint fingerprint overlaps Liberty's foot.

Trade Dollar PR63. Rich gunmetal-blue and silver-gray toning drapes the mirrors, and dots of deeper color are splashed about. Light hairlines in the fields, though the mildly frosted devices are free of all but the most minor contact marks.
From The Boca Collection, Part I. (Total: 8 coins)

A 15% BUYER'S PREMIUM ($14 MIN.) APPLIES TO ALL LOTS.

Eight-Piece 1876 Proof Set
The Famous Centennial Year

2021   1876 Eight-Piece Proof Set NGC. As the nation celebrated its centennial, more proof coins were minted than in any previous year, with at least 1,150 proofs struck of each silver denomination. Demand was heightened by those who sought souvenirs of the U.S. centennial. Now as then, the year 1876 holds importance for collectors, and the historical value of the 1876 coinage ensures that demand remains at high levels today.

Only minor varieties are known among the different denominations. Proof Trade dollars exist in two different hub combinations. The last 50 proof 1876 Trade dollars in our recent auctions include 47 examples of the Type One obverse, Type Two reverse combination, and only three examples of the Type Two obverse, Type Two reverse variant.

As each silver denomination has a slightly different mintage, it is possible that some individual coins were sold to centennial celebrants. It is also highly probable that a larger number of minor proof coins were minted, possibly as many as 2,000 examples of each denomination.

Cent PR63 Red and Brown. The obverse is light copper-yellow and green-gold with elements of salmon and violet, while the reverse has richer orange coloration. This charmingly toned Select piece shows a contact mark on Liberty's cheek, and a handful of hairlines are visible when the fields are closely inspected.

Three Cent Nickel PR64 Cameo. Occasional faint nickel-gray and blue elements visit gleaming fields that are otherwise brilliant. The portrait is richly frosted, and both sides show stronger contrast than the typical "Cameo" example of this issue has to offer.

Five Cent Nickel PR65 Cameo. Green-gold toning visits most of each side, with elements of nickel-gray, sage, and olive also present. The toning highlights the coin's cameo effect; rather than dulling the contrast, the patina lets the strongly mirrored fields stand out from the sharply struck devices.

Dime PR66 Cameo. Frosted snow-white devices and gleaming silver-white mirrors are the immediate attractions of this Cameo Premium Gem, and the scattered dots of gold and violet peripheral toning enhance the coin's essential contrast. Crisply struck and carefully preserved.

Twenty Cent PR65. A colorful Gem specimen of the second and last twenty cent proof date paired with a business strike. The obverse is split between electric-blue and green-gold color, while the reverse has bold royal-blue toning with violet and mint-green accents. Through the deep patina, a modicum of contrast persists.

Quarter PR65 Cameo. A hint of gold-orange toning at the left obverse rim adds a touch of color to this starkly contrasted Gem. Both sides have lovely fields, slightly watery on the obverse with more direct reflectivity on the reverse.

Half Dollar PR64. Both sides show considerable contrast, with the obverse distinctly Cameo in appearance, though this specimen's mint-accented gray-gold toning is deeper on the reverse, muting the effect there. Strongly mirrored fields show a few faint hairlines and points of contact.

Trade Dollar PR64. Type One Obverse, Type Two Reverse. Rich gold-gray toning overall with patches of deeper umber and blue. A few shallow flaws hidden beneath the toning preclude Gem status, but the eye appeal is strong for the grade.
From The Boca Collection, Part I. (Total: 8 coins)

A 15% BUYER'S PREMIUM ($14 MIN.) APPLIES TO ALL LOTS.

Important Eight-Piece 1877 Proof Set
Includes Cent, Three Proof-Only Issues

2022   Eight-Piece 1877 Proof Set NGC. Nationally, the economic crisis that began in 1873 continued through this year, and adversely affected business strike production and sales of proof coins at the Mint. Lack of demand for smaller denomination coinage created several rarities for collectors. The 1877 Indian cent had a sub-million coin mintage, while the nickel three cent piece and the Shield nickel were each only coined in proof format for collectors with an unknown actual mintage. The small or nonexistent mintage of the minor coins was a reflection of the Mint's huge stockpile of such coins.

Another proof-only denomination was the twenty cent piece, though unlike its three cent and five cent counterparts, it would never again be made for circulation. Unlike most other years, the mintage of silver proofs dated 1877 varied from 350 twenty cent pieces to 880 quarter dollars, but the number of pieces to actually leave the Mint is unknown. While 510 silver proof sets were actually delivered in 1877, according to Breen's *Proof Encyclopedia,* the number of sets actually *dated* 1877 is likely lower, with the 350 twenty cent coins providing a guideline.

In general, proof coins of 1877 and some later years were lower quality than in previous years. Finding high grade pieces and especially examples with cameo contrast can be a challenging endeavor. This set includes three such Cameo selections.

Cent PR65 Red and Brown. Thanks to the key-date status of this proof issue's associated business strike, demand is unceasing for this date. This Red and Brown Gem specimen is attractive and uncommonly colorful, with bold peach, magenta, and violet-blue shadings evident on each side. The first color prevails on the obverse, while the last dominates the reverse.

Three Cent Nickel PR64 Cameo. The first of three proof-only issues in this set, the 1877 is the most valuable three cent nickel proof in virtually all grades. This Choice coin has subtle but distinct contrast beneath layers of light lavender-pink and gold patina.

Five Cent Nickel PR65 Cameo. Brightly reflective with elements of gray-gold color over otherwise nickel-white surfaces. This proof-only date is the second most challenging proof Shield nickel issue, after the famously low-mintage 1867 With Rays pieces.

Dime PR63. The obverse has broad toning coverage with gold-gray, champagne, and blue-green colors, while the reverse has brighter centers and similar but bolder colors at the upper right periphery. Modestly hairlined for the grade.

Twenty Cent PR64. The first of two proof-only issues to end the denomination and the lowest-mintage proof, at just 350 pieces struck. This piece shows a delightful melange of blue-green and champagne-sunset toning over a gleaming silver-white base, with the color on the reverse slightly deeper.

Quarter PR64. Mildly contrasted but boldly appealing, this near-Gem offers impressive reflectivity beneath a thin veneer of cloud-white and liquid-gold toning. Small hairlines and a few points of contact are scattered in the fields.

Half Dollar PR65 Cameo. Strongly contrasted and beautifully patinated. Outer emerald toning fades through blue and violet into a rose-orange center on the obverse, a pattern repeated on the reverse and continued through gold and silver-white. A fantastic Gem specimen.

Trade Dollar PR64. The light blue-violet patina that appears in patches at parts of the margins becomes dotty as it spreads into the gleaming fields, which are silver-white elsewhere. A small contact mark is noted below star 8 on the obverse.
From The Boca Collection, Part I. (Total: 8 coins)

Memorable 1878 Silver-Minor Proof Set

2023   1878 10-Piece Proof Set NGC. The year 1878 saw a surge in proof coin production from the previous year, reflecting the Mint's anticipation of a large increase in demand from the growing number of coin collectors. Indian head cent, three cent nickel, and Shield nickel proof coinage amounted to 2,350 pieces each in 1878, up from 900 cents, 510+ three cent nickels, and the same number of Shield nickels in 1877. At least 800 of each denomination were included in the silver-minor proof sets assembled by the Mint for public sale. The remaining 1,550 of each base-metal coin were likely sold in three-piece minor coin proof sets or individually.

The number of proof dimes, quarters, and half dollars coined increased from 510 each in 1877 to 800 in 1878. Twenty cent pieces grew from 350 in 1877 to 600 in 1878, while the Trade dollar increased to 900 from 510 in 1877. The Morgan dollar, introduced in 1878, was initially minted with eight tail feathers (500 proofs), then with seven tail feathers (figures vary from 50 to 250 proofs). The Morgan dollar, according to Robert Julian in an article titled "The Silver Proof Coinage of 1878" published in the December 1986 *The Numismatist*, was excluded from the regular 1878 proof sets, but could be purchased separately beginning in mid-March.

Julian indicates that by January 29, 200 proof sets were delivered to the Mint treasurer for public sale at $4.50 each. The sets included one, three, five, ten, twenty, twenty five, and fifty cent pieces, and a Trade dollar. They sold quickly. The Mint coiner delivered another 100 sets on February 7, followed by 100 more on February 19 and 200 on March 18. Despite the brisk sales, Philadelphia Mint Superintendent James Pollock, believed the price was too high, and requested permission from Mint Director Henry Linderman to reduce it to $4. Pollock's request was granted on April 15.

The coiner delivered another 200 proof sets on May 17. That delivery included all coins except the twenty cent piece, which Congress had eliminated on May 2. At that point, however, sales slowed dramatically. Mint records indicate that 123 proof sets remained unsold at year's end.

Cent PR65 Red and Brown. Beginning in 1878, mintages for minor proof coinage were published in the Annual report of the director of the Mint. Richard Snow writes in his *Guide Book of Flying Eagle and Indian Head Cents* that:

"Earlier, mintages of Proof minor coins were calculated from sales records of minor coin sets plus the production of silver sets (which had been recorded since 1859), or simply guessed at."

Copper-gold luster endows this wonderful Gem, freckled with reddish-tan on the obverse and reddish-orange on the reverse. The design elements are sharply struck, including virtually full definition on the feather tips, diamonds, and the reverse leaf ribbing. Each side is devoid of marks or carbon and exhibits a good deal of field-motif contrast at various angles. Census: 56 in 65 Red and Brown, 6 finer (10/09).

Three Cent Nickel PR64. David Bowers, in his *United States Three-Cent and Five-Cent Pieces*, says of the proof-only 1878 nickel three cent pieces that they:

"... often occur with a full frosty 'Uncirculated' or business strike appearance, but as these were originally struck as Proofs and were included as part of the Proof sets of that year, they are designated as Proofs by cataloguers today."

Exquisitely struck design features, squared-off rims, bold dentilation, and mirrored fields conclusively affirm the proof status of this near-Gem specimen. Its motifs display considerable frost, and pronounced variance with the fields is evident over both sides, each of which is covered with a veneer of soft ice-blue and beige patina and devoid of mentionable contacts or flecks.

Five Cent Nickel PR66. Walter Breen in his proof encyclopedia writes of the 1878 proof-only nickel: "Only one variety seen; rare earliest state has shaft of 7 in lower loop of last 8." Gloria Peters and Cynthia Mohon (*Shield & Liberty Head Nickels*), on the other hand, state: "Experts do not agree that a genuine 'overdate' of this date exists." And Edward Fletcher opines in *The Shield Five Cent Series*: "Repunching is seen WEST inside the lower loop of the second 8," and further says: "This variety is repeatedly mistaken for an overdate."

The lower loop of the 8 of this Premium Gem does indeed show strong remnants of another figure to the right. Both sides show a combination of satiny luster and semiprooflike surfaces, which is typical for the issue. The essentially untoned obverse cedes to barely discernible ice-blue and beige on the reverse, and each side is impeccably preserved. The design elements are boldly defined throughout.

Dime PR64 Cameo. All 1878 proof dimes have a Type Two reverse, which shows the E in ONE significantly farther from the wreath than Type One, where the E nearly touches it. Cobalt-blue and purple toning gravitates to the obverse margin on this near-Gem while the same color palette is lighter in hue but more extensive on the reverse. Mirrored fields highlight the sharply struck design features. Census: 13 in 64 Cameo, 11 finer (10/09).

Twenty Cent PR65 Cameo. Counting from the left, the second and fourth leaves on the reverse are stemless and detached from the branch, a characteristic of the proof-only 1878 twenty cent. The fifth leaf on the current Gem displays a partial, but very faint stem. The frosty devices appear to float over deep watery fields and have benefited from a decisive strike. A small obverse rim mark at 9:30 and another on the left (facing) wrist are well within the parameters of the numerical grade and might help to identify the coin. Census: 13 in 65 Cameo, 7 finer (10/09).

Quarter PR64. Deep electric-blue, lavender, and orange toning covers most of the obverse fields leaving the center light champagne-gold, while most of the reverse takes on the latter coloration accented with deep electric-blue, lavender, and orange at the lower right border. A powerful strike leaves bold detail on the design features, enhancing even more the coin's delightful eye appeal. An occasional stray hairline joins the several light die polish lines on the obverse. Really a beautiful piece for a PR64. Census: 50 in 64, 30 finer (10/09).

Half Dollar PR64 Cameo. Type Two Reverse, with a pointed (not split) berry above the H in HALF; the vast majority of proofs, including the present near-Gem Cameo, are of this variety. It is worth mentioning, however, that another variety of proof half dollar was recently discovered with a Type One reverse that shows poorly defined leaves, an open bud above the H in HALF, and a die scratch in the shield on the extreme right side.

A solid strike manifests itself with nearly complete definition on the design elements that appear to be suspended above the deeply mirrored fields. Only the left (facing) claw and the arrow feathers exhibit minor softness. Whispers of gold patina around the margins is a tad deeper on the reverse. A few wispy handling marks barely prevent the attainment of PR65. Census: 23 in 64 Cameo, 22 finer (10/09).

Trade Dollar PR63 Cameo. Trade dollar mintage at Philadelphia in 1878 was limited to proofs. This is the first proof-only Trade dollar, and its 900-piece mintage is the lowest of the proof series (with the exception of the rare 1884 and 1885). All Trade dollars of 1878 and later years are Type Two/Two (the obverse ribbon-ends point downward and there is no berry under the claw).

David Bowers, in his *Silver Dollars and Trade Dollars of the United States*, writes that by early 1879 there were 219 unsold 1878-dated proof Trade dollars. He goes on to say: "These were distributed, presumably for bullion value or possibly face value, probably to coin dealers." Additionally, Bowers asserts: "Most of the 900 original Proof pieces still survive." This estimate may be somewhat high as NGC and PCGS have certified a little under 600 pieces, a number of which are undoubtedly resubmitted or cross-overed coins.

Both sides of this Select proof display excellent Cameo contrast, and each is nearly color free except for a couple of golden-tan toning streaks, the obverse ones accented with blue and purple. A well executed strike imparts sharp detail to the design features, including squared-off rims and bold dentils. Fine hairlines and a few minute marks in the fields define the numerical grade as does a minor reverse rim bruise at 10:30.

Morgan Dollar Eight Tail Feathers PR64. VAM-14.3. Attributed by the following: doubling on the upper underside of the date digits, numerous die polishing lines inside the recess of the cap, a die scratch between the left (facing) leg and tail, and doubling on bottom of reverse right leaves. Beautiful cobalt-blue, reddish-orange, and beige-gold patina exhibits slightly deeper hues on the obverse. Exquisitely struck, including the hair over Liberty's ear. While cameo contrast is minimal on this issue, this particular near-Gem specimen displays a fair degree of variance, especially when the coin is tilted slightly under a light source. A few trivial handling marks deny Gem classification. Census for Eight Tail Feathers: 34 in 64, 29 finer (10/09).

Morgan Dollar, Seven Tail Feathers, Reverse of 1878 PR65 Cameo. The arrow feathers are parallel and the eagle's breast is flat on this reverse. Leroy Van Allen and George Mallis (*Encyclopedia of Morgan and Peace Dollars*) write:

"Only 200 7 TF flat breast proofs were struck according to the coiner's daily delivery records. All of these are the VAM 131 variety with normal dies that did not have the doubling so common with this design type. Generally these proofs have only moderate contrast and are scarce."

Along a similar vein, David Bowers (*A Guide Book of Morgan Silver Dollars*) says:

"Striking is sometimes light above the ear. Medium to low cameo contrast. This variety will challenge you, not only to find one in the first place, but beyond that, to get one with good eye appeal. No wonder gems are apt to make auction bidders sit straight up in their chairs!"

Regarding Bowers' last point, the Gem Cameo in this set will do just that! Both sides yield stunning field-motif contrast, and an exacting strike delivers full delineation to both obverse and reverse devices. Hints of light gold color gravitate to the borders, but the coin initially presents as color free. A few wispy handling marks in the fields likely preclude an even finer numerical grade. Liberty's cheek and neck are remarkably smooth. All in all, this piece generates outstanding eye appeal. Census: 9 in 65 Cameo, 2 finer (10/09).
From The Boca Collection, Part I. (Total: 10 coins)

Seven-Piece 1879 Proof Set
Complete Save for Quarter

2024   Seven-Piece 1879 Proof Set NGC. The passage of the Bland-Allison Act of 1878 mandated the Treasury purchase between 2 and 4 million ounces of newly mined silver each month for conversion into coinage. The striking of silver dollars used more silver bullion than the production of smaller denomination coins. As a result, to satisfy the requirements of the Bland-Allison Act the various mints generated enormous numbers of silver dollars which were generally not needed for commercial transactions and ended up in storage, some for decades.

Consequently, the number of circulation strike quarters and halves produced between 1879 and 1890 is usually between 10,000 and 20,000 pieces. This lack of circulation strikes has led to great confusion over the years between early business strikes from newly polished dies and actual proofs-a problem that persists throughout the decade of the 1880s.

The actual number of 1879 proof sets struck and sold is unknown, as seen from this passage from Breen's 1988 *Complete Encyclopedia*: "Internal records of the Mint insist that only 250 proofs [quarters] were coined, but more survive; the older figure of 1,100 proof sets for the year is likely to include interpolated business strikes and/or mixed dates."

Note: This proof set has seven of the eight minor and silver issues. It does not include the quarter.

Cent PR65 Red and Brown. Decidedly more Red than Brown, with copper-orange and ruby shadings first and second in prominence. Sufficient quantities of olive and mahogany are present to preclude a fully Red designation. Well-defined overall, if a trifle weak on the diamonds, and pleasingly preserved.

Three Cent Nickel PR65. Elegant sky-blue and powder-blue shadings prevail over much of each side, though the upper obverse also displays a measure of sea-green. Attractively mirrored with appreciable contrast on the obverse, though the reverse falls short of a Cameo designation.

Five Cent Nickel PR66 Cameo. Both sides show toning accents, with golden glints visiting the obverse and small patches of cloud-white floating on the reverse. Appealingly contrasted with impressive fields and strongly struck devices that stand out despite a general lack of frost.

Dime PR64 Cameo. Lightly gold-toned in the same manner as the nickel, but with a silver-white base instead of nickel-white. A small spot is noted just above Liberty's left (facing) elbow, and the fields show minor hairlines and contact. Still, a highly appealing specimen for the grade.

Quarter not included.

Half Dollar PR62. Struck from heavily polished dies, as shown by the incomplete drapery off Liberty's arm. The surfaces show a few contact marks, including one below Liberty's left (facing) elbow, as well as numerous hairlines. The mirrors and peripheral toning redeem the eye appeal, however, especially the latter, which has shades of blue and gold.

Morgan Dollar PR66. Captivating patina is core to the eye appeal of this exquisite Premium Gem. Rich blue outer bands fade through violet and gold to pale pearl-gray centers. Frost on the inner devices hints at this specimen's past contrast.

Trade Dollar PR64 Cameo. Light silver-gray color overall with streaks of gold on both sides that deepen to orange at parts of the rims. The strongest contrast of any coin in this set, thanks to the intense mirrors and contrasting frost. Small contact marks are visible in the reverse fields.
From The Boca Collection, Part I. (Total: 7 coins)

Impressive Eight-Piece 1880 Proof Set
Featuring PR67 Cameo Morgan Dollar

2025   Eight-Piece 1880 Proof Set NGC. Silver dollar mintages remained high in 1880, and consequently the production of quarters and halves for circulation remained low. Proof sets were available from the Mint in several combinations. Minor sets were offered of the cent, three cent nickel, and nickel, with 2,600 of these sets sold outside the silver proof sets. Many of these minor coin proof sets were broken up for the nickel as the Shield nickel reached a series-low of 16,000 pieces in 1880, thus placing strong date pressure on the proofs of this date. Silver proof sets included a dime, quarter, half, Morgan dollar, and Trade dollar, and 1,355 of these sets were sold. Of course, gold sets were available also, but only 20 sets were coined.

In 1879 and 1880 there was a brief flurry of interest in speculating in proof Trade dollars. In June of this year Trade dollars were offered for retail sale for $2 apiece, while other proof sets were still available from the Mint at issued prices. This increased demand accounts for the significantly higher mintage of 1880 Trade dollars (1987 pieces), which was a series high, compared to 1,355 proofs of the Morgan design. This increase in collector and investor interest was commented on in *Mason's Coin Collectors' Herald*: "Some idea of the extensive interest taken in the collection of coins and medals may be gathered from the fact that in the year 1880 there were thirty-seven sales of coin collections in the city of New York alone. The total value of the sales was about $50,000. When to this is added the sales by regular dealers the total value of the sales of coins and medals foots up $100,000 a year."

Cent PR65 Red and Brown. Both sides show an appealing mixture of olive-brown, mahogany, and dusky copper-orange. A strongly struck and attractive Gem specimen.

Three Cent Nickel PR66 Cameo. Pale golden tints accent the otherwise nickel-white fields. The devices are snowy, which sets up excellent contrast with the fields. From heavily polished dies, as evidenced by the lapping on the reverse ribbon.

Five Cent Nickel PR66. Canary-yellow and nickel-gray shadings combine on this shining Premium Gem. Above-average definition and preservation translate into powerful eye appeal.

Dime PR62. Boldly struck and richly toned. Outer sea-green color cedes to a mixture of blue and violet on each side. A number of scattered hairlines in the fields preclude Select status.

Quarter PR65 Cameo. First in a series of four silver pieces with amazing contrast. Light golden tints over otherwise silver-white surfaces add color to the piece, though a few splashes of milky patina are also present. The devices are beautifully frosted.

Half Dollar PR65 Cameo. More colorful but no less contrasted than its Cameo fellows, this piece has blue, violet, and gold outer toning around minimally patinated centers. Exquisitely frosted devices offer impressive design definition.

Morgan Dollar PR67 Cameo. The star of the set, without question. The obverse contrast borders on black-and-white, and that of the reverse is nearly its equal. Gleaming mirrors are untoned save for a few small dots of milky toning that are generally unobtrusive. A stunning Superb Gem.

Trade Dollar PR63 Cameo. Both sides offer an impressive cameo effect with minimal toning visible. The reverse shows a long, thin line in the lower right field that contributes to the grade assigned.
From The Boca Collection, Part I. (Total: 8 coins)

A 15% BUYER'S PREMIUM ($14 MIN.) APPLIES TO ALL LOTS.

Attractive 1881 Proof Set
Six of Eight Pieces Cameo

2026   1881 Eight-Piece Proof Set NGC. As with 1880, many of the three-coin bronze and copper-nickel proof sets issued by the Mint were broken up for the Shield nickel. The nickel had a circulation mintage of only 68,800 pieces—a far cry from the 16,000 coins struck the previous year, but it was still a difficult coin to locate in circulation. In the 19th century, collectors took little note of proofs or business strikes, just as they little noted mintmarks. If a collector needed a date for a set, a proof would do as well as a circulation strike. This thinking persisted until recent decades when more in-depth studies were made and relative rarities of both proofs and business strikes were published. As a result, most original proof sets were broken up decades ago for the low mintage silver coins which were generally not available as circulation strikes.

As with most dates in the 1880s, it is difficult to distinguish between proofs and prooflike business strikes. Because of the low mintage of coins struck for circulation the initial die polish remained on many of these pieces. As noted in Breen (1977), the number of complete silver proof sets with both the Trade and Morgan dollar is not definitely known. Possibly as few as 925 sets were struck that contained both, and this number presumably also includes the minor coins.

Cent PR64 Red and Brown. Considerable copper-orange remains on the obverse, while the reverse's dusky mahogany color is almost uniform. Crisply detailed with a small flyspeck noted to the left of Liberty's forehead.

Three Cent Nickel PR66 Cameo. While this issue is not under the same pressure from date collectors as some other later three cent nickel years, the appeal of an attractive Cameo specimen like this Premium Gem cannot be denied. Both the watery fields and amply frosted devices show peach and gold accents.

Nickel PR65 Cameo. Aside from a few tiny flyspecks in the fields, this Cameo Gem is largely problem-free. Each side combines strong mirrors and boldly struck, moderately frosted devices for pleasing contrast.

Dime PR65. Strongly frosted devices hint at past contrast, but it is the patina, electric-blue at the borders with amethyst and rose centers, that defines this Gem's eye appeal. Pleasingly preserved beneath the toning.

Quarter PR64 Cameo. While the dime is wildly toned, the rest of the silver coins in the set have pale to moderate tan-gold patina. This quarter is faintly toned at the margins, yielding to a strongly contrasted center in silver-white. Well-preserved save for a few faint scuffs and contact marks in the obverse fields.

Half PR64 Cameo. Slightly broader peripheral toning than seen on the quarter, with additional dusky gray elements in a vertical stripe at the left reverse. Strongly mirrored with great eye appeal despite the presence of a few hairlines.

Morgan Dollar PR65 Cameo. Profoundly reflective with a slight golden cast to the fields. Sharply struck devices are moderately frosted. On the reverse, a small planchet flaw below the G in GOD does not affect the grade.

Trade Dollar PR63 Cameo. The champagne toning that bathes the fields helps the immensely frosted devices stand out. Strongly appealing for the Select designation, though light hairlines running through the obverse fields render the grade accurate.
From The Boca Collection, Part I. (Total: 8 coins)

A 15% BUYER'S PREMIUM ($14 MIN.) APPLIES TO ALL LOTS.

Attractive Eight-Piece 1882 Proof Set
All Pieces PR64 or Finer

2027   Eight-Piece 1882 Proof Set NGC. Low mintages for business strike coins continued in 1882 as over the past several years; and in fact, this year marked a series low for half dollar coinage with only 4,400 pieces struck (a mintage that was duplicated two years later). The shortage of circulating coins of this year was noted in the June issue of *Mason's Coin Collectors' Magazine*:

"The year 1882 is creeping on towards the end, and yet there are no U.S. silver half dollars, quarters or dimes coined for general circulation this year, and it is not likely there will be, and but a few thousand struck off for collectors in December; hence, the reflective collector will perceive the necessity of keeping the matter in mind, else he will pay twice the intrinsic value of the coins in January, 1883, when they can be had at par in December, 1882."

For most contemporary collectors, proofs were the only alternative for coinage dated 1882. Breen states that some 2,000 minor proof sets were sold separately, and another 1,100 minor coin sets were included with the silver proof sets.

Cent PR64 Red. Vibrant copper-gold surfaces show lovely lemon and orange accents. A strongly struck specimen that is immensely appealing for the grade, though a few flecks are visible and a handful of hairlines preclude an even finer designation.

Three Cent Nickel PR66. Strong gold and peach overtones influence the small areas of nickel-gray still visible on this lovely Premium Gem. Well-defined overall with only slight softness on Liberty's hair. Surface quality is excellent, as is the visual appeal.

Five Cent Nickel PR66. The obverse alone would be a strong candidate for a Cameo designation, but the green-gold toning that graces much of that side becomes thicker on the reverse. Solid design definition, including on the often-weak reverse stars.

Dime PR64. A gleaming near-Gem specimen with surprisingly strong contrast for a coin not designated as Cameo. The centers are essentially silver-white, while the margins show elements of blue, gold, and violet. On the reverse, a few small contact marks are scattered among the widespread planchet flaws.

Quarter PR65 Cameo. Incredible mirrors fuel this Gem's classic Cameo look, heightening the texture on the attractively frosted devices. Both sides exhibit a light golden peripheral aura, which extends slightly into the fields on the reverse.

Half Dollar PR64 Cameo. Both sides show a progression from silver-white to champagne color, generally top to bottom on the obverse and right to left on the reverse. Strongly struck with slightly watery fields that show a handful of faint hairlines.

Morgan Dollar PR64 Cameo. Gold and orange patina of varying intensity visits the margins of this gleaming near-Gem, while the centers are minimally toned save for suggestions of cloud-gray color. Sharply struck with a bold cameo effect.

Trade Dollar PR65. A colorful Gem that retains its sense of frostiness on the devices, and though the deep patina (variously violet, gold-gray, rose-orange, and blue) obscures most of the fields, the lighter areas hint at the piece's past contrast. Excellent preservation and eye appeal.
From The Boca Collection, Part I. (Total: 8 coins)

Memorable 1883 10-Piece Proof Set

2028   1883 10-Piece Proof Set NGC. This year is noteworthy for the three variants of nickels produced. The year began with the final issue of the Shield design with 5,419 proofs struck. Curiously, Shield nickel proofs were struck and delivered at the same time as the new No CENTS design by Charles Barber, and a slightly smaller number were produced with 5,219 proofs coined of this initial Liberty nickel type. Lacking a denomination proved a major design oversight for the newly introduced nickel, and an altered design with the word CENTS on the lower reverse rim was introduced later in the year. An even larger number of these were minted with 6,783 proofs believed struck. According to Breen (1977):

> "Apparently the earliest minor sets had only the shield nickels, and those of fall and winter had all three. In the A.M. Smith hoard, obtained by this veteran Mint publicist directly from the Mint, there were 34 minor sets, of which two had only the shield nickel, 6 only the shield and No CENTS, and the other 26 all three nickels."

The most reliable figure for silver proof sets (10 coins, including the cent and nickels) is 1,039 sets. At least 52, possibly more, of these sets lacked the Trade dollar. Proofs from 1883 are important to the collector as so few circulation strikes were made, as in previous years. Again, Mint resources were diverted to striking mostly silver dollars that were required under the Bland-Allison Act.

Cent PR64 Red and Brown. The pink-orange of the obverse is only slightly muted, though the reverse has much deeper mahogany and pumpkin hues. Sharply impressed with only a few modest flaws in the fields that account for the grade.

Three Cent Nickel PR66. With a proof mintage greater than that of the corresponding business strike, the 1883 is best known as a proof type issue, but this gold-kissed Premium Gem specimen is easily appreciated on its own merits. Uncommonly strong mirrors for the series.

Shield Nickel PR66. Light peach toning over each side, slightly stronger on the obverse. Pleasingly luminous with mild field-to-device contrast. An excellent strike by the standards of the issue with eye appeal to match.

No Cents Liberty Nickel PR66. Pastel-yellow and cloud-white toning graces the fields, while the sharp devices show minimal patina. Distinctly contrasted, almost to a Cameo level, as shown by comparison with the next coin.

With Cents Liberty Nickel PR65 Cameo. A lovely Cameo coin with splashes of peach-gold over faintly nickel-blue surfaces. Strongly struck and appealing, this Gem shows only a few tiny flaws in the fields that preclude an even finer designation.

Dime PR66 ★ Cameo. Each side is beautifully contrasted beneath concentric blue, peach, and champagne toning. Exquisitely detailed with marvelous frost on the figure of Liberty, a flat-out gorgeous specimen. One of just four Cameo proofs for the year awarded the Star designation by NGC (10/09).

Quarter PR66 Cameo. Minimally toned centers give way to reddish-orange at the obverse periphery and a touch of gold on the reverse. Strongly contrasted with a small planchet flaw noted near star 13 on the obverse. NGC has graded just six numerically finer Cameo coins (10/09).

Half Dollar PR65. Though rich, faintly gold-gray toning drapes each side of this Gem proof, frost on the devices suggests this coin's original contrast. Boldly impressed with excellent eye appeal for the grade.

Trade Dollar PR66 Cameo. A whisper of champagne graces the rims of this Trade dollar, from the last proof-only issue made available to the wider collecting audience. Profoundly mirrored with a small planchet flaw visible in the field over the eagle's neck.

Morgan Dollar PR66 ★ Cameo. This boldly contrasted Premium Gem proof makes a fantastic capstone to the set. Profoundly mirrored fields show only a few tiny dots of milky toning, and Liberty's broad cheek has rich and unbroken frost. NGC has graded just six numerically finer Cameo specimens, none of which were awarded the Star designation (10/09).
From The Boca Collection, Part I. (Total: 10 coins)

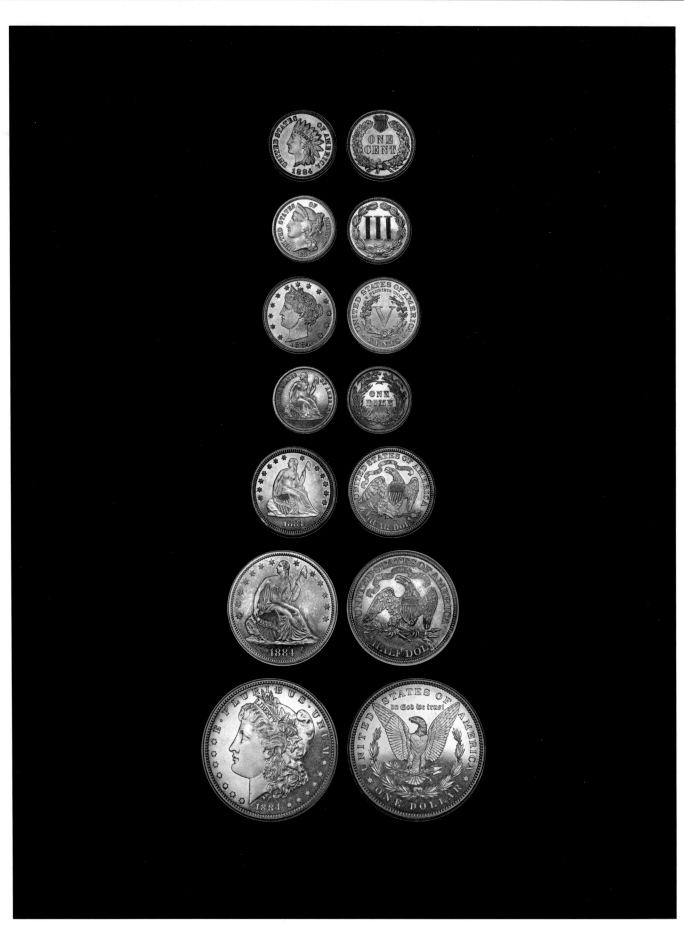

Seven-Piece 1884 Proof Set
Featuring a PR66 ★ Half

2029   1884 Seven-Piece Proof Set NGC. As the mints continued to churn out silver dollars, much-needed quarters and half dollars languished with extremely low mintages. Half dollar production equaled the number struck two years previously with a mere 4,400 coins minted for commercial usage. Quarters were also limited in number with just 8,000 circulation strikes. In each case, only 875 proofs were coined, a number equal to the quantity of silver proof sets of this year. Minor (three-coin) proof sets were struck in considerably larger numbers with a total of 3,942 pieces made of each of the denominations. Those not included in the silver proof sets were sold as minor coin proof sets.

Because the output of business strike quarters and halves was so low in 1884, date pressure was considerable and most of the silver proof sets were broken up for these two denominations. Early circulation strikes and proofs can be confusing, and diagnostics are not conclusive on the half dollars. It appears that both proofs and business strikes may have been produced from the same dies as each show minute repunching on the base of the 4 and above the base of the 1.

Cent PR64 Red and Brown. Both sides have intense copper-orange color with only slight evidence of turning, though there is enough violet, olive, and mahogany to warrant a Red and Brown designation. Boldly impressed with a faint fingerprint visible above the headdress.

Three Cent Nickel PR65. Both sides show pale blue patina with an underlying layer of faint nickel-gray. The obverse shows strong contrast between the watery mirrors and the delicately frosted portrait of Liberty, but the reverse falls short of compelling a Cameo designation.

Five Cent Nickel PR65. Swaths of light gold color also show hints of lemongrass. This Gem proof is well-defined in the centers, though the peripheral stars on the obverse show significant striking softness. Still, a carefully preserved coin beneath the patina.

Dime PR64. An intriguing near-Gem proof that is attractively, if asymmetrically toned. The obverse has a traditional concentric look, with grass-green at parts of the borders that fades through blues into plum and dusky rose shadings. On the reverse, bold sapphire and amethyst jewel-tones are present at the left and right margins. These fade into gold with a hard stop at the brilliant center.

Quarter PR63. The devices show appreciable frost, but only the obverse approaches cameo contrast. That side has a light gold wash overall that deepens into peach-tan and blue-green at the right obverse. The reverse has a broad center in faded baby-blue that yields to green near the rims.

Half Dollar PR66 ★. Fantastic toning is key to this Premium Gem proof's eye appeal. On the obverse, an outer band of jade-green leads into a ring of blue surrounding a center that combines violet and gold elements. The reverse has electric-blue peripheral toning surrounding pink and white patina. Carefully preserved and all-around outstanding.

Morgan Dollar PR65 Cameo. This set ends with the Morgan dollar, since the Trade dollars dated 1884 were not included in the year's proof sets (and only 10 were struck, likely well after that year). This distinctly contrasted Gem offers thickly frosted devices that post a stark contrast with the gleam of the fields. Peripheral gold-orange (and on the obverse, also blue) patina highlights the contrast of the nearly untoned centers.

From The Boca Collection, Part I. (Total: 7 coins)

A 15% BUYER'S PREMIUM ($14 MIN.) APPLIES TO ALL LOTS.

Pleasing 1885 Silver-Minor Proof Set

2030   1885 Seven-Piece Proof Set NGC. As in the previous year, 1885 proof sets were broken up because of date pressure from low-mintage business strikes. The best known is the series-key Liberty nickel. Only 1.4 million circulation strike nickels were produced, which gave it the lowest mintage (to that point) and the coin to have in the new and widely collected series. This demand also placed tremendous date pressure on the 3,790 proof strikings. Similarly, the three cent nickel is almost only available as a proof as there were only 1,000 business strikes coined. This same date pressure was seen on the quarters and halves, as in previous years. Only 13,600 circulation strike quarters and 5,200 circulation strike halves were produced vs. 940 and 930 proofs, respectively. The usual blurring of appearance is seen on early circulation strikes and proofs of this low-mintage year. Unlike in 1884, though, diagnostics for all denominations of proofs are well known. According to Breen (1977) a total of 3,790 minor proof sets were struck, and 930 of those sets were included in the silver proof sets for the year.

One Cent PR65 Brown. Deep bluish-purple patination dominates this glossy Gem, accented with olive-green at the margins. As with many 1884 proof cents, this interesting coloration on 1885 pieces likely came from Wayte Raymond's stock in mint wrappers (Breen 1977). An exacting strike imparts sharp detail to the design motifs, including the feather tips, diamonds, shield, and leaf ribbing. Well cared for surfaces are free of mentionable contact marks or spots.

Three Cent Nickel PR65. Both sides of this Gem three cent nickel specimen display considerable field-motif variance at various angles and possess a thin coat of soft ice-blue and violet color. A decisive strike manifests itself in sharp definition on the design elements, including the lines of the III denomination. A few tiny flecks are undisturbing.

Five Cent Nickel PR66 Cameo. Reflective fields highlight the frosty devices, all of which exhibit a sharp strike, including the hair above Liberty's ear and the leaves and ear of corn left of the bow knot. Freckles of light gray are visible under high magnification and well cared for surfaces reveal no mentionable blemishes. A readily available issue right through Premium Gem. Cameos, however, are difficult to acquire in all grade levels. Census: 27 in 66 Cameo, 15 finer (11/09).

Dime PR65. Breen (1977) writes of 1885 proof dimes that "mediocre strikes" are frequent. This lovely Gem offers an above average impression. Liberty's gown and shield detail are strong. Only the hair atop Liberty's head and a few elements in the upper left part of the wreath are a tad incomplete. Splashes of cobalt-blue, lavender, and gold-brown are a bit deeper in hue and more extensive on the obverse. Nicely preserved throughout.

Quarter PR63. Deep electric-blue, lavender, and golden-orange toning greets the observer of this Select quarter. This color palette covers the entire reverse, while being confined to the left and bottom border of the obverse. Luminous surfaces exhibit sharply struck devices, though the centrils of the stars along the right margin are soft. Reflective fields highlight the motifs at most angles, particularly on the obverse. Faint hairlines in the right obverse fields barely prevent the attainment of a finer grade.

Half Dollar PR61. Aqua-blue and deep violet patina concentrates around the borders of this half leaving the central areas brilliant. Only the hair on the top of Liberty's head and the eagle's left (facing) claw reveal a touch of incompleteness, and mirrored fields yield mild yet pleasing contrast with the lightly frosted devices. Fine hairlines in the fields appear to preclude a finer grade. Nevertheless, a rather attractive coin. That said, one might wonder whether this piece has claims to a finer grade.

Morgan Dollar PR65. Breen (1977) says of the 1885 Morgan dollar proof that many have been excessively scrubbed. Happily this Gem is a notable exception. Its surfaces are completely devoid of even the hint of hairlines or abusive contact marks. Indeed, Liberty's cheek and neck are remarkably smooth. Splashes of cobalt-blue, lavender, and gold-tan patination visit each side and a solid strike delivers strong definition to the design elements. These factors combine to generate outstanding eye appeal.
From The Boca Collection, Part I. (Total: 7 coins)

Eight Piece 1886 Proof Set Including
Both Indian Cent Varieties

2031   Eight-Piece 1886 Proof Set. This year, like all the other years from this decade, is notable for low mintage business strikes that drive demand for proofs. Once again the Liberty nickel had an impressively low mintage, this time 3.3 million pieces were struck. This was more than twice as many as the 1885 business strike nickels, but still low enough to place this date in the key category and subject extra date demand on the proofs. The three cent nickel is only available with this date in proof format as there were no circulation strikes produced. Once again, the quarters and halves were low mintage issues as business strikes, each had only 5,000 pieces produced. A new hub was introduced for the Indian cent, and each variant is known as a proof (and represented in this set).

A record-breaking 4,290 three-coin minor proof sets were struck in 1886, most of which were obviously broken up for the nickel and three cent nickel. Of the four-coin silver proof sets, only 886 sets were produced. Walter Breen states that the silver sets produced in the fourth quarter (261 sets) "went as Christmas presents, that being then an apparently common pattern."

Cent (Type 1) PR64 Brown NGC. The more accessible of the two proof cent issues for the year, offered here with glimpses of copper-orange at the obverse margins but dusky violet and cinnamon-brown color elsewhere. Sharply struck and decidedly appealing.

Cent (Type 2) PR66 Brown NGC. Easily the most expensive proof Indian cent issue after 1877, and arguably the most important, though an exact mintage figure is unknown. Though both sides show deep peach, blue, and sienna color overall, the obverse also shows a dramatic, near-vertical streak of copper-gold.

Three Cent Nickel PR66 Cameo NGC. The last of the proof-only three cent nickel issues, the 1886 was more heavily minted than its two predecessors put together. Still, high-end specimens such as this Cameo Premium Gem are highly prized. Gleaming nickel-white surfaces show just a hint of golden color and a few scattered flyspecks.

Five Cent Nickel PR66 NGC. Dappled green-gold, baby-blue, and lavender hues drape this charming example. Sharply struck but with a certain level of rotational luster in addition to the reflectivity, which might allow this specimen to better pass as a business strike in an otherwise circulation-finish set.

Dime PR64 PCGS. Boldly impressed and fantastically mirrored through rich cloud-white toning that takes on glints of gold. Well-defined devices have considerable frost, though the patina dampens this specimen's potential contrast.

Quarter PR65 Cameo NGC. A charming Gem, largely untoned through the fields with fantastic reflectivity and delightfully contrasting frost over the portrait and eagle. Splashes of umber and violet-gold are visible at parts of the upper rims.

Half Dollar PR62 NGC. Sharply struck with antique-gold color overall that thickens to khaki-tan and violet at parts of the margins. The moderately hairlined reverse is edged in cobalt-blue.

Morgan Dollar PR65 NGC. Remarkably strong contrast for a coin not recognized as Cameo. Perhaps the gauzy patina over the obverse fields accounts for this, but even that side has excellent mirrors through the toning, not to mention impressively frosted devices.
From The Boca Collection, Part I. (Total: 8 coins)

Seven-Piece 1887 Proof Set Including
1887/6 Three Cent Nickel

2032   Seven-Piece 1887 Proof Set NGC. The 1887 proof set is a seven-coin grouping that is in many ways a microcosm of the coinage activities in the United States as a whole during the year. It is one of the more popular and interesting of the decade, containing one of two three cent nickel varieties (1887/6 overdate or the non-overdate) along with the popular Seated Liberty quarter and half dollar, both of which have low-mintage business-strike counterparts.

This was another year in which the Philadelphia Mint was churning out unwanted millions of Morgan silver dollars, to the detriment of most other coinage denominations. Accordingly, the business strike Seated Liberty quarter and half dollar have minuscule mintages of 10,000 and 5,000, respectively. While the business strikes of both denominations can be found in high grades, their scarcity does exert moderate upward pressure on proofs of the year. The proof silver coins, dime through silver dollar, each were issued to the extent of 710 pieces. The minor coinage sets, Indian cent, three cent nickel, and Liberty five cent nickel, saw production of 2,960 coins apiece.

As mentioned, the 1887/6 three cent nickel is an overdate produced only in proof format and comprising a majority of proofs, with the non-overdate 1887 proof correspondingly rarer. Breen comments:

"The earliest die state of this popular proof-only overdate is quite rare, showing plain impressions of both 8's and *almost the entire* 6 in addition to the final 887, respectively at bases of 8's and within them, occupying almost the entire space below arm of 7. I have seen very few of these. Dies clashed and were drastically repolished. The vast majority, struck after repolishing, show only part of left curve of 6 below arm of 7, sometimes only a small fragment, sometimes also with part of loop of 6, but always weak in this state. Probably 3/4, possibly as many as 4/5 of the extant proof 1887 3¢ nickels are from this obverse die, in its later states."

Interestingly, the Philadelphia and New Orleans Morgan dollars also have popular 1887/6 varieties, but conversely to the three cent nickel, the overdates are unknown as proof strikings. While the business-strike 1887-Ps had a bank-bag-busting production of 19.9 million pieces, the proofs had a mere 710 coins struck. Most show little to no contrast, but offer a strong strike.

Cent PR64 Brown. Dusky mahogany surfaces show glimpses of rose and pumpkin-orange. A luminous and pleasing Choice proof that shows a handful of faint but grade-defining hairlines.

Overdated Three Cent Nickel PR65. Prominently overdated with a bold "wedge" from the 6 visible in the space not taken up by the 7. Impressively mirrored with areas of canary-yellow over otherwise nickel-white surfaces.

Five Cent Nickel PR66. A well struck and attractive Premium Gem proof. The centers are minimally toned, while the margins show slight patina in the gold-to-orange spectrum, most visible and deepest along the rim to the left of the date.

Dime PR66 ★ Cameo. A star of this set, boldly contrasted with wonderful eye appeal. The mirrors are stunning, as is the frostiness of the devices. The peripheral toning, blue and gold-orange on the obverse with champagne echoes on the reverse, enhances the cameo effect and the visual appeal.

Quarter PR64. Strongly contrasted on the obverse, though the blue and violet patina that covers most of the obverse fields also appears across virtually the entire reverse, including the devices. Small hairlines are hidden under the toning.

Half Dollar PR64 Cameo. Antique-gold and blue peripheral shadings frame minimally toned centers that present delightful contrast. Strongly sculpted, thickly frosted devices stand out from the impressively reflective fields.

Morgan Dollar PR65. While the frost on the devices is not heavy, this coin has immediately apparent contrast, making the lack of a Cameo designation something of a mystery. Rich orange-gold patina gives way to silver-white at the centers, after passing through an intermediate band of champagne on the reverse.
From The Boca Collection, Part I. (Total: 7 coins)

Choice and Better Seven-Piece 1888 Proof Set
Featuring PR67 ★ Quarter

2033   Seven-Piece 1888 Proof Set NGC. By 1888 the three cent nickel had long since outlived its usefulness, and in the following year it would be eliminated entirely. Interestingly, the 1888 and 1889 three cent nickels had *higher* business-strike and proof mintages than the corresponding numbers for 1887. For 1888 there were 36,501 three cent nickel business strikes produced, along with 4,582 proofs. The Indian cents of this year are somewhat carelessly struck up as a rule, and full Red coins are quite elusive. Some of the Liberty nickel proofs show a doubled date.

The proof silver coins, dime through dollar, had mintages of 832 coins each. The proof Seated dime's corresponding circulation strikes had a plentiful mintage of nearly 5.5 million pieces. On the other hand, the proof Seated quarter and half dollar proofs are always popular, due to the low mintages of their business-strike counterparts: 10,001 and 12,001 coins, respectively. This continues a long string of low-mintage Seated quarters and halves that began in 1879, the year after the introduction of the Morgan dollar.

Bowers' Morgan dollar *Guide Book* (third edition) notes that one of the "at least two" obverse dies used in this year shows slight repunching of the date. More cogently, Bowers writes of the proof Morgan: "Lightly struck at the centers. Low contrast. About this time the Mint became sloppy in the making of Proofs, and not long afterward dealer Harlan P. Smith filed a formal complaint. Still, Proofs of the era beginning about now are not on a visual par with those earlier in the decade."

Cent PR64 Brown. Captivating for a Brown coin with iridescent toning that includes dusky peach as well as light sea-green, blue, and deep plum. Sharply struck with immense eye appeal for the grade.

Three Cent Nickel PR66. Pale aqua and golden tints embrace each side of this elegant Premium Gem proof. Well struck overall with a hint of elegant satin on the portrait.

Five Cent Nickel PR66. Thin veils of cloud-white toning show glints of gold-green close to the rims. A sharply struck and immensely reflective beauty of undeniable quality.

Dime PR64 ★. A few tiny hairlines and contact marks are visible on this near-Gem, but the coin's sheer eye appeal renders these flaws all but irrelevant. The obverse has stunning cobalt and gold-orange peripheral patina around a near-brilliant center, with the latter color echoing at the reverse margins.

Quarter PR67 ★. Exquisitely preserved and stunningly toned. The obverse's peripheral blue and central gold-orange shadings offer a window into the coin's original contrast, but the reverse is toned all the way across in cobalt and sunset-orange. The sole PR67 example in the NGC *Census Report* awarded the Star designation, with none finer in the contrast category (11/09).

Half Dollar PR65 Cameo. Unlike the previous two silver pieces, which were toned too heavily to earn a Cameo designation, this Gem specimen has only light green-gold and mint shadings which extend into the fields. Away from the strongly contrasted centers, deeper ruby-plum color appears on parts of the rims.

Morgan Dollar PR66 Cameo. The pale blue shadings over the strongly mirrored reverse fields enhance the inherent contrast of this stunning example. Icy white devices have substantially above-average definition for the issue.

From The Boca Collection, Part I. (Total: 7 coins)

Seven-Piece 1889 Proof Set
Four Pieces Gem or Better

2034   Seven-Piece 1889 Proof Set. The 1889 minor proof set contains the Indian Head cent and the last of the three cent nickel issues, along with the Liberty five cent nickel. Only 18,125 three cent nickel business strikes were produced, as compared with 3,336 proofs each of the cent and Liberty nickel—and 3,436 of the three cent nickel proofs, concerning which Breen says that "the extra hundred appear to mark the final issue of this denomination."

The Indian cent business strikes had an enormous production of nearly 50 million pieces, but the proof cents of 1889 are rare either in full Red or with Cameo designation. Some of the three cent nickel proofs show bold recutting on the 1 in the date. Breen comments concerning both the 1888 and 1889 Liberty nickel issues that they seldom show brilliant mirrors, being possibly from a slightly different crystalline structure in the nickel alloy that prevents such an appearance.

The Seated quarter and half dollar, as in recent years past, had few circulation strikes produced, a situation that increases the price pressure on nice proofs of the year. The 1889 Seated quarter and Seated half each saw only 12,000 business strikes made. The Morgan silver dollar, as in other years, was the culprit, which under the inflexible Bland-Allison Act of 1878 was responsible for nearly 35 million pieces coined in this year, at four different mints. Bowers writes that the Morgan dollar proofs of this issue show an average strike that is usually weak at the centers, with medium to low contrast.

Cent PR65 Red and Brown PCGS. A charming Gem offering a range of colors, from pale copper-orange through sunset and into mahogany with occasional splashes of mint-green. Excellent strike and surface preservation.

Three Cent Nickel PR65 NGC. This Gem offers a fitting end to the run of proof three cent nickels. Both sides are pale pearl-gray with whispers of golden color. The portrait is softly frosted, though the fine hair detail found on the sharpest specimens is absent here.

Five Cent Nickel PR64 NGC. Highly appealing for a "mere" near-Gem proof. Light nickel-blue surfaces show distinct green-gold accents at the lower reverse. Both sides show a handful of hairlines and flyspecks, and there is a tiny contact mark above the V on the reverse.

Dime PR66 NGC. Both sides offer colorful and contrasting toning. The obverse is deep blue to the left and predominantly silver-white on the right, with a faint fingerprint visible there. The reverse has golden color over the inner field with deeper blue-influenced hues on the wreath and beyond.

Quarter—Improperly Cleaned—Proof NGC. Better eye appeal than the Improperly Cleaned designation might suggest, though there are strong hairlines in the mirrored fields. Surfaces are largely silver-white with splashes of orange. A broad but shallow planchet flaw is noted to the left of the date.

Half Dollar PR64 NGC. An attractive Choice proof with significant contrast, though not quite to the Cameo level. Gold and orange peripheral tints yield swiftly to near-brilliance in the fields, while the well-defined devices are mildly frosted. Minor hairlines and contact marks, most noticeably to the right of Liberty.

Morgan Dollar PR65 NGC. A captivating Gem with considerable frostiness on the devices. While the obverse's blue-accented surfaces show dappled orange and silver-white color not conducive to contrast, the reverse, toned only with gold-orange at the margins, offers a fully Cameo experience.
From The Boca Collection, Part I. (Total: 7 coins)

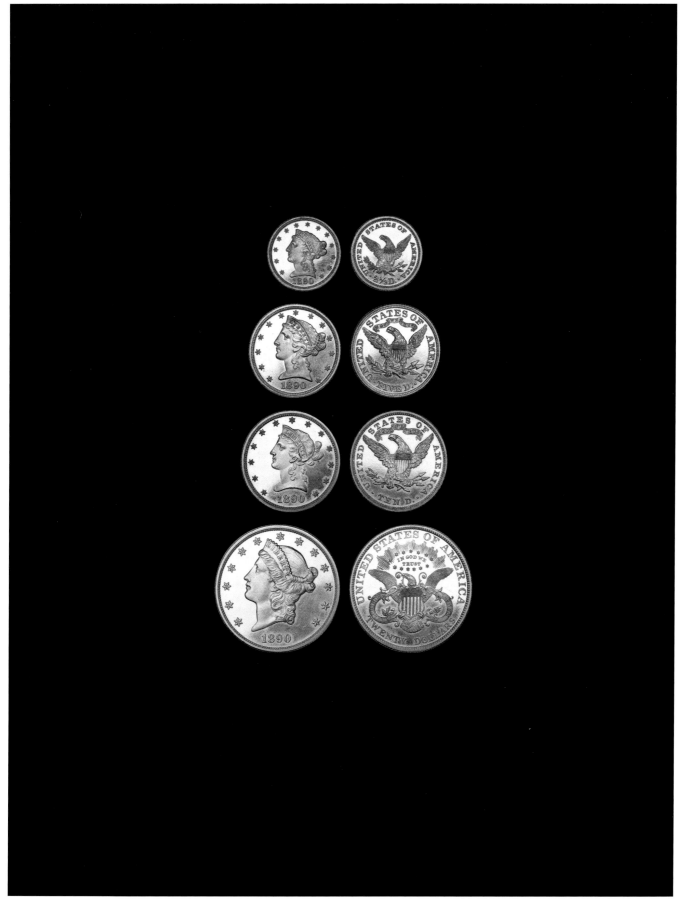

Complete NGC Certified 1890 Proof Set with Gold

2035   1890 10-Piece Proof Set NGC. The minor proof sets of 1890 contain only the Indian cent and Liberty nickel (as the three cent nickel had been discontinued a year earlier), both produced to the extent of 2,740 pieces. Richard Snow's Indian cent *Guide Book* makes an interesting comment regarding 1890 proof cents:

> "This date is readily available in most grades except in full red. The number of Proofs minted during the 1890s slides to new lows. Collectors mistakenly equate the more common dates struck for circulation as being common in Proof as well. The truth is that many of the dates in the 1890s and 1900s are very tough to find in gem Proof."

Breen's *Proof Encyclopedia* notes that the Liberty nickels of 1890 are "not found with the intractable dullness of 1888-9. The mint must have found another supplier of nickel blanks." The Seated dime, quarter, and half dollar each saw a proof mintage of only 590 pieces. And as before, the Seated dime proof had a plentiful number of business-strike counterparts—which was not at all the case for the Seated quarter or half dollar. Seated quarters struck for circulation would total only 80,000 coins, along with 12,000 Seated halves. Proof Morgan dollars produced in this year again feature slight to moderate contrast, although the strike is a bit better on average than the year before.

The present proof set also includes the gold proofs, including the quarter eagle, half eagle, eagle, and double eagle. (The gold dollar and three dollar were discontinued by the Act of September 26, 1890, the same Act that discontinued the three cent nickel.) As even many casual numismatists know, proof gold of the 19th century is the *crème de la crème* of U.S. numismatics, and among the most in-demand types of American coinage. Heritage is proud to offer this complete 10-piece 1890 proof set. To say that we expect fierce bidding for this lot is a considerable understatement.

The quarter eagle gold proof has a recorded mintage of 93 pieces, and a number of attractive, high-grade examples of the issue survive. Perhaps 35 to 40 survive in all proof grades. Circulation strike quarter eagles were produced to the extent of only 8,720 pieces, so many such pieces show prooflike surfaces. True proofs, as opposed to prooflike business strikes, show the date slanting upward to the right, with the left base of 1 in the date left of center and horizontal die-polishing lines visible in MERIC.

The proof half eagle, despite a similar mintage recorded at 88 coins, is much more elusive than the quarter eagle. Garrett and Guth (2006) comment that only 20 to 25 coins are known, an estimate that we believe to be fairly accurate. Despite the considerably larger totals of certified coins at NGC and PCGS, we believe there are an inordinate number of duplicates in those figures. Again, due to a small mintage of only 4,240 circulation strikes, many of those coins have prooflike surfaces.

The eagles of 1890 have a recorded proof mintage of 63 pieces, of which nearly half survive today. Fortunately many of the 1890-dated proof gold coins have pleasing Cameo or Deep/Ultra Cameo surfaces. The double eagle proof mintage is only 55 coins, and we doubt that more than a dozen exist today in high grades from a total population of less than 30 survivors. (Garrett and Guth put the number at 15, including examples in museum collections and permanently off the market.) For many collectors, being able to acquire, hold, and admire this largest denomination of classic proof gold coinage is a once-in-a-lifetime experience.

Do not let this *remarkable and memorable opportunity* pass you by.

Cent PR65 Red and Brown. Slight steel-blue and iridescent toning in the fields prevents a Red designation to this beautiful Indian cent. The strike is excellent, the fields fully mirrored, and the devices satiny. Only trivial spots prevent a higher grade. A highly attractive piece with excellent eye appeal. NGC Census: 37 in PR65 Red and Brown; 2 finer (10/09). NGC has also certified one in PR65 Red and Brown Cameo, 11 in PR65 Red, and one in PR66 Red.

Nickel PR65. A tiny raised projection just above the bust point appears to be the serif from an errant 1, and that feature appears to be previously unpublished. We find no record of any variety of 1890 proof nickel in currently available literature.

This gorgeous Liberty nickel has pale gold, blue, and salmon toning over moderately reflective mirrors. The devices are lustrous, and faint cameo contrast is present on both sides. Scattered spots on each side are entirely trivial, and have no affect on the grade.

Dime PR65 Cameo. Fortin-101. Gerry Fortin has identified four different varieties of 1890 Seated dime proofs at his website, www.seateddimevarieties.com. The die pair of the present proof was initially used for business strikes, and later for proofs as determined through die state evidence. The rarity of the four proof varieties remains undetermined.

The present Gem Cameo proof is intriguing, with a blend of cobalt blue, turquoise, and magenta on the obverse. The reverse is apple-green at the center, with a frame of lemon-yellow. Both sides have fully mirrored fields with lustrous devices and excellent cameo contrast that is visible through the toning. NGC Census: 10 in PR65 Cameo; 20 finer (10/09). The finer examples include three high grade Ultra Cameo proofs.

Quarter PR67. Briggs 3-C, the single proof die combination that Briggs' describes in *The Comprehensive Encyclopedia of United States Liberty Seated Quarters.* A stunning Superb Gem with contrast equal to that of the dime in this set, although the quarter has no designation. Both sides are mostly brilliant silver-white, with delicate gold and magenta toning over the lower obverse, and subtle gold toning on the reverse. The strike is sharp and the surfaces are pristine. NGC Census: 14 in PR67; 3 finer (10/09). In addition, NGC has certified 37 pieces in PR67 Cameo or finer.

Half Dollar PR65 Ultra Cameo. No varieties are recorded in the Wiley-Bugert *Complete Guide to Liberty Seated Half Dollars,* and this piece displays no unusual die characteristics. Every individual die characteristic is boldly defined on this lovely Gem. A few faint hairlines are evident in the fields, preventing a higher grade. This incredible example, with its amazing eye appeal, will easily satisfy the connoisseur. NGC Census: 2 in PR65 Ultra Cameo; 7 finer (10/09).

Morgan Dollar PR67 Cameo. A stunning, sharply struck Superb Gem Cameo proof, this piece is entirely brilliant with white-silver surfaces and subliminal champagne toning on the reverse. The fields are extremely deep and the devices are frosty and lustrous, resulting in a borderline Ultra Cameo example. Both sides have pristine, unblemished surfaces. The NGC census data suggests that quite a number of high grade proofs survive, although it is a certainty that some of the figures represent resubmissions. NGC Census: 13 in PR67 Cameo, 5 finer (10/09). NGC has also certified six PR67 Ultra Cameo or finer examples.

Quarter Eagle PR65 Cameo. This delightful Gem Cameo proof has yellow-ochre devices and brown-ochre fields, with excellent contrast between the two elements. All of the devices are boldly detailed, and the fields exhibit the watery or wavy appearance usually or always present on proof gold of this era. A faint original haze adheres to both sides. NGC Census: 7 in PR65 Cameo; 3 finer (10/09). NGC has also certified 14 PR65 or finer Ultra Cameo specimens.

Half Eagle PR65 Cameo. The spaces between the vertical shield stripes are mostly filled with die polishing lines, and show little reflective proof surface. Faint glimmers of pale green toning are evident near the borders. All four proof gold coins in this 1890 set have a nearly identical appearance with frosty yellow devices and fully mirrored brownish-yellow fields. A splash of reddish-orange toning is visible over the letters LI at the top of the coronet. The surfaces are pleasing with few flaws of any type. NGC Census: 6 in PR65 Cameo, 2 finer (10/09). NGC has also certified 14 examples in PR65 or finer Ultra Cameo.

Eagle PR64 Cameo. A few faint hairlines in the fields separate this piece from Gem quality. However, it retains the same exceptional, hazy and original appearance of the other gold proofs in this set. All four pieces are remarkably well matched, undoubtedly remaining together for a long time and possibly since 1890. Faint green and iridescent toning accompanies the yellow devices and yellow-brown fields. NGC Census: 3 in PR64 Cameo; 3 finer (10/09). NGC has also certified 10 submissions in PR64 or finer Ultra Cameo.

Double Eagle PR64 Cameo. Like the eagle, the presence of faint hairlines prevent a higher grade. This gorgeous double eagle has exceptional contrast between its frosty and brilliant yellow devices, and brownish-ochre fields. Both sides have fully mirrored and reflective fields that are covered with a faint haze. NGC Census: 3 in PR64 Cameo, 3 finer. The three finer NGC certified pieces are each recorded as PR68 Cameo NGC, suggesting resubmission of a single coin. NGC has also certified five coins in PR65 or finer Ultra Cameo.
From The Boca Collection, Part I. (Total: 10 coins)

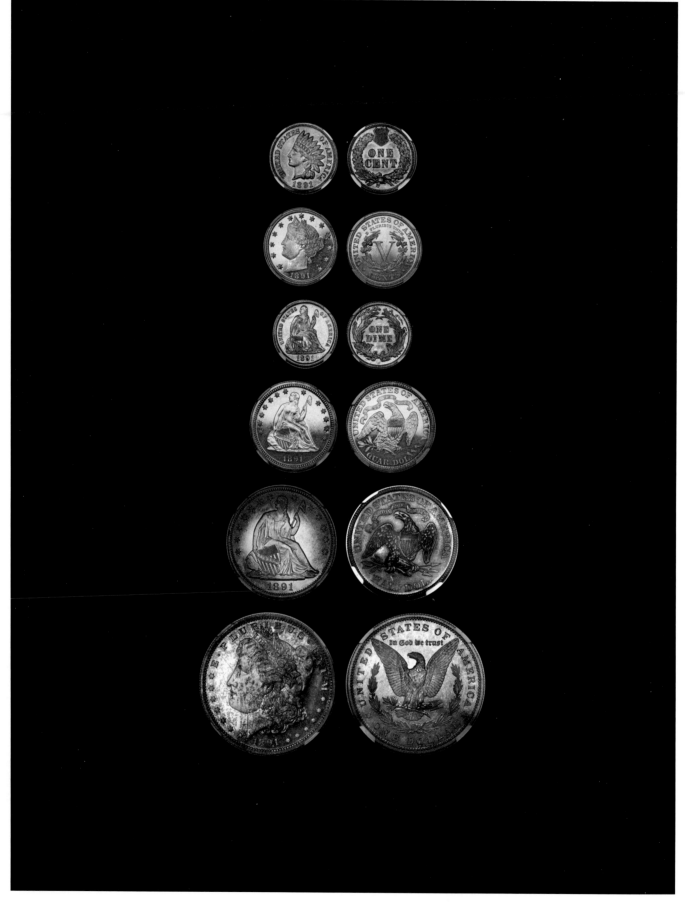

A 15% BUYER'S PREMIUM ($14 MIN.) APPLIES TO ALL LOTS.

Six-Piece 1891 Proof Set
Five Coins Gem or Better

2036   Six-Piece 1891 Proof Set NGC. Christian Gobrecht and James Longacre dominated American coinage during the second half of the 19th century. The Seated Liberty design by Gobrecht was used on all silver coins from half dime to silver dollar, while his Liberty Head could be seen on essentially all gold coins. Even the short-lived twenty cent piece, the gold dollar, and the double eagle would feature slightly modified versions of Gobrecht's Seated Liberty (for the twenty cent) or Liberty Head (for the gold dollar and double eagle). It is not surprising that by the 1870s many, including Mint Director Henry Linderman, called for a redesign of America's coinage.

Charles Barber, Chief Engraver since 1879, introduced the "V" nickel in 1883, but the other denominations were untouched. A design competition was planned for 1887, but the Attorney General determined that only Congress could change coin designs. After several changes to coinage laws, another competition was to be held in 1891 and ten artists were invited to participate.

The artists, however, felt that there was not enough time and compensation, and they sent Mint Director Edward Leech a list of demands. Rather than accede to the artists' wishes, Charles Foster, the Secretary of the Treasury, decided to hold a public competition, which turned out to be a complete failure. Over 300 entries were received, but the three judges—seal engraver Henry Mitchell, Augustus Saint-Gaudens, and Charles Barber—dismissed all of them as unsuitable.

Leech, probably frustrated and a little embarrassed, gave the commission to Barber, who created a design reminiscent of the French coins of the era. The year 1891 brought the final coins to feature the long-lived Seated Liberty design. After more than 50 years, dimes, quarter, and halves would have a new design.

Cent—Altered Color—Proof. A well-defined specimen with small, scattered hairlines. NGC has judged the coin's mahogany and muted copper-orange color to be altered, but the toning is neither garish nor particularly distracting.

Five Cent Nickel PR65 Cameo. Both sides have solid contrast, but the obverse is particularly laudable, almost Ultra Cameo in appearance on its own. The light golden toning that visits that side thickens over the reverse, with a fade to mint-green within the wreath.

Dime PR65. Green-gold and blue patina is visible on each side, but in different configurations. The shining obverse shows mostly the former color with just a touch of blue along the bottom, while the reverse is edged in green-gold with a broad blue core. Dynamic eye appeal.

Quarter PR65 Cameo. Lightly gold-toned with intensely reflective fields. The margins show a degree of orange color, most noticeably at the right reverse, and the rims have rich umber and violet patina. A gorgeous Gem.

Half Dollar PR66. Deep plum, blue, and amber shadings dominate the eye appeal of this Premium Gem. While the obverse has a gleaming center of pale silver-gray, the reverse is toned all the way across.

Morgan Dollar PR65. An incredible Gem proof with outlandish, divergent patina. The obverse has translucent, dappled champagne and silver patina edged in blue, while the reverse has deeper, duskier versions of the two colors that show a more even blend.
From The Boca Collection, Part I. (Total: 6 coins)

Notable Six-Piece 1892 Proof Set
First Year of Barber Silver Design

2037   Six-Piece 1892 Proof Set NGC. After attempts at a competition proved futile, the Mint opted to instead have Charles Barber create a new design to appear on the dime, quarter, and half dollar. The benefits of using Barber were twofold: first, as Chief Engraver he would not receive any additional compensation; secondly, his experience with engraving and minting would ensure that all of the coins would be struck properly. As Mint Director Edward Leech wrote in 1891 to *Century Magazine* art critic R. W. Gilder, "Artistic design for coins, which would meet the ideas of any art critic like yourself, and artists generally, are not always adapted for practical coinage.... My only object is to improve the appearance of our coins, and if I find that this can be done satisfactorily within the mint service I see no good reason to go beyond it."

Barber's design was used on the dime, quarter, and half dollar beginning in 1892. Although often criticized as unimaginative and scarcely an improvement over the Seated Liberty design, the Barber coins were excellent from a technical perspective. Besides the relative ease with which the Barber coins were struck, they retained a significant amount of detail even after extensive circulation. Proofs were issued each year from 1892 to 1915, and only in the first year was the distribution of silver proofs higher than 1,000 specimens.

Cent PR64 Red and Brown. Copper-gold, mustard, and yellow ochre shadings prevail on this Red and Brown cent. Moderately reflective mirrors and attentively struck devices attest to this specimen's quality, though a few faint hairlines on each side preclude a finer designation.

Nickel PR65. Pale lavender-blue and canary-gold shadings visit each side of this Gem proof, though in a reversal of this collection's usual pattern, the lavender-blue appears largely at the margins and the canary-gold occupies the centers. Profoundly reflective and undeniably appealing.

Dime PR67 Cameo. This PR67 Cameo specimen is tied with 13 other Cameo coins for the finest in the category certified by NGC (11/09). Decisively struck, richly frosted devices stand out from the fields, which show watery reflectivity beneath thin layers of gold and orange toning. Considerable silver-white color is also present. Amazing preservation and eye appeal, as demanded of the grade.

Quarter PR65 Cameo. A thin veil of light cloud-gray toning drapes much of the fields, while pale golden color extends just beyond the rims. The boldly impressed devices are wonderfully frosted, with the eye-catching portrait especially so. Pleasingly preserved for the grade.

Half Dollar PR64 Cameo. The last of the three Cameo Barber pieces in this set and the most colorful of the three, with blue and mustard-gold color over much of each side, including parts of the devices. Strongly contrasted and immensely reflective through the toning with top-notch eye appeal for the grade.

Morgan Dollar PR65. A richly toned Gem proof that must have been beautifully contrasted before the gold-gray, dusty-rose, and aqua patina settled over each side. Crisply detailed devices show evidence of their original frostiness, while the fields have strong reflectivity through the toning.
From The Boca Collection, Part I. (Total: 6 coins)

A 15% BUYER'S PREMIUM ($14 MIN.) APPLIES TO ALL LOTS.

Delightful 1893 Silver-Minor Proof Set

2038   1893 6-Piece Proof Set NGC. The second year of a series is often scarcer than the first because the novelty of the design has since worn off and fewer examples were saved by collectors. This was the case with the Barber coins, and proof mintages dropped precipitously in 1893. Only 2,195 proof cents and nickels were struck, compared to 2,745 specimens the previous year, and just 792 proof dimes, quarters, halves, and dollars were issued, as opposed to 1,245 examples in 1892.

The 1893 Morgan dollar had a relatively low business strike mintage of 378,000 pieces and prior to the 1950s this issue was considered to be very rare. Consequently, proofs were especially desirable and virtually all of the original sets were broken up by collectors seeking just the dollar. Although the dollar is no longer considered as rare as it once was, there is still significant demand for proof examples.

In 1893 the Philadelphia Mint installed a hydraulic press to strike proofs, which replaced the antiquated screw press that was still used at the Mint to strike medals and most proofs. Regular issues, however, had been struck on a steam press beginning in 1836. Nonetheless, there does not seem to be any difference in appearance between the proofs struck on a screw press versus those struck on a hydraulic press. By slowly squeezing the two dies together on the hydraulic press, as opposed to the rapid striking of regular issues, the Mint was able to impart razor-sharp definition on virtually every proof struck. This method of production remains essentially the same well over a century later.

Cent PR65 Red and Brown. Proof cents of 1893 in the Gem level of preservation are very scarce in all three color designations. Crimson and gold-orange dominate the obverse of this Red and Brown Gem accented with wisps of mint-green and sky-blue, while the same color scheme assumes deeper shades on the reverse. A well directed strike leaves strong definition on the design elements except for minor softness on the first couple of feathers. Well preserved surfaces reveal no marks or spots worthy of mention. Census: 38 in 65 Red and Brown, 7 finer (11/09).

Nickel PR64 Cameo. Walter Breen (1977) lists three 1893 proof nickel varieties. The specimen in this set features a repunched 1 in the date, of which Breen in his 1988 *Complete Encyclopedia* says: "Very rare. Comprises only a tiny minority of proofs."

An occasional whisper of light tan color visits the obverse of this near-Gem and a well executed strike delivers bold definition to the design features, including the hair over Liberty ear and the intricacies of the wreath elements. Both sides display pleasing Cameo contrast. A few small marks are visible on the obverse.

Dime PR65 Cameo. Stunning field-motif contrast is evident on both sides of this Gem Cameo that becomes even more pronounced when the coin is turned just slightly under a light source. Delicate cobalt-blue and beige-gold on the obverse cede to slightly deeper shades on the reverse, though neither palette interferes with the reflectivity in the fields. The design elements are moderately frosted and sharply defined. These attributes, when combined the blemish-free surfaces, add up to exemplary eye appeal.

Quarter Dollar PR66. Aqua-blue, lavender, and golden-brown gravitate to the obverse borders while a medley of sky-blue, reddish-gold, and beige-gold traverses the reverse. The obverse displays nice field-device contrast and all design features exhibit full delineation. A light graze is noted on Liberty's cheek as are a couple of hair-thin marks. Census: 53 in 66, 33 finer (11/09).

Half Dollar PR66. A mix of cobalt-blue, reddish-gold, lavender, beige, and white-gold patination on the obverse cedes to soft reddish-gold with blue-gray accents on the reverse. The design elements exhibit sharp details except for the often seen softness in the upper right corner of the shield. A degree of field-device contrast is more noticeable on the obverse. Well preserved throughout. Census: 29 in 66, 19 finer (11/09).

Morgan Dollar PR67. This Superb Gem Morgan dollar proof displays absolutely stunning eye appeal resulting from a combination of the following factors: spectacular patination consisting of delicate lavender and sky-blue on the obverse that takes on deeper hues of this color palette on the reverse; excellent field-motif contrast that is more noticeable on the obverse; and immaculately preserved surfaces. The centers exhibit a weak strike, however, as always seen on 1892 and 1893 proof dollars (David Bowers, 1993, p. 2516). Census: 17 in 67, 7 finer (11/09).
From The Boca Collection, Part I. (Total: 6 coins)

Engaging 1894 NGC Certified Proof Set

2039 1894 Six-Piece Proof Set NGC. Due to the scarcity of the 1894 dollar in business strike format (only 110,000 pieces were minted), proofs have long brought a premium from date collectors. Walter Breen (1977) also notes that many of these proofs were harshly cleaned. Therefore, despite a decent distribution of 972 silver proof sets, this year can be quite challenging to locate and attractive examples sell for sizeable sums.

Although not issued as part of any sets, the proof 1894-S dime deserves a special mention. Its story is well known and will not be repeated here, but it is important to note that these pieces are now considered to be proofs. Nonetheless, there is some difference in appearance between the S-Mint dimes and the Philadelphia proofs. Unlike the regular proofs, the 1894-S dimes do not exhibit the same level of sharpness and the fields are less reflective.

As with most years, nearly all of the original 1894 proof sets were broken up decades ago. Besides the scarce 1894 dollar, many of the other denominations are also conditionally rare as business strikes, placing added demand on the proofs. While proofs are easily located in lower grades as many were improperly handled, the astute collector will realize the importance of a carefully preserved set.

Cent PR65 Red and Brown. A bold strike is demonstrated through the sharpness of each individual design element on both sides of this lovely Gem proof. Full, deeply mirrored fields and satiny devices create a noticeable contrast, especially on the obverse. Many observers will feel that a Cameo designation should be assigned to this highly attractive and appealing Indian cent. The fields exhibit minor blemishes that prevent an even higher grade. Those most apparent are in the left obverse field, and even they require magnification to observe. Both sides have brilliant orange devices with deeper reddish-orange fields and iridescent toning highlights. NGC Census: 37 in PR65 Red and Brown; 11 finer. NGC has also certified 20 examples in PR65 Red or finer.

Nickel PR67. The 4 is doubled below its final position. It appears that this Repunched Date is quite a bit rarer than the Normal Date proof. Incredible design definition is evident on both sides of this Superb Gem, with each individual detail sharply impressed. The brilliant obverse and slightly hazy reverse are remarkable, with deeply mirrored fields on both sides. The devices are lustrous and the overall appearance is borderline cameo. Both sides are pristine and mark-free. Subtle champagne toning is barely visible over the brilliant nickel-gray surfaces. NGC Census: 8 in PR67; 2 finer. NGC has also certified five examples as PR67 Cameo.

Dime PR67. The reverse border shows slight merging of the dentils, indicative of less than a full strike, but all other details are bold and sharp. Highly lustrous, satiny devices are framed by deeply mirrored fields on this Superb Gem. The contrast is equal to the Barber quarter and half dollar in this set, both assigned a Cameo designation. Delicate gold and light blue toning are found near the borders of this otherwise brilliant and untoned Barber dime. NGC Census: 27 in PR67; 9 finer. NGC has also certified 12 examples in PR67 Cameo or finer.

Quarter PR65 Cameo. Slight weakness is evident along the top edge of each wing on the reverse, but the overall appearance is that of a bold strike. A few trivial marks and lines on Liberty's cheek and neck prevent a higher grade, but the visual presentation clearly supports the Gem grade assigned to this delightful quarter. The fields are fully mirrored and the devices are lustrous with scintillating mint frost. Both sides have pale yellow toning with peripheral rose and sea-green highlights. NGC Census: 13 in PR65 Cameo; 26 finer. NGC has also certified three pieces as PR65 Ultra Cameo or finer.

Half Dollar PR66 Cameo. Most design elements are boldly details, with some weakness at the junction of the wing and right shield border, a point that is often ill-defined on Barber half dollars, proofs and business strikes. The tiny marks on Liberty's cheek appear to be mint made planchet flakes that have no affect on the grade. Highly lustrous and satiny devices are surrounded by fully mirrored fields. This amazing piece has brilliant silver centers, surrounded by considerable magenta and cobalt-blue closer to the borders. NGC Census: 18 in PR66 Cameo; 13 finer.

Morgan Dollar PR66. Every design feature on both sides of this Premium Gem illustrates the design exactly as George T. Morgan intended. The motifs, lettering, and border are fully defined. Both sides have deeply mirrored fields and satiny devices with at least as much contrast as found on the Cameo designated Barber half dollar in this set. Dark yellow-brown toning accompanies peripheral gold, lilac, and blue on each side, deeper on the reverse.
From The Boca Collection, Part I. (Total: 6 coins)

NGC Certified 1895 Six-Piece Proof Set
Featuring the King of Morgan Dollars, PR66 ★

2040   1895 Six-Piece Proof Set NGC. The 1895 Morgan dollar is one of the most important proof issues in the history of U.S. coinage. While there have been persistent rumors that a business strike 1895 dollar exists, it appears that none were ever struck-although that is still debated from time to time. As a proof-only issue, it is one of the most challenging and desirable dates in the widely collected Morgan dollar series. The dollar is undoubtedly the highlight of this proof set.

The other denominations in this set are less significant than the dollar, but they are still popular because of the aura of the 1895 date. For example, the cataloger of the Eliasberg collection wrote the following about the dime. "This is a very important date from the fact that related business strikes are major rarities. This *should* place a strong demand upon Proofs, and among the cognoscenti it does, although the subtlety is often lost on the 'investor' buyer. Regardless, the 1895 dime is of great historical importance..." The remaining denominations are more plentiful but still important.

It is exciting to see the 1895 dollar in a set with all of the other denominations. The dollar alone would attract fierce competition from bidders, but as a set it is particularly noteworthy. This is just one of the many significant opportunities represented by this fabulous collection. Just 880 silver proof sets were issued and it may be years before another 1895 proof set is sold intact.

Cent PR64 Brown. Repunched Date from the dies of Snow-1 and FS-301. The 8, 9, and 5 are each dramatically doubled. All design features, from the feathers in the headdress to the leaves in the wreath, show outstanding definition. Reflective, lightly mirrored fields frame the lustrous devices of this near-Gem. A few faint hairlines and tiny contact marks on each side are consistent with the grade. Reddish-brown surfaces on both sides are accompanied by mauve and turquoise-green toning on the obverse.

Nickel PR63. Exceptional detail is present on both sides, with no weakness of any element. Even the ear of corn left of the ribbon bow is well detailed. This Select proof has faint hairlines and other minor blemishes that limit the grade. Traces of old lacquer are visible on the reverse. Both sides have brilliant, untoned nickel-gray surfaces.

Dime PR64 Cameo. This boldly detailed dime has full design definition on each side, including the leaves at the lower reverse. Excellent field to device contrast is evident with full mirrors around the lustrous motifs on each side. A few non-distracting hairlines are present in the fields. Both sides have pale cerise at the centers, with peripheral magenta toning. NGC Census: 7 in PR64 Cameo; 39 finer (10/09).

Quarter PR66 Cameo. A sharply defined Barber quarter, this piece has exquisitely detailed design elements. The stars, hair, and leaves on the obverse are all full. The reverse has a bold eagle with complete wing, neck, and tail details. This is an exemplary specimen showing exceptional contrast between the mirrored fields and lustrous, frosty devices. Both sides have a lovely blend of light blue, magenta, reddish-orange, and greenish-yellow toning. NGC Census: 12 in PR66 Cameo; 25 finer (10/09).

Half Dollar PR66 Cameo. Like the other coins in this set, the Barber half dollar is fully detailed. Even the right edge of the shield is sharp and crisply defined. This distinctive 1895 Barber half dollar exhibits fully lustrous devices and exceptional mirrored fields. The obverse and reverse each have significant areas of silver-white with accompanying blue, green, yellow, violet, and iridescent toning. NGC Census: 21 in PR66 Cameo; 21 finer (10/09).

Morgan Dollar PR66 ★. A few hair strands over Liberty's ear are merged together as usual, but all other design motifs are crisp and sharp. An exquisite beauty, this "King of Morgan Dollars" deserves a Cameo designation in addition to its NGC assigned ★ designation. Faint lines on the reverse are the only distractions on this otherwise pristine piece. The central motifs have pale salmon toning with rings of ultramarine, lemon-yellow, bright purple, and emerald. This "album toning" ranks among the most desirable color presentations ever achieved.

NGC Census: 1 in PR66 ★; 0 finer (10/09). In all grades, NGC has certified 583 submissions of 1895 Morgan dollars but only three coins, including the piece in this 1895 proof set, have been assigned the ★ designation. The other two are certified PR64 ★ Cameo and PR67 ★ Ultra Cameo.
From The Boca Collection, Part I. (Total: 6 coins)

A 15% BUYER'S PREMIUM ($14 MIN.) APPLIES TO ALL LOTS.

Delightful 1896 Six-Piece Proof Set

2041 **1896 Six-Piece Proof Set NGC.** The debate between proponents of the gold standard and those who favored free coinage of silver reached a fevered pitch in 1896. William Jennings Bryan, an outspoken supporter of Free Silver and the common man, waged an intense campaign against William McKinley, who wanted to maintain the gold standard that had been in place since the Coinage Act of 1873. This election, which many historians consider to be the pivotal moment in defining the modern political parties of the United States, had the potential to greatly change the nation—and its coinage.

Bryan, memorable for his "Cross of Gold" speech, narrowly lost to McKinley, and the gold standard remained in place until it was effectively ended by Franklin Roosevelt in 1933. Ultimately no changes were made to the silver coins then circulating. Nonetheless, this important year sparked an outflow of souvenir medals and tokens relating to the debate and these pieces are widely collected today. Never again have coins taken such a prominent position in a presidential election.

Breen (1977) wrote that many of the proof 1896 nickels were broken out and hoarded, but he does not give further details or an explanation why this would have occurred. The mintage of 1,862 proof minor coins was the lowest since 1877, which may have fueled demand from speculators. Regardless, the 1896 proof set represents a significant year in the history of the United States and its coinage. The proof coins from this year are generally regarded as the best produced (perhaps only rivaled by 1898) of the proofs struck in the latter half of the 19th century.

Cent PR65 Red and Brown. The bright surfaces of this pretty Gem display splashes of crimson, lime-green, sky-blue, and orange-gold on the obverse, while yellow-gold imbued with wisps of light green resides in the reverse center flanked by reddish-gold and electric-blue at the margins. Sharp definition is visible on the design elements, though the first couple of feather tips are soft. Neither side reveals mentionable contact marks. Census: 38 in 65 Red and Brown, 9 finer (11/09).

Nickel PR64. David Bowers writes in his *Shield and Liberty Head Nickels*: "At least one obverse die was heavily repolished; Proofs struck from this die have some stars with flat centers and show prominent lint marks from debris." The present near-Gem obviously was not struck with this obverse die as all of its design features, including the star centers, are boldly impressed, and just one unobtrusive lint mark is visible. The reverse devices are also sharp. Soft champagne-gold patina bathes both sides, each of which displays whispers of light bluish-violet and is nicely preserved.

Dime PR66 Cameo. Mirrored fields highlight frosty motifs on this highly attractive Premium Gem. Aqua-blue and soft reddish-orange patina gravitates to the margins, and an exacting strike imparts crisp detail to the design features. Both sides are immaculately preserved. Census: 16 in 66 Cameo, 11 finer (11/09).

Quarter Dollar PR64 ★ Cameo. NGC's coveted Star confirms the majestic eye appeal of this wonderful near-Gem Cameo, one of only six 1896 proof quarters given this designation (11/09). Frosty, exquisitely struck design elements seem to float over the deep watery fields, and both sides are essentially untoned and devoid of mentionable marks.

Half Dollar PR60. Fully brilliant surfaces with essentially indiscernible wisps of peripheral gold color reach out to the observer and a solid strike leaves strong definition on the design elements. Only the upper right corner of the shield reveals minor softness, which is typical for the issue. Occasional faint hairlines appear under high magnification, nevertheless this coin generates considerable appeal for the designated grade.

Morgan Dollar PR66 Cameo. This Premium Gem displays a dramatic Cameo effect, which is typical for the issue. Indeed, David Bowers (1993) cites Wayne Miller, saying: "... Proof dollars of 1896-1898 evidence the most awesome cameo contrast of any Proofs in the Morgan series." This contrast is enhanced by the nearly untoned surfaces. Only a hint of light tan occasionally appears under magnification. Additionally, a well executed strike delivers sharp detail to the design elements, generating even greater eye appeal. Finally, close examination reveals beautiful blemish-free surfaces.
From The Boca Collection, Part I. (Total: 6 coins)

A 15% BUYER'S PREMIUM ($14 MIN.) APPLIES TO ALL LOTS.

Lovely 1897 Six-Piece Proof Set

2042   1897 Six-Piece Proof Set NGC. The number of silver proof sets issued in 1897 declined from the previous year to just 731 pieces for each denomination, with a nearly identical output in 1898. Although not as elusive as some of their 20th century counterparts, the 1897 dimes, quarters, and half dollars are probably the scarcest proof Barber issues from the 1890s. The other issues-namely the cent, nickel, and dollar-are not particularly noteworthy, but all six pieces are seldom sold as a complete set.

By many accounts 1897 was a slow year for numismatics. In December 1896, after a period of diminished activity, *The Numismatist* and the American Numismatic Association separated. Editor George B. Heath wrote that the ANA "is not dead, but seemingly sleepeth; somnolently, solemnly, silently, sweetly ... This magazine cannot, however, afford to remain with the inactive body longer, and until it arises with new habiliments and energy, shall remain detached and independent." It was also noted that the previous two ANA conventions were "flops."

The Numismatist would not regain its position as official organ of the ANA until 1899. The two years that the ANA was dormant coincided with the lowest proof mintages since 1891.

The 1897 proof set was issued at an interesting time for the hobby, and its relatively scarcity is not fully appreciated by collectors today.

Cent PR65 Red and Brown. Bright greenish-gold with splashes of reddish-purple adorns the obverse of this Gem, ceding to crimson and electric-blue on the reverse. An impressive strike lends strong detail to the design elements, save for minor softness in the second feather. Both sides are devoid of mentionable marks or spots. Census: 53 in 65 Red and Brown, 18 finer (11/09).

Nickel PR64 Cameo. Nearly untoned surfaces display the slightest hint of color at the reverse periphery, and reflective fields yield pleasing contrast with the satiny design motifs. A powerful strike imparts crisp definition to the design features, including the corn ear left of the ribbon bow that is sometimes incomplete. A couple of trivial minute marks in the lower right obverse field barely deny Gem classification.

Dime PR66 Cameo. Walter Breen (1988) writes that proof and business strike 1897 dimes come with the 7 either touching the truncation or free of it, and that one variety with the 7 free has an incomplete wreath from drastically repolished dies. The 7 on this Premium Gem is free of the bust and has a complete wreath. Splashes of violet, yellow-gold, and golden-orange bathe both sides, each of which displays excellent Cameo contrast. Frosty devices are boldly impressed. Devoid of mentionable marks.

Quarter Dollar PR64 Cameo. Soft reddish-tan patination fails to impede the stunning field-motif contrast on this wonderful near-Gem. An exacting strike leaves strong delineation on the design elements and both obverse and reverse are nicely preserved. A couple of tiny flecks on the lower reverse do not distract.

Half Dollar PR66 Ultra Cameo. Frosty devices appear to be suspended over the deep water fields on this marvelous Premium Gem Ultra Cameo. Untoned surfaces reveal immaculate preservation and sharply struck design elements. Splendid overall eye appeal.

Morgan Dollar PR66. As mentioned in Breen (1977) and seen on the current Premium Gem is repunching on 1 below the upper serif. Whispers of golden-orange color are slightly more prevalent and possess somewhat deeper hues on the reverse. The design elements are sharply struck, including the hair above Liberty's ear and the eagle's breast feathers. An occasional hairline is interspersed with die polish lines on Liberty's cheek and neck. Great overall eye appeal. Census: 22 in 66, 18 finer (11/09).
From The Boca Collection, Part I. (Total: 6 coins)

Desirable Six-Piece 1898 Proof Set
Outstanding Quarter and Dollar

2043   Six-Piece 1898 Proof Set NGC. The proof coins of 1898 are among the best produced issues prior to the start of the modern proof series in 1936. These pieces typically show deeply mirrored fields and razor-sharp definition, along with outstanding cameo contrast. For the collector who desires coins of the utmost quality, an 1898 proof set would be an excellent choice.

While the dime, quarter, and half dollar had received a new design in 1892, the other issues had been passed over. The "V" nickel design had been issued since 1883, the Morgan dollar since 1878, and the Indian Head cent since 1859 (save for a few minor changes). Only the cent had been in circulation for more than the congressionally mandated 25 years, so none of the other denominations could legally be changed without an Act of Congress. Nonetheless, there were persistent calls for a revitalization of American coinage.

In 1898 a member of the Congressional Committee on Coinage, Weights and Measures remarked, "The designs on some of our coins are not artistic or beautiful. On some the significance and appropriateness of the design has been destroyed in an unsuccessful effort to improve its appearance. On most of them there is too much work, the devices are too elaborate and the effort for artistic effect is overdone ... It is submitted as proper that the Secretary of the Treasury should have the authority to seek new and more attractive designs for our coins, but not to be adopted until first submitted to Congress for its approval." Despite this recommendation, the designs would remain until Theodore Roosevelt became obsessed with the idea several years later. The Barber coins would continue to circulate until their eventual replacement in 1916.

Cent PR65 Red and Brown. Both sides show a blend of pale copper-gold and mint-green color. The devices are boldly impressed, and the fields exhibit a level of reflectivity not often associated with Red and Brown specimens. Indisputably Gem-level eye appeal.

Nickel PR65. Boldly struck and attractive, a proof with watery reflectivity beneath delicate patina, lavender on the obverse with outer green-gold and inner blue on the reverse.

Dime PR62. Strongly reflective with a modicum of contrast. Pearl-gray centers give way to green-gold and orange toning at parts of the margins. The obverse appears clean for the PR62 designation, though a number of hairlines are visible within the reverse wreath.

Quarter PR68 Cameo. Exquisitely preserved with gorgeous toning, translucent champagne and peach-gold over most of the centers with blue and violet peripheral shadings that are more overt on the reverse. Each side is impressively contrasted through the patina. Census: 9 in 68 Cameo, 2 finer (11/09).

Half Dollar PR63. Both sides show definite contrast, though the blue and gray shadings over the obverse dampen the cameo effect just enough to preclude a designation. On the reverse, where the toning is lighter, the fields display wonderful reflectivity.

Morgan Dollar PR66 ★ Ultra Cameo. A stunning Premium Gem that exemplifies all the possibilities for the issue. The razor-sharp devices are thickly frosted and the near-brilliant mirrors gleam beautifully. Only a few hints of gold and gray appear close to the rims. Among Star-designated Ultra Cameo pieces, this is the sole PR66 certified by NGC with four finer (11/09).
From The Boca Collection, Part I. (Total: 6 coins)

Six-Piece 1899 Proof Set

2044   1899 Six-Piece Proof Set NGC. The low-mintage 1899 dollar was once considered very scarce in business strike format and proof examples were especially desirable. However, due to the great Treasury releases of the 1960s, thousands of Uncirculated examples flooded the market. Proofs are now significantly more elusive than their regular issue counterparts. Nonetheless, the former rarity assigned to the dollar meant that many proof sets were broken up and the dollars are seldom seen as part of a complete set.

Unlike the proof issues from 1896 to 1898, the 1899 can be difficult to locate with full details, cameo contrast, and excellent eye appeal. Although many of the silver proof 1899 issues show minor contrast between the fields and the devices, they seldom come close to matching the appearance of the three previous years. The cents and nickels were typically better produced, but they are often found with tiny blemishes. The proofs of 1899 often demand considerable trade-offs from the would-be collector.

The population data from NGC and PCGS support this conclusion. While the 1899 proofs are plentiful at the PR63 and PR64 level, the number of survivors drops substantially in Gem and finer grades. Only a select few proofs have received a Cameo designation from either service, and these rare pieces are highly desirable. Due to the level of connoisseurship that the date demands, the 1899 proof set is the perfect choice for a value-seeking specialist.

Cent PR65 Red and Brown. Bright copper-orange and lemon-gold are the most prominent colors on this cent, though the obverse also shows green shadings at the right obverse and the reverse exhibits mahogany tints. A sharply struck and highly appealing Gem.

Nickel PR66. Both sides show pale nickel-blue and bolder chartreuse toning, with the former color prevailing on the obverse and the latter more prominent on the reverse. Exactingly struck with moderate mirrors that show the greatest depth of reflectivity to either side of the portrait.

Dime PR66. Splashes of violet and emerald toning supplement the golden patina that covers most of the obverse and the upper left reverse. The lowest part of the latter side shows a degree of contrast, thanks to frostiness on the sharply impressed wreath. The mirrored fields show excellent surface quality.

Quarter PR67. Considerable frostiness is evident on the devices, though the deep blue, green, violet, and gold-orange shadings across each side have precluded the possibility of a Cameo designation. The mirrors remain strong, particularly on the reverse, and the preservation is wonderful.

Half Dollar PR65. A starkly beautiful Gem that comes the closest in the set to a Cameo designation, and judging from the well-contrasted obverse, that side alone would have ample credentials for such an honor. Golden-brown and canary-yellow peripheral shadings fade into near-nothingness as they progress toward the center.

Morgan Dollar PR64. This amply toned Choice proof has deep violet and dusky lavender toning elements over most of each side, with small cores of lighter color near the centers; that on the obverse is pearl-gray, while the one on the reverse is nearly silver-white. Razor-sharp striking definition with only a few faults that are partly hidden by the toning.
From The Boca Collection, Part I. (Total: 6 coins)

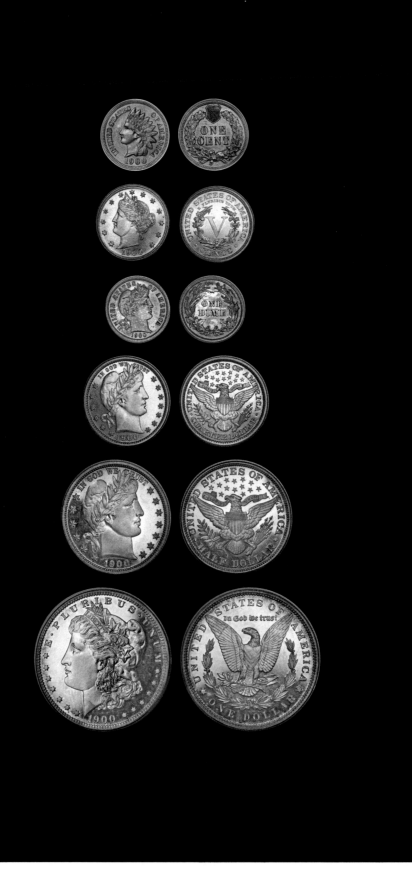

Six-Piece 1900 Minor and Silver Proof Set

2045 **Six-Piece 1900 Proof Set NGC.** In *The History of United States Coinage as Illustrated by the Garrett Collection*, Q. David Bowers writes, "A survey in 1900 showed that there were 21 full-time and part-time rare coin dealers in the United States. There were several thousand serious collectors, many of whom ordered Proof coins from the Mint each year." The Mint released 912 silver proof sets in 1900, which was above-average, and production would fall in later years until it reached a low in 1914.

Walter Breen (1977) apparently believed that the reported distribution of 2,262 minor proof sets was a typographical error, and that the actual number was 2,062, as recorded in his *Proof Encyclopedia*. However, he fails to provide any evidence to support this reasoning, and it is now generally accepted that 2,262 proof examples were struck of each denomination in the minor proof set, the cent and the nickel. On the other hand, Breen's note that many of the proof coins of the 1900s show numerous spots, which resulted in many examples being harshly cleaned over the years, is better supported by empirical evidence. Carefully preserved specimens represent only a tiny minority of the 1900 proofs seen today.

Cent PR65 Red and Brown. A sharply struck Gem with smooth and charming luster. While the obverse is mostly blue and violet with only a pale copper-gold fringe at the lower and right margins suggesting the coin's original color, the reverse is generally gold and orange with occasional lavender accents. Carefully preserved with great eye appeal for the grade.

Nickel PR65. Excellent design definition overall with the only perceptible striking softness present on the lower left ear of corn. A thin layer of green-gold and sky-blue patina drapes moderately reflective surfaces that are otherwise pale nickel-gray. The right obverse rim shows a pair of tiny flecks.

Dime PR65. This Gem, the third consecutive PR65 coin in the set, must have been strongly contrasted once, though the rich blue, violet, and gold patina over each side has dampened the cameo effect. The fields show the various colors in separate areas, while the portrait shows the same colors dappled.

Quarter PR66. A Premium Gem proof and the highest-graded coin in the set, this quarter has readily appreciable contrast, though the portrait is not thickly frosted enough to meet typical Cameo standards. Light gold and pale silver-blue colors cover most of each side. The obverse fields are flashy, while the reverse mirrors are a trifle subdued.

Half Dollar PR63 Cameo. Impressively frosted devices on both obverse and reverse lend this Select Cameo piece strong eye appeal. Strong golden overtones inform each side, while the margins also show elements of blue-green and violet that dissolve into iridescence. Distinctly appealing despite a handful of grade-defining hairlines.

Morgan Dollar PR64 Cameo. The gold-orange field toning of this near-Gem, strongest at the rims but present all the way up to the devices, heightens the contrast between the mirrors and the frosted devices, which are snow-white save for a patch of tan at the bottom of Liberty's neck. Strongly struck and modestly flawed for the grade.
From The Boca Collection, Part I. (Total: 6 coins)

A 15% BUYER'S PREMIUM ($14 MIN.) APPLIES TO ALL LOTS.

Six-Piece 1901 Proof Set

2046   Six-Piece 1901 Proof Set NGC. The non-gold proof sets of the early 1900s are more notable for their lack of variety than for any other outstanding characteristics. Each set contains the cent through silver dollar (half dollar after 1904 when Morgan dollars took a 17-year hiatus), with no missing issues or lack of business strike counterparts *á la* the 1895 Morgan dollar. This is not to say that no changes occurred; for example, 1901 did see a minor obverse hub redesign for the Barber dime, quarter, and half dollar, and 1902 saw lessened cameo contrast on most proof coins. But overall, the early years of the decade are those of uniformity, if not downright monotony.

The new obverse hub for the Barber dime design of 1901 shows longer leaves and the N in UNITED "notably farther from the ribbon" (Breen *Proof Encyclopedia*). The quarter and half dollar also have longer leaves and larger berries, with "more details in the ear and part of the hair." Breen calls all three redesigns "type coins," a point that many collectors would find debatable. Breen records 1,985 minor proof sets produced (Indian cent and Liberty nickel), along with 813 of the silver sets, containing the three Barber coins plus the silver dollar.

The 1901 Morgan dollar proof deserves special mention, as the 1901-dated business strikes in high Mint State grades are among the rarest of the entire series. This phenomenon exerts considerable upward pressure on the 1901 proofs.

Cent PR65 Red and Brown. The bright copper-gold of the broad centers is tempered only slightly at the margins, where glimpses of mahogany and magenta-violet appear. A sharp and gorgeous Gem that is decidedly more Red than Brown.

Nickel PR66. This delightful Premium Gem has delicate, exquisite patina over gleaming mirrored surfaces. Pale lavender-blue centers give way to yellow-green at the margins, with the latter color intermittent on the obverse but continuous on the reverse. Strongly appealing.

Dime PR64 Cameo. The 1901 silver proofs are among the last in the Barber series to be found routinely with Cameo-level contrast. This dime has a light golden cast overall with deeper orange color at the date area on the obverse. The icy portrait of Liberty emerges from liquid mirrors.

Quarter PR66. Through the rich patina, this quarter offers suggestions of past contrast. In parts of the fields, reflectivity pierces the veil of gold-orange, violet, and blue toning. A carefully preserved and immensely appealing specimen.

Half Dollar PR66 Cameo. The most starkly contrasted specimen in the set, this piece is profoundly mirrored with richly frosted devices and subtle toning. Hints of champagne and khaki color visit the rims, while the fields show subtle whispers of cloud-gray.

Morgan Dollar PR65 Cameo. As noted above, the rarity of high-grade business strike 1901 Morgan dollars puts added pressure on proofs, but this Cameo Gem is just as easily appreciated on its own terms. Glimpses of golden peripheral toning give way to near-brilliant mirrors, and the devices, while lightly frosted, offer more than enough contrast for the Cameo designation.
From The Boca Collection, Part I. (Total: 6 coins)

Six-Piece 1902 Proof Set Featuring
PR67 ★ Liberty Nickel

2047   Six-Piece 1902 Proof Set NGC. The Philadelphia Mint in this year implemented subtle changes in the texture or surface finish of all proof coinage denominations. The most obvious difference is seen on proof gold. Dr. Robert Loewinger's *Proof Gold Coinage of the United States* says lackadaisically, "Proofs from 1902-7 have semi-brilliant devices rather than frosty devices." Breen uses the same term in describing the cent and nickel issues of the year: "From now on ... devices are semi-brilliant, though less noticeably so than in higher denominations."

Snow's *Guide Book of Flying Eagle and Indian Head Cents* is a bit more specific on the issue: "During this year, and the next two, a change in die preparation eliminated the cameo contrast on most denominations. Only the first couple of coins minted from a die will have any contrast between the devices and field. Coins of this date designated as cameos are very rare." The Bowers *Guide to Shield and Liberty Head Nickels*, while commenting specifically on the five cent denomination provides more explication for the 1902 issues as a whole: "The portrait is in low contrast, reflecting changes at the Mint, which had just recently moved into a new building."

The generally accepted mintage figures for 1902-dated proofs are 2,018 for the minor proof set coins, the cent and nickel, and 777 for the pieces in the silver proof set, the dime through the Morgan dollar. There are no significant rarities for the year.

Cent PR64 Red and Brown. A strongly impressed near-Gem with generally lemon-gold and orange shadings on the obverse. The reverse has bold violet and magenta hues in the center which account for the Red and Brown designation. A faint fingerprint is noted in the space above the headdress.

Nickel PR67 ★. Though it does not have the Cameo contrast seen on many proofs from prior years, this Superb Gem specimen has amazing eye appeal on its own terms. The gleaming mirrors are carefully preserved with only a few flecks, and a planchet flaw near the point of the V is hardly distracting.

Dime PR63. A generally silver-white piece with champagne-gold patina visible at the right obverse and around the reverse rim. This faintly hairlined Select coin shows above-average frostiness on the portrait of Liberty, though the reverse is closer to brilliant.

Quarter PR65. As with the dime, this Gem quarter is better-contrasted than usually seen for the issue, though not to the extent of a true Cameo coin. Occasional green-gold whispers visit the margins, but the surfaces are near-brilliant otherwise.

Half Dollar PR64. The upper peripheral obverse and the reverse margins show echoes of pale yellow, while the rest of the coin is gleaming silver-white with occasional small milky spots. A few small hairlines scattered in the fields preclude a finer designation.

Morgan Dollar PR64. This Choice proof is strongly but not flawlessly struck, with a few strands of hair over Liberty's ear showing incomplete definition. Modestly hairlined mirrors are primarily silver-white with occasional glints of yellow, though the left obverse rim and peripheral reverse show deeper sage and antique-gold shadings.
From The Boca Collection, Part I. (Total: 6 coins)

Appealing 1903 Proof Set Featuring
Superb Gem Half Dollar

2048   1903 Six-Piece Proof Set NGC. The 1903 proof set is the next-to-last containing a Morgan dollar, along with the five small-denomination coins from cent through half dollar. The generally accepted mintage for the minor coinage sets including the Indian cent and Liberty nickel is 1,790 sets, with 755 for the four-coin silver sets. As in 1902, most of the denominations have little to no field-device contrast. In fact, concerning the 1903 proof Morgan dollars, Q. David Bowers' *Guide Book of Morgan Silver Dollars* contributes this: "Medium to subpar strike plus no cameo contrast. The portraits and certain other recessed parts of the die were polished—what student of the series Michael Fuljenz calls 'the chrome look.' "

In other denominations, the small proof production of 755 each of the Barber coins (a mintage also shared by the Morgan dollar) is in stark contrast to the business strike coinages in Philadelphia for the years, which, relative to their respective series, were at abundant if not record levels. Walter Breen notes that the 1903 Liberty nickel is occasionally found with the reverse oriented 180 degrees from normal rotation, i.e. in medal turn rather than coin turn.

Cent PR64 Red and Brown. The copper-orange color on the obverse remains fresh, but the reverse has mellowed just enough, most noticeably in a violet arc along the inner wreath, to preclude a fully Red designation. Strong striking definition with only a handful of minor hairlines and flyspecks.

Nickel PR65 Cameo. Though the Mint procedures for striking proof coinage greatly reduced the likelihood of any one coin being a Cameo, such pieces were still produced, as this boldly contrasted Gem amply demonstrates. Lemongrass toning drapes each side, with that of the reverse slightly lighter. The broad mirrors are free of overt flaws.

Dime PR60. Gold, orange, and umber peripheral elements give way to near-brilliant centers. While the obverse shows a number of hairlines as well as potential slide marks on the cheek, the reverse is comparatively clean. Overall, an attractive coin by PR60 standards.

Quarter PR66 Cameo. A rewarding Premium Gem that sports rich frost across the portrait of Liberty and the eagle, with a small hollow below the ear the only point on the devices showing readily perceptible brilliance. Both sides show a light champagne-gold cast, with the obverse's toning slightly more intense. Carefully preserved beneath the patina and thoroughly attractive. Census: 13 in 66 Cameo, 20 finer (10/09).

Half Dollar PR67. Highly appealing with significant contrast for a coin not designated as a Cameo. Glimpses of golden peripheral toning frame nearly unpatinated centers. With its sharp strike and potent mirrors, this Superb Gem specimen has all the ingredients for undeniable eye appeal. Census: 18 in 67, 3 finer (10/09).

Morgan Dollar PR63. The well-defined devices on each side are of distinctly different texture from the gleaming fields, though this difference does not add up to clearly defined contrast. Dappled gold and blue-gray toning elements scarcely impede this Select dollar's natural reflectivity. Light, scattered hairlines account for the grade.
From The Boca Collection, Part I. (Total: 6 coins)

Attractive 1904 Proof Set

2049   1904 6-Piece Proof Set NGC. The 1904 proof sets are the last to contain a Morgan dollar, which went on a 17-year hiatus until the business strikes of 1921. (Certain rare "Chapman" and "Zerbe" proof Morgan dollars exist, dated 1921, but were not part of proof sets.) As in 1903, the Morgan dollars have a glassy, chromelike quicksilver appearance, produced by a near-total lack of contrast from polishing the recesses of the die.

A total of 1,817 minor proof sets were produced for 1904, along with 670 sets containing the silver dime through dollar. Breen comments concerning the Indian Head cent that "quite a few of these show flaming golden brilliance, the untarnished original color." His *Proof Encyclopedia* also mentions the Barber coinage as being the "lowest proof mintage of the design so far, but not really rare nor favored by speculators."

In December 1904, President Theodore Roosevelt wrote a letter, addressed to Treasury Secretary Leslie Mortier Shaw but aimed foursquare at Mint Chief Engraver Charles Barber. In it he penned the famous remark about American coin designs being "artistically of atrocious hideousness." The Breen *Proof Encyclopedia,* marginally more charitable, places the proof sets of this era in its chapter titled, "Stereotypy Rules, 1890-1906."

Cent PR65 Red and Brown. Soft crimson and yellow-gold patina bathes both sides of this lovely Gem. A well executed strike leaves sharp definition on the design elements, save for the usual minor softness in the first couple of feather tips. A few tiny reverse flecks take nothing away from the coin's gorgeous eye appeal. Census: 34 in 65 Red and Brown, 4 finer (11/09).

Nickel PR64. Freckles of golden-tan patina dominate the luminous surfaces of this near-Gem, accented with occasional splashes of bluish-gray and lavender. A solid strike imparts sharp detail to the design features, including the hair above Liberty's ear and the corn ear left of the bow knot. A couple of trivial handling marks preclude Gem classification.

Dime PR64. Whispers of electric-blue, purple, and orange-gold, somewhat more extensive on the obverse, gather at the peripheries yielding to light champagne-gold in the central areas. A powerful strike results in full delineation on the design elements, rounding out the coin's exceptional eye appeal. Examination under a loupe reveals a few unobtrusive hairlines.

Quarter PR64. Mild frost on the devices results in a degree of contrast with the deeply mirrored fields. Essentially untoned surfaces exhibit sharply struck design motifs, including fullness on the arrow feathers and nearly complete detail on the upper right shield corner and eagle's right (facing) claw. A few very faint obverse hairlines mingle with die polish lines.

Half Dollar PR66. Breen (1977) writes of 1904 proof half dollars: "Most specimens have been cleaned to death." Not so the Premium Gem in this lot! Its impeccably preserved surfaces are devoid of mentionable hairlines or other blemishes. The obverse is nearly color free while wisps of light reddish-brown make occasional visits to the reverse, joined by sky-blue in its lower right quadrant. Outstanding detail shows on the design features, save for the often seen minor softness on the upper right shield corner. Census: 34 in 66, 14 finer (11/09).

Morgan Dollar PR64. This 1904 Morgan has a closed 9, which Breen (1977) calls VAM-1. Blushes of russet gather at the borders of this near-Gem, joined on the obverse margin by splashes of sky-blue. The design elements are exquisitely brought up except for a touch of softness in the hair over Liberty's ear. Faint short vertical marks of unknown origin are visible on Liberty's cheek.
From The Boca Collection, Part I. (Total: 6 coins)

Captivating 1905 Five-Piece Proof Set
NGC Certified

2050   1905 Five-Piece Proof Set NGC. Although the minor and silver proof sets of this year contain no Morgan dollar and neither the cent nor nickel changed one iota, proof coinage showed considerably larger mintages than in the previous year. There were 2,152 sets made containing the Indian cent and Liberty nickel, along with 727 silver three-coin sets of the Barber dime through half dollar. The proof Indian cents of this year are still fairly common in the market today, many showing striations from die polishing.

In his *Proof Encyclopedia,* Walter Breen remarked concerning the dime that "the peculiar marks within the 5 on proofs and on unc. examples of all mints are *not* evidence of overdate; they are characteristics of the date logotype made for the year." Bowers' *Guide Book of Shield and Liberty Nickels* comments that "proofs have deeply mirrored fields and are usually well struck and attractive."

The proof Barber half is a popular issue, occasionally substituting for the low-mintage 1905 business strike, produced to the extent of only 662,000 coins.

Cent PR65 Red and Brown. The design elements are well-defined, indicating a sharp strike, with only slight merging of details in the tips of some feathers in the headdress. The reflective, mirrored fields combine with satiny devices to create excellent eye appeal. Only the slightest mellowing of the original orange mint color prevents a full Red designation to this lovely Gem.

Nickel PR66. A bold strike is confirmed through the intricate details on both sides. Only slight weakness is noted left of the ribbon bow, although the ear of corn is sharp. Full and deeply mirrored fields surround satiny, lustrous devices, resulting in excellent contrast, although insufficient for a Cameo designation. This Premium Gem is untoned with brilliant nickel-gray surfaces. NGC Census: 64; 23 finer (10/09).

The Barber dime, quarter, and half dollar in this 1905 proof set have exceptional cameo contrast, and they also exhibit well matched toning. There is no doubt that they have remained together for the last 105 years. In the early years of the 20th century, coins with any degree of cameo contrast were considered undesirable. As a result, Mint officers instructed employees to create proofs without any contrast, making true Cameo proofs especially elusive today.

Dime PR67 Cameo. The strike is unquestionably full and complete, with every detail from the original dies found on this Superb Gem. This exquisite Barber dime has unending mirrored fields around fully lustrous devices. Both sides are virtually perfect. The obverse has delicate yellow-orange with traces of new blue and mauve at the lower border. The reverse has nearly identical toning along the upper left and right border. NGC Census: 8 in PR67 Cameo; 1 finer (10/09). Only 10% (20 of 194) of all NGC certified 1905 proof dimes are given the Cameo designation, with no Ultra Cameo pieces certified.

Quarter PR68 Cameo. A detailed microscopic examination of this Superb Gem fails to show any evidence of less than a full and complete strike. A stunning Superb Gem, this piece has extraordinary contrast between the fully and deeply mirrored fields, and the lustrous, satiny devices. The central motifs are brilliant white, with peripheral yellow-orange, new blue, and mauve toning. The same colors are splashes across much of the reverse. NGC Census: 3 in PR68 Cameo; 0 finer (10/09). Only 5% (12 of 232) of all NGC certified 1905 proof quarters are given the Cameo designation, with no Ultra Cameo pieces certified.

Half Dollar PR67 Cameo. All design elements on each side are full and complete, including the hair, leaf, and star details on the obverse, and the eagle and shield details on the reverse. Like the dime and quarter, the Barber half dollar has satiny devices and deeply mirrored fields. As the largest coin in this set, the Barber half dollar has the most surface area to accumulate imperfections, yet this amazing piece is void of any but the tiniest blemishes. The half dollar has similar toning to the quarter, although much of the reverse is untoned with only small splashes of color. NGC Census: 6 in PR67 Cameo; 0 finer (10/09). Only 6% (12 of 201) of all NGC certified 1905 proof half dollars are given the Cameo designation, with no Ultra Cameo pieces certified.
From The Boca Collection, Part I. (Total: 5 coins)

A 15% BUYER'S PREMIUM ($14 MIN.) APPLIES TO ALL LOTS.

Quality Five-Piece 1906 Proof Set
All Coins PR64 or Finer

2051   Five-Piece 1906 Proof Set NGC. There were 1,725 two-coin minor proof sets made in this year containing the Indian Head cent and Liberty nickel. The Indian cents are seldom seen with full Red color, although Cameo coins are more available than previously. The proof Liberty nickels are usually sharply struck with deep mirrors.

A smallish 675 minor silver proof sets were struck, containing the Barber dime, quarter, and half dollar. As is the case with most post-1902 proof coinage, relatively few Barber proofs of the year, of any denomination, show appreciable field-device contrast. Even those certified as Cameo are usually not heavily contrasted, which makes the dime in the present set all the more special. Of course, no Morgan dollars in proof (or any other) format had been produced since 1904.

The cent and nickel proofs of the mid-1900s, despite their relatively low mintages, are nonetheless always available for a price, no doubt due to greater survival rates compared to proof coinage from earlier decades. The proof coinage of this year featured four coins bearing two of the same uninspired designs by Charles Barber that had lingered for decades. But great change was in the wind, in the form of wholesale coinage design, first plotted out in 1905, that would commence in 1907; ironically, this change, which is widely praised today, would turn collectors even more firmly from proofs bearing the Barber design and contribute to the first cessation of proof sets in 1916.

Cent PR64 Brown. At first glance, this piece appears completely Brown, with dusky mahogany and umber shadings dominant. At certain angles, however, the surfaces come alive, and rich copper-orange and pumpkin hues appear, as well as violet-magenta accents at the reverse rims. A handful of faint hairlines in the fields contribute to the grade.

Nickel PR65. A lightly toned Gem proof that shares its patina with a number of other nickels in this collection, with pale green-gold outer toning that gives way to delicate lavender-blue in the centers. Sharply struck with considerable charm and potent mirrors that bring the colors to life.

Dime PR66 Cameo. As noted above, Cameo examples of the proof 1906 dime are elusive, and often weakly contrasted by the standards of past years. This specimen seems like a remarkable throwback, with crisp delineation between the frost of the devices and the clear and striking mirrors. A whisper of golden peripheral toning completes the eye appeal. Census: 5 in 66 Cameo, 6 finer (11/09).

Quarter PR66. While not designated as a Cameo by NGC, this Premium Gem quarter nonetheless offers appreciable field-to-device contrast. The mirrors are strong with a touch of champagne close to the rims, and the boldly impressed devices are faintly frosted, which creates a pleasing effect.

Half Dollar PR66. Like the quarter, the half dollar shows a degree of contrast, particularly on the obverse, but not at the Cameo level. Light green-gold rim toning takes on an added orange element at the lower reverse. A captivating specimen with undeniable eye appeal. For the contrast category, Census: 31 in 66, 23 finer (11/09).
From The Boca Collection, Part I. (Total: 5 coins)

A 15% BUYER'S PREMIUM ($14 MIN.) APPLIES TO ALL LOTS.

Prized 1907 Five-Piece Proof Set
Featuring PR68 ★ Cameo Quarter

2052 1907 Five-Piece Proof Set NGC. The five lower-denomination proof coins of 1907 consisted of the Indian cent and Liberty nickel, produced to the extent of 1,475 pieces each, and the Barber dime through half dollar, totaling 575 examples of each. Many of the proof 1907 cents are found with prominent die-polishing lines. The Liberty nickel issue is the lowest proof mintage of the entire series. This low production most likely reflects collector disenchantment with the staid and long-running series more than possible effects of the financial Panic of 1907. Bowers' Liberty nickel *Guide Book* notes that "quality of striking and appearance can vary widely among 1907 nickels in both circulation strikes and Proofs." The production figures on the three Barber silver proof coins are consistent with other proof issues of the 1900s, although proof mintages would plummet in 1914 and 1915 as the series' end approached.

Although it did not affect the minor denominations (yet), the introduction of the Augustus Saint-Gaudens-designed twenty and ten dollar gold pieces in 1907 would usher in a new (and unfortunately all too short-lived) era of artistic excellence in U.S. coinage, one that would extend to all denominations in the ensuing decade and a half. Saint-Gaudens would not live to see it, however, succumbing to cancer on August 3 without ever seeing his masterpieces in circulation. It fell to his artistic heirs to carry the torch, distinguished artists such as Bela Pratt, James Earle Fraser, Victor David Brenner, Adolph Weinman, and Hermon MacNeil.

Cent PR64 Brown. Strong violet and blue overtones are immediately eye-catching, but this coin also sports salmon hues on the obverse and considerable faded copper-orange on the reverse. Sharply struck with bright luster and undeniable eye appeal despite the faint hairlines that preclude a finer designation.

Nickel PR64 Cameo. This coin's considerable contrast is unusual, though not unheard-of. Hints of gold and blue patina visit the strongly mirrored fields, while the frosted devices show less toning. A handful of tiny contact marks are present in the portrait area.

Dime PR62. While the obverse shows a clear cameo effect, the reverse has more muted contrast, due to light silver-gray toning that shows a tendency to green-gold near the rims. The portrait side has more vibrant color at the margins, as well as considerable frost on the devices. Close inspection reveals a few wispy slide marks.

Quarter PR68 ★ Cameo. The most prominent piece in the set, this quarter offers simply breathtaking eye appeal, with its strong contrast only one component. The fields are powerfully mirrored beneath dappled champagne and gold-orange patina that lets in occasional hints of bright silver-white. Exquisitely preserved and instantly memorable.

Half Dollar PR66 Cameo. Of the three Barber coins in this lot, the half comes the closest to brilliance in the fields, though a touch of silver-gray toning is present. Both portrait and eagle are amply frosted, an uncommon state for this largest denomination. On the reverse, the right (facing) wing shows the effects of overzealous die polishing, with a row of inner feathers lost.
From The Boca Collection, Part I. (Total: 5 coins)

Desirable 1908 Proof Set Featuring
PR66 Cameo Dime

2053   1908 Five-Piece Proof Set NGC. The 1908 proof mintage is recorded at 1,620 pieces for the Indian cent and Liberty nickel, along with 545 each of the Barber dime, quarter dollar, and half dollar. The proof Indian cents are, of course, the next-to-last in the series, and although a lower-mintage date, when found they are apt to be well struck and attractive. The Bowers *Guide Book* calls 1908 proof Liberty nickels "among the rarest in the series. When found, they are usually attractive. Pristine, undipped Proofs of this era often have delicate, bluish toning, probably from the tissue-paper wrappers in which they were housed when sold by the Mint."

The 1908 proof Barber dime is one of the rarest in the series in high grades, due to the low original production. Most examples are fully struck. The 1908 Barber quarter and half dollar, both of which had a mintage of only 545 proofs (the same as for the dime), were saved in only average quality when compared to other proof issues with larger productions. Cameo and Deep/Ultra Cameo examples, however, are quite rare and seldom encountered.

Cent PR65 Brown. Bewitching violet and blue overtones are core to the eye appeal of this wonderful Gem specimen. While the dominant color is chocolate-brown, appreciable faded orange can be found at the obverse margins. Decisively struck and thoroughly appealing with excellent surface quality for the grade.

Nickel PR64 Cameo. Rather than the aforementioned blue, this specimen shows faint champagne and sea-green overtones, with a small streak of deeper color starting in the left obverse field and traveling through Liberty's hair, almost to her coronet. Sharply struck with only a few tiny flaws in the fields that preclude an even finer designation.

Dime PR66 Cameo. The star attraction of the lot, this Cameo Premium Gem proof dime combines outstanding contrast, a rarity for the issue, and high overall surface quality. The frost on Liberty's portrait is particularly noteworthy, sparkling and silver-white. The exquisitely detailed reverse also shows readily appreciable contrast, though the intensity of the mirrors plays more of a role on that side. Hints of green-gold peripheral toning add color to the piece. NGC has graded only 14 Cameo examples of this issue, with none as Ultra Cameo; this is one of two PR66 Cameo coins with four Cameo examples finer (10/09).

Quarter PR62. The patina is the most rewarding facet of this well-mirrored proof Barber quarter. The margins show a mix of green-gold, orange, and plum shadings, with the former two colors more prominent on the obverse and the latter heavily represented on the reverse. Lightly hairlined in the fields with a few wispy slide marks on the cheek, which combine to account for the grade.

Half Dollar PR65. A melange of rose, violet, blue, and gold-orange shadings embraces each side of this delightful Gem proof. The reverse shows an appreciable degree of frost on the eagle, which suggests that that side must have shown considerable contrast once. Overall, a gorgeous and pleasingly preserved specimen that shows no overt distractions.
From The Boca Collection, Part I. (Total: 5 coins)

A 15% BUYER'S PREMIUM ($14 MIN.) APPLIES TO ALL LOTS.

Seven-Piece 1909 Proof Set
All Three Cent Varieties

2054   Seven-Piece 1909 Proof Set. With seven different types across six distinct designs and five denominations, 1909 was the high point of 20th century proof minor coinage diversity until the advent of the Statehood quarters in 1999. While the Liberty nickel and Barber dime, quarter, and half all enjoyed design stability in 1909, the cent went through three distinct phases, all captured in proof format: the Indian Head, the VDB Reverse Lincoln, and the Lincoln design with VDB removed.

The final proof Indian cent issue enjoyed higher production than many of its peers, with collector acknowledgement of the design's upcoming end a likely influence. Its mintage of 2,175 pieces was the largest tally for a proof cent since 1900, and that figure follows three consecutive years with proof cent mintages well below the 2,000 mark. The 1909 Indian cent would be the last date for the denomination struck with a brilliant proof finish until 1936, since the beginning of the Lincoln cent brought a change in finish along with the change in design.

Drawing from its experiences with the proof gold coinage of 1908, the Mint chose to issue Lincoln cent proofs with matte surfaces. Only a limited number of matte proof Lincoln cents were struck, however, before yet another design change occurred: the designer's initials were removed, separating the year's output into two subtypes, those with and without the VDB on the reverse. Among proofs of the VDB type, only a limited number were released, a figure traditionally given as 420 pieces but one that is perhaps a shade too low.

Since the Liberty nickel was often sold along with the cent in two-coin sets, it benefited from the smaller denomination's design-change excitement, and 4,763 specimens were struck, a figure very close to the sum of the Indian and no-VDB Lincoln cent proof mintages. The silver proofs languished by comparison, with just 650 sets sold.

Indian Cent PR64 Red NGC. Sharply struck with pale copper-peach surfaces that are practically unturned. The left obverse field shows a faint fingerprint.

Lincoln VDB Cent PR63 Red and Brown ANACS. Sharply struck with the finely granular surfaces characteristic of this initial matte proof cent issue. Most of each side is copper-gold, though the faintly disturbed surfaces also show olive, mahogany, and violet accents. Housed in a small-format holder.

Lincoln Cent (No VDB) PR65 Brown NGC. Deep chocolate and mahogany shadings prevail over much of each side, but rich orange-gold peripheral tints still remain. A sharp and satiny Gem matte proof with textured yet smooth surfaces, an elegant paradox.

Nickel PR66 NGC. Light golden toning covers much of the profoundly mirrored fields of this crisp Premium Gem proof. Carefully preserved with glints of nickel-white present mostly on the devices and at the margins.

Dime PR66 NGC. An unusual specimen that once must have had considerable contrast, though patchy gold-orange and blue patina covers most of each side. The portrait retains considerable frostiness.

Quarter PR67 Cameo NGC. An outstanding Superb Gem with watery gold-graced mirrors that show specks of blue-green close to the rims. Moderately contrasted, though the frost is light, as is usual on Cameo representatives of the post-1902 Barber issues. Census: 10 in 67 Cameo, 1 finer (11/09).

Half Dollar PR65 Cameo NGC. Aside from a whisper of gold-gray toning, the fields of this Gem proof are essentially brilliant, and the devices are snow-white. Pleasingly contrasted, though the brilliant hollow in the space below Liberty's ear reveals how thin the frost is on the devices. Nonetheless, an immensely appealing specimen.
From The Boca Collection, Part I. (Total: 7 coins)

Important 1910 Proof Set
With Cameo Dime and Quarter

2055 1910 Five-Piece Proof Set NGC. Just as the Liberty nickel enjoyed its high mark for 20th century proof production in 1909, the matte proof Lincoln cent took its turn for generous production in 1910, with a mintage in excess of 4,000 specimens. Sources differ on the exact figure; the one listed in the Q. David Bowers reference *A Guide Book of Lincoln Cents* is 4,083 pieces. Yet significantly fewer Liberty nickel proofs (2,405 examples) were released. Why the discrepancy?

Bowers cites personal correspondence with coin dealer William L. Pukall. According to Bowers, "The Mint is said to have kept quantities of these [matte proofs] on hand after 1910, eventually selling them to dealers including" Pukall. Around 40% of all matte proof Lincoln cents for the year were sold outside the two-coin minor proof sets, but the exact number that were sold past the year of issue must remain a mystery.

Following the one-year increase in silver proof set strikings that came in 1909, production settled down again in 1910, to 551 pieces versus a proof mintage of 545 coins for the various silver denominations in 1908. The Barber design had long experienced collector disapproval, but after the Morgan dollar's suspension in 1904, the silver proof set experienced a far more pernicious effect: flat-out indifference. The mid-500s mintage level is a common sight from 1907 on, though the lowest mintages for proof Barber coinage sets would not begin until 1914.

Cent PR65 Brown. As noted above, the most accessible matte proof Lincoln cent when sought on its own, though its status as part of a set is far more elusive. The present piece has considerable orange for a "Brown" example, particularly on the otherwise mahogany-and-magenta obverse, though the blue-tinged surfaces on the reverse are toned much more deeply with a walnut hue for a base.

Nickel PR64. Sharply struck with delicate golden tints over otherwise pale nickel-gray surfaces. This mildly contrasted Choice proof shows only a few minor faults in the fields, though these are sufficient to preclude an even finer designation.

Dime PR65 Cameo. One of only 19 Cameo examples of this issue certified by NGC (10/09), this dime is colorfully toned in addition to its strong contrast. Green-gold, apricot, violet, and blue toning elements converge in the fields, though the frosty portrait has largely resisted patina. Crisply struck and carefully preserved.

Quarter PR64 Cameo. This coin's outstanding contrast is key to its winning eye appeal. The thickly frosted portrait stands out from the deep mirrors almost to an Ultra Cameo level, and if the reverse contrast were stronger, this coin could well have received such a designation. The strong yellow toning elements on the obverse carry over to the reverse, which also shows splashes of blue.

Half Dollar PR66. While not as strongly contrasted as either of its Cameo counterparts in the set, this Premium Gem proof half still shows a mild version of the effect, particularly on the obverse. Small splashes of cloud-gray toning visit the intense mirrors, and the upper obverse rim shows a hint of blue.
From The Boca Collection, Part I. (Total: 5 coins)

1911 Proof Set With Highlight
PR67 Cameo Half Dollar

2056   1911 Five-Piece Proof Set NGC. Landing as it does between the rapid-fire design changes of the cent in 1909 and the nickel in 1912 and 1913, the year 1911 seems relatively peaceful for the minor copper and nickel proof coinage, and for those two issues, the impression is correct. There is a difference of only eight pieces between the year's proof cents and nickels (1,725 specimens for the former versus 1,733 examples for the latter), and while these figures represent declines from the prior year, they also suggest that no after-year cent-selling shenanigans went on with 1911-dated coins (as seen in 1910).

Similarly, the initial view of the Barber silver proof issues for the year is not immediately jarring. David Lawrence, in his *The Complete Guide to Barber Halves,* describes the proof halves of 1911 as "readily available," thanks to high survival and certification rates. His note that the 1911 half dollar's "543 proofs made is third lowest for the series," however, deserves further examination. (While Mr. Lawrence was writing specifically of half dollars, the note is equally applicable to dimes and quarters.)

It is true that the mintage of 543 proofs for the various silver denominations is third-lowest for the Barber design, albeit not by much; 1908 saw a universal mintage of 545 proofs, for example. While the difference between them is trifling, it is the low mintage itself, rather than any relative comparison, that is significant; in the following four years of proof Barber coinage, two years of slightly elevated production give way to the design's two lowest-mintage dates.

Cent PR65 Brown. Frankly, for a coin showing as much lemon-gold and pumpkin-orange as this Gem proof does on the obverse, a "Brown" designation is absurd. While the sharply struck reverse has far more muted brown shadings, even it shows faded elements of original color.

Nickel PR65 Cameo. Pale golden tints enhance the contrast of this outstanding Gem proof, a decidedly Cameo coin with strongly reflective fields. Broadly appealing and without overt hairlines or contact marks, though a single tiny flyspeck is noted on the left foot of the I in AMERICA.

Dime PR64 Cameo. Only a small minority of the proof 1911 Barber dimes in the NGC *Census Report* have received a Cameo (or in one case, an Ultra Cameo) designation. This specimen, with its pale aquamarine and mauve shadings over light silver-gray surfaces, is one of the fortunate few. The toning helps the obverse's richly frosted portrait stand out from the adjacent mirrors.

Quarter PR61. A mildly contrasted specimen with muted mauve and green-gold toning elements over moderate mirrors. A single contact mark is noted close to Liberty's ear, and small scuffs and contact marks on the obverse contribute to the grade.

Half Dollar PR67 Cameo. The issue is readily available in lower and midrange grades, but this is no run-of-the-mill coin; it is a powerfully contrasted Superb Gem with stunning eye appeal and almost unapproachable quality. The thin veil of gold-gray toning that drapes each side does nothing to halt the impressive field-to-device contrast. Census: 5 in 67 Cameo, 1 finer (10/09).
From The Boca Collection, Part I. (Total: 5 coins)

Noteworthy 1912 Proof Set With
Stunning PR67 ★ Cameo Dime

2057   1912 Five-Piece Proof Set NGC. Walter Breen's *Proof Encyclopedia* comments tersely on the proof Liberty Head nickels of 1912: "Popular final year of the design; subject to type collector demand and also to some hoarding. Brilliant, of course." All of his listed thoughts warrant further explanation. First, the 1912 does enjoy last-of-its-kind popularity, more so now than at the time, since it is the last proof Liberty Head nickel to be sold in sets. (The infamous 1913 Liberty Head nickels were sold *as* a set, but that is a completely different topic.)

Not only did 1912 mark the last year for proof Liberty Head nickels, it also marked the last year for brilliant proof nickels of any design until 1936, since the early years of Buffalo nickel proofs were made in matte format. As for Breen's comment about the date's popularity for type purposes, almost every proof Liberty Head nickel after 1887 can be treated more or less the same in that regard, and the year's mintage of 2,145 proofs is neither wildly high nor abnormally low. Practically the only difference between the 1912 and a 19th century date of similar mintage is that the former is significantly less likely to show cameo contrast.

In other denominations, proof Lincoln cent production hews closely to that of the nickel, with 2,172 specimens struck for the former. Among the Barber silver denominations, the year's 700 silver proof sets marks a localized high, in that the previous year to top that figure was 1905 and the design would not see so high a mintage again.

Cent PR64 Brown. Deep brown color with violet and gold undercurrents, muted on the obverse but significantly more prominent on the reverse. Though a few tiny disturbances preclude a finer designation, this coin offers remarkable visual appeal for the grade.

Nickel PR66. An outstanding Premium Gem that comes close to a Cameo designation. Light golden toning overall with occasional whispers of peach and green. The flashy fields are virtually undimmed by the patina, and the frost on the portrait and wreath remains sparkling. Great surface quality with eye appeal to match.

Dime PR67 ★ Cameo. NGC has graded just three examples of this issue as PR67 Cameo, with no Cameo coins finer, and of the three, this is one of two to have received the Star designation (10/09). The certified grade, however, merely supplies a number; this Superb Gem's eye appeal speaks for itself. Minimally toned, outstandingly contrasted centers give way to gold-orange peripheral patina that then fades into violet and blue. Fantastic preservation completes this incredible specimen.

Quarter PR63. Mildly contrasted on each side, though the portrait's frost is too subtle for a Cameo designation. A thin wash of green-gold patina covers much of each side, with a touch of pale blue at the lower right reverse. Broadly reflective fields show a handful of scattered hairlines.

Half Dollar PR63. Light silver-gray toning over each side with subtle rose and gold tints. This Select proof has excellent eye appeal for the grade assigned, though close inspection reveals a number of hairlines, with the most prominent ones in the right obverse field.
From The Boca Collection, Part I. (Total: 5 coins)

Popular 1913 Proof Set Containing
Type One and Type Two Nickels

2058   1913 Six-Piece Proof Set NGC. Beginning in 1913, the two-coin minor proof set turned into an all-matte affair, as the James Earle Fraser-designed Buffalo nickel replaced the Liberty Head motifs. Like the Lincoln cent (and the Saint-Gaudens and Pratt gold designs) before it, the Buffalo nickel was not designed with brilliant proofs in mind, and a matte technique was used instead. The matte proofs proved unpopular, and mintages steadily deteriorated from 1913 to 1916.

The two varieties of Buffalo nickel struck in 1913, the Type One with the bison on raised ground and the Type Two with the same bison on flat ground, are also reflected in the year's matte proofs. Mintages for Type One and Type Two proofs are close (1,520 specimens for the former versus 1,514 pieces for the latter), though the Type One is in greater demand since it is the only proof issue bearing its particular design. The year's minor proofs must have been sold virtually exclusively as two-coin sets both before and after the design change, as suggested by the cent and nickel proof mintages; while the two nickel varieties together sum up to a little over 3,000 pieces, there were just *under* 3,000 proof Lincoln cents coined.

Unlike many prior years, the mintages of silver proof dimes, quarters, and halves in 1913 do not match one another. The dime has a listed mintage of 622 pieces, with 613 quarters and 627 halves rounding out the stated figures. The lowest-mintage quarter denomination, which creates the cap of 613 possible silver proof sets, enjoys an additional popularity boost thanks to a mintage of fewer than half a million circulation strikes, the lowest for any Philadelphia Barber quarter issue.

Cent PR65 Red and Brown. Both sides show a luxurious blend of orange and coffee-brown color, and the surfaces are smoothly satiny. Exactingly struck with just a couple of minor flyspecks visible in the obverse fields. Census: 48 in 65 Red and Brown, 28 finer (10/09).

Type 1 Nickel PR65. Light nickel-blue color overall with arcs of pale peach-champagne gracing parts of the rims. This Gem specimen, with its rugged definition and exquisitely textured surfaces, bears a striking resemblance to Fraser's initial ideal for the Buffalo nickel.

Type 2 Nickel PR67. An exquisitely detailed representative of the modified Buffalo nickel type with reworked reverse. Pale sky-blue patina drapes most of the obverse, while the apricot accents on that side blossom into full-on coverage on the reverse. Outstanding preservation and visual appeal. Census: 38 in 67, 5 finer (10/09).

Dime PR64 Cameo. Distinctly contrasted, an unusual state for the later years of proof Barber coinage. The devices are attractively frosted, particularly the portrait. Light silver and gold-gray color on each side with occasional dots of deeper toning at the rims. Census: 5 in 64 Cameo, 12 finer (10/09).

Quarter PR66 Cameo. Strongly contrasted like the dime, with the effect amplified by deep blue-green toning that drapes much of the mirrors but leaves most of the frosted devices untouched. Along with the Type 2 nickel, a showcase coin in the set. Census: 7 in 66 Cameo, 11 finer (10/09).

Half Dollar PR65. Both sides are immensely reflective, though contrast is minimal. Liquid gold-orange luster across each side shows glimpses of aquamarine at the margins. A decisively struck Gem.
From The Boca Collection, Part I. (Total: 6 coins)

Wonderful 1914 Proof Set
All Coins Gem or Better Quality

2059   1914 Five-Piece Proof Set NGC. The most memorable feature of the proofs of 1914 is the mintage for the silver proof set; no more than 380 proof sets could have been produced (borrowing the verbiage so particular to Walter Breen) and that figure was the lowest for a year since 1858. While the 1914 proof dimes have a stated mintage of 425 pieces, the quarter and half share the lower figure of 380 coins. Of the three denominations, the half dollar is of special interest because the lowest-mintage proof date in the Barber series coincides with the lowest-mintage *business strike* date.

As with other proof dates associated with key-date business strikes, this creates added price pressure on the proofs and also might have induced the break-up of a number of sets in the past. A lesser version of the same effect took place the year before. However, with 627 proof halves minted in 1913, there was a significant supply to absorb the spillover demand from business strike collectors. By contrast, the 380 proofs struck in 1914 (and the 450 proofs struck in 1915) have much less flexibility to meet the needs of those who are not proof specialists.

Among minor matte proofs, production was close between cents and nickels, with 1,365 specimens for the former and 1,275 pieces for the latter. These mintages continue a trend of decline for the proof nickel and begin one for the cent; the smallest denomination had enjoyed an uptick in 1913, thanks to its pairing with the two first-year varieties of Buffalo nickel proofs, but 1914 saw matte proof mintages come crashing down again.

Cent PR66 ★ Brown. This spectacularly eye-catching cent specimen leads off the set. The bold magenta, cherry-red, and heather overtones on this matte proof nearly overshadow the light brown base color. Exquisitely detailed and carefully preserved, a winner in every respect.

Nickel PR65. Subtle gold and pink tints visit otherwise nickel-white surfaces. Neither side shows any faults readily visible to the unaided eye, and this crisply struck Gem proof has outstanding eye appeal for the grade, particularly on the obverse with its original "Fraser" texture.

Dime PR66. The three Barber silver proofs in this set are remarkably well-matched in appearance. The dime sets the tone, with liquid green-gold peripheral toning around muted lavender-blue centers. Two elongated silvery dots underline the letters AME of AMERICA. Both the portrait and wreath are lightly frosted, lending a touch of contrast to each side.

Quarter PR66. At first glance, the toning on the quarter is highly similar to that of the dime, but on closer inspection, a few differences emerge. A hint of orange is mixed into the green-gold at the periphery, and the much larger lavender-blue centers show mint-green hues as well. Small splashes of silver color appear at the obverse margins.

Half Dollar PR66. Rounding out the trio of Premium Gems is this impressive half. The obverse shows a clear delineation between the outer green-gold and inner blue shadings, but the reverse shows the former color and peach intermixed. Of the three Barber pieces, the mirrors are perhaps the most impressive on this coin. Wonderful eye appeal.
From The Boca Collection, Part I. (Total: 5 coins)

Strong 1915 Proof Set
Last of the Barber Series

2060   1915 Five-Piece Proof Set NGC. The year 1915 marks the end of the first era of high-distribution silver proof sets. It had not been the Mint's intent to strike Barber coinage in the early part of 1916, the traditional season for proof strikings at that time. Even when the Barber design was continued into 1916 on the dime and quarter, as delays in the finishing of those denominations' new designs ran into the needs of commerce, proofs were not struck. As discussed under 1916, complications with the new silver designs contributed to the end of the Mint's proof program. Thus, the brilliant proof Barber silver coins of 1915 were the end of the line, at least until the resumption of proof sets in 1936.

Production of silver proof sets in 1915 was low, though not so depressed as in 1914; proof strikings for the three silver denominations amounted to 450 pieces each in 1915, a figure that seems downright healthy compared to the 380 proof quarters and halves struck the year before. Still, between collector distaste for the design on the silver proofs and disdain for the matte proof finish on the cents and nickels, signs of purchasing fatigue are easy to read.

Today, the silver proofs of 1915 experience considerable demand, particularly the half dollar, which (like the 1914 proof half) is associated with a low-mintage business strike of the same date. In his *Proof Encyclopedia,* Walter Breen makes the intriguing note: "Numerals on all 1915 dimes cruder than on any preceding years." Among matte proof issues, cent production beat that of the nickel, 1,150 pieces to 1,050 specimens; but in both cases, the numbers are part of a continuing decline that would not stop until the terminal issues in 1916.

Cent PR65 Red and Brown. Copper-orange color, faded on the reverse but bright on the obverse, puts a distinctive accent on this otherwise violet-brown Gem proof, which is decisively detailed and attractively preserved for the grade. A few small splashes of bluish color are noted in the field just above the date.

Nickel PR66. Glimpses of peach, pink, and champagne patina visit parts of the margins, leaving the rest of this gorgeous proof virtually nickel-white. Exactingly struck with a few tiny flyspecks visible at the upper reverse that are mentioned strictly for accuracy.

Dime PR64. A subtly but delightfully toned near-Gem with light blue, emerald, and forest-green shadings over intensely mirrored surfaces. The portrait shows a pleasing level of frost, and a few dots of deeper color are present within the reverse wreath. A handful of tiny hairlines account for the grade.

Quarter PR64. Far more boldly toned than the dime, with blue, orange, and lavender peripheral shadings that are at their most intense along the lower obverse rim. Faintly silver-gray centers show a degree of contrast. Two small contact marks, one near Liberty's jawline and the other close to the truncation of the bust, contribute to the grade.

Half Dollar PR64. This coin shows a return to colors close to those of the dime, with muted olive-gold and blue most prevalent. The obverse has an untoned core, while the reverse is almost completely patinated. A faint fingerprint is visible below the eagle's tailfeathers. *From The Boca Collection, Part I.* (Total: 5 coins)

Two-Piece 1916 Proof Set
Last Year of Issue Until 1936

2061   Two-Piece 1916 Proof Set NGC.

"Effective at once, you will please discontinue the manufacture of proof coins."

—Mint Director Fredrich von Engelken, October 18th, 1916, as quoted in Roger W. Burdette's Renaissance of American Coinage 1916-1921

The end of the Barber design for silver coinage indirectly brought with it the end of the first era of American proof sets as well. With the Barber design officially on the way out and the numerous well-known difficulties in adapting the MacNeil and Weinman designs to coinage, manufacturing proofs of the silver denominations was a low priority for the Philadelphia Mint.

Complaints from collectors and coin dealers mounted, matched by Philadelphia Mint employees' increasing frustration with their demanding customers, yet no silver proofs were forthcoming. Only the cent and nickel, which had already experienced their "growing pains" as matte proofs, were offered as a two-coin set. Just 600 such sets were produced, and some may have gone unsold.

Roger W. Burdette, writing in his *Renaissance of American Coinage 1916 - 1921,* assigns responsibility for the demise of proof coinage to Philadelphia Mint Superintendent Adam Joyce, who wrote a letter to Mint Director Fredrich von Engelken dated October 17, 1916, laying out his case for the end of proof production. Burdette sums up Joyce's argument and von Engelken's reaction: "It didn't take von Engelken long to make a decision - the mint was losing money on each proof coin made, collectors were complaining, and paperwork had become a nuisance. Rather than look for ways to correct problems, the director decided to eliminate all proof coins."

Two decades would pass before the proof set tradition rose again.

Cent PR63 Brown. A strongly appealing Select specimen of the last standard-issue matte proof Lincoln cent, primarily violet and blue-brown overall but with considerable magenta intermixed. The obverse margins and a horizontal streak at the central reverse show muted copper-orange.

Nickel PR66. The most challenging and most costly of the widely distributed Buffalo nickel proofs, offered here as a gorgeous Premium Gem. Exquisitely detailed with wonderful satiny luster that graces textured surfaces, pale nickel-pink with broad gold elements and occasional orange accents.

From The Boca Collection, Part I. (Total: 2 coins)

Famous 1936 Proof Set With
Brilliant Finish Cent and Nickel

2062   1936 Five-Piece Proof Set NGC. William Woodin, first Secretary of the Treasury under Franklin Delano Roosevelt, is the most famous coin collector associated with that administration, but another, more behind-the-scenes player also had considerable impact on the story of American coinage. Louis McHenry Howe, a reporter turned FDR campaign manager who became the president's personal secretary and ultimate confidant, spent nearly the last eight months of his life hospital-bound, yet remained a meaningful influence.

Howe may be little-remembered outside historical and political-science circles, but a near-contemporary document makes his power clear. The June 1936 edition of *The Numismatist* quotes a "press dispatch" discussing the return of proof coinage: "Secretary [of the Treasury Henry] Morgenthau has announced he had authorized the mint to resume the practice of issuing "proof" coins ... It was understood at the Treasury that the resumption of such minting was ordered on a suggestion of Louis M. Howe, secretary to President Roosevelt, a few weeks before his death."

What Howe wanted was made so, but collectors, not having learned their lesson from two decades earlier, immediately complained about the satiny finish found on the early runs of proof cents and nickels, prompting the editor of *The Numismatist* to write to the Mint about the newly restarted proof striking process. Mint Director Nellie Tayloe Ross replied, forwarding information from the Superintendent of the Mint. Her reply appeared in the July 1936 edition of *The Numismatist*. The Barber silver and Liberty gold denominations' dies had been prepared by "basining" the fields; as expressed by Ross, "the field was polished to a perfect radius on a revolving disc," creating strong "definition between motif and field."

By contrast, "All the present coins [i.e. coins current in 1936] are made from sculptured models without retouching with a graver in any way ... This gives a more or less uneven background with less sharpness in the details." Further, "With the present coins, the models were never prepared with the intention of 'basining' and it could not be done without many radical alterations to the present design."

The Director's statements notwithstanding, brilliant proofs did come about later in the year, creating two distinct varieties for proof cents and nickels. David Lange writes in his *Complete Guide to Mercury Dimes* that while both satin and brilliant proof dimes were struck in 1936, the satin pieces are both rare and rarely distinguished from their brilliant peers: "Since silver is among the more reflective of metals, the visible difference between satin proofs and brilliant proofs is too subtle for the hobby to make an official distinction."

A last important note is that starting with 1936, the various proof denominations were offered individually, with each piece commanding its own premium. Whereas pre-1936 proof coins had matching mintages or nearly so, the mix-and-match nature of proof ordering in 1936 resulted in disparate production: 5,569 proof cents were struck versus 5,769 nickels, 4,130 dimes, 3,837 quarters, and 3,901 halves. The quarter's mintage of 3,837 specimens places a hard cap on the number of possible five-coin proof sets issued.

Brilliant Finish Cent PR64 Red. This coin's bright copper-orange surfaces also show a slight lemon cast. Decisively detailed with only a few stray hairlines accounting for the grade.

Brilliant Finish Nickel PR66. Faint blue and lavender toning elements over otherwise pale nickel-gray surfaces. An exquisitely struck and carefully preserved specimen with remarkable visual appeal.

Dime PR65. Exactingly struck with gleaming mirrors, this Gem proof offers outstanding eye appeal. Green-gold toning elements stick largely to the rims, leaving the centers minimally toned.

Quarter PR64. Echoes of pale green-gold toning visit the rims, but the centers are bright silver-white on this first-year Washington quarter specimen. Decisively detailed and thoroughly appealing, though light hairlines preclude a finer designation.

Half Dollar PR64. Both sides show appreciable contrast, though not enough for a Cameo designation. Strongly mirrored, faintly hairlined surfaces are silver-white save for dots of rose and sage that are present close to the rims.
From The Boca Collection, Part I. (Total: 5 coins)

A 15% BUYER'S PREMIUM ($14 MIN.) APPLIES TO ALL LOTS.

Outstanding 1937 Proof Set
All Coins PR66 or Finer

2063   1937 Five-Piece Proof Set NGC. The proof sets issued in the 1936 to 1942 era are considered by many numismatists to be in a class by themselves. The mintages of this group were extremely small by today's standards, increasing only slightly each year. Moreover, published mintage figures for 1936-1942 sets are listed for each denomination rather than the number of five-coin sets sold. For example, the 2010 *Guide Book* shows the 1937 proof mintages at 9,320 cents, 5,769 nickels, 5,756 dimes, 5,542 quarters, and 5,728 half dollars. These were sold singly over the counter and by mail at 15 cents over face value for each coin. A complete set cost $1.81 (including 23 cents for postage and insurance). The *Guide Book* lists the mintage of the 1937 proof set at 5,542 pieces-the number of quarters made, which is the lowest of all five denominations.

The packaging of the 1936-42 proof sets left much to be desired. Arno Safran, in an article titled "Is the 1937 Proof Set Underrated?" published in the December 2007 *Augusta Coin Club Monthly Newsletter*, writes: "Each coin was inserted into a brittle cellophane envelope. The envelopes were then stapled at the top to the others; then placed into a small square cardboard box."

Inadequate packaging resulted in problems over the years, such as rusted staples or the cellophane envelopes ripping, causing corrosion or damage to some coins. Also, some pieces, especially the larger denominations, which were issued during the Depression, were spent. These factors combined to leave the population of attractive, problem-free 1937 proof sets significantly diminished, and are considered by many greatly undervalued.

Cent PR67 ★ Red and Brown. Pale copper color fades into fiery yellow-orange, peach, blue, and green at the margins of this stunning Superb Gem. Remarkable preservation combines with stunning toning for flat-out fantastic eye appeal. A wonderful coin to start the set.

Nickel PR66. The final proof Buffalo nickel issue, since the denomination switched over to Jefferson nickel proofs in 1938 (there are no P-mint 1938 Buffalo nickels). Strongly reflective fields and boldly defined devices show faint, dappled pink and gold toning overall. An incredibly attractive Premium Gem.

Dime PR66. A gleaming specimen, virtually brilliant save for a faint halo of gold close to the margins. The devices are exactingly defined, revealing many nuances of the Weinman design. Outstanding preservation that does credit to the PR66 designation.

Quarter PR66. The light gold-gray toning that has settled over each side does not dim the intensity of the mirrors. Definition is strong in general, though overzealous polishing has lapped away parts of the ribbon at the back of Washington's head. On the reverse, the eagle is faintly frosted.

Half Dollar PR67. The set began with a Superb Gem, and it ends with a Superb Gem in this stunning PR67 half. With whispers of sky-blue and sea-green patina touching the obverse and faint canary-yellow glints gracing parts of the eagle's feathers, this example is not brilliant, but the reflectivity of the fields is potent nonetheless. Incredibly appealing.
From The Boca Collection, Part I. (Total: 5 coins)

Attractive 1938 Proof Set

2064   1938 Five-Piece Proof Set NGC. The proof coins of 1938 had a higher mintage than their 1937 counterparts, with the difference most noticeable for the one and five cent denominations. The cent mintage was 14,734 coins, the five cent 19,365 specimens, the dime 8,728 pieces, the quarter dollar 8,045 examples, and the half dollar 8,152 coins. Thus, a maximum of 8,045 proof sets could have been issued; however, Walter Breen (1977) writes that probably fewer sets were actually assembled. He also indicates that they were "Much speculated in, like the 1937's."

The 1938 proof coinage is significant because it included the new Jefferson nickel. An editorial comment in the June 1938 *The Numismatist* says: "The new Jefferson nickel has the distinction of being the first coin of the United States the designs for which were selected in an open competition." The obverse is much like creator Felix Schlag's original conception, but the reverse shows a front view of Monticello, a far cry from the sculptor's initial design.

Breen lists two varieties of the Jefferson nickel: the first has normal letters and an irregularly-shaped star. According to Breen, it was greatly hoarded as the first year of issue. The second variety has extremely thin, wispy ERTY letters, and the star shows as a mere dot. Breen says this variety is "very scarce."

Cent PR65 Red. Bright yellow-orange color lends itself to excellent mirrors on this Gem proof, a boldly executed coin with praiseworthy surface quality. There are no hairlines or contact marks of any particular note, though a small flyspeck visible above the T in LIBERTY may have contributed to the grade.

Nickel PR66. Breen's first variety, which apparently shows less extensive die polishing than its scarcer counterpart. Both sides are boldly mirrored beneath light but rewarding patina, which appears as waves of pink and pale yellow. Curiously, the area on Jefferson's coat nearest the truncation of the bust shows a number of die scratches; it should be noted that these were a part of the coin from the moment of striking and have zero influence on the grade.

Dime PR67. The strike is absolute on this Superb Gem, which offers a chromelike gleam in its small but attractive mirrors. While the obverse is virtually brilliant, the reverse exhibits small splashes of sage and sea-green patina above and to the right of the fasces. An attractive coin and the highest-graded specimen in the set.

Quarter PR65. Pale gray patina is the rule in the fields, though the obverse also shows a touch of golden toning that is most visible in the area of Washington's neck. On the reverse, a tiny dot of deep crimson is visible at the rim to the right of the R in DOLLAR. A solidly struck Gem with noteworthy visual appeal.

Half Dollar PR66. Pale silver-gray toning over most of each side with light but distinct green and gold toning visible at parts of the margins. Additional crimson elements are present at the upper obverse, with the most readily visible dot of color present just to the right of the E in LIBERTY. Magnificent eye appeal aided by strong definition on Liberty's branch hand.
From The Boca Collection, Part I. (Total: 5 coins)

Exquisite 1939 Silver-Minor Proof Set
All Coins PR66 Or Finer

2065   **1939 5-Piece Proof Set NGC.** There was only a slight increase in the number of proof sets from the previous year. The quarter had the lowest number of pieces struck with only 8,795 coins. This limits the number of possible proof sets to the quarter's mintage, but since proof coins could be ordered from the Mint singly the actual number of sets is certainly less than this figure. The only scarce variant in the 1939 proof set is the nickel. The hub was changed in 1939, and proof nickels were struck from both the Reverse of 1938 and the Reverse of 1940. The Reverse of 1938 shows Monticello with the so-called "Wavy Steps." The hub of 1940 has straight steps and shows a heavier and thicker top step. The Reverse of 1940 nickels are much scarcer than their Reverse of 1938 counterparts. As with all years from 1936 through 1942, proofs are seldom seen with any degree of contrast between the fields and devices.

Cent PR66 Red. David Bowers writes in his *Guide Book of Lincoln Cents* that while 1939 proof cents are "readily available ... pristine undipped gems are in the minority." The fully Red Premium Gem housed in this set qualifies as one of the minority that Bowers alludes to. Its brilliant coppery-orange surfaces are imbued with hints of light green and are devoid of mentionable contact marks or spots. A decisive strike leaves shaper definition on the design elements. This piece exudes phenomenal overall eye appeal.

Five Cent Reverse of 1938 PR66. The "waviness" of Monticello's steps identifies the 1938 Reverse discussed in the introductory section. This Premium Gem is noteworthy in that it is very well struck, displaying about 5 1/2 steps. David Bowers notes in *A Guide Book of Buffalo and Jefferson Nickels* that Reverse of 1938 proof nickels with 5 full steps are "scarce" and those with 6 full steps are "very rare." Additionally, hues of delicate bluish-violet, beige-gold, and lilac patina drapes the impeccably preserved surfaces on both sides. Truly an exceptional coin in all respects.

Dime PR67. While this Superb Gem appears color free with the unaided eye, magnification brings out a melange of soft ice-blue, violet, and gold patination. A powerful strike imparts bold definition to the design features and luminous surfaces reveal exquisite preservation.

Quarter PR67. An assemblage of powder-blue, beige-gold, and violet coloration adorns bright surfaces on both sides of this lovely Superb Gem quarter, each of which has been well cared for. All of the design elements are well brought up.

Half Dollar PR66. Both sides of this Premium Gem half dollar display full brilliance that appears to reach out to the observer. The only discernible color is a handful of light violet freckles in the reverse fields, and an impressive strike leaves crisp delineation on the design features. A few minuscule ticks are of no consequence.
From The Boca Collection, Part I. (Total: 5 coins)

Attractive 1940 Proof Set

2066 **1940 Five-Piece Proof Set NGC.** In 1940 the United States was on the brink of war, which had broken out in Europe in September 1939 with the German invasion of Poland. The United States provided material support to the Allies, most notably to the United Kingdom during the Battle of Britain, but would not itself declare war on an Axis nation until December 1941.

In the years from 1936 to 1942, the Mint sold proof coins individually to collectors based on the number of orders, so recorded mintages for the various denominations differ. Proof coin totals for the cent and nickel decreased in 1939 compared to 1938, while the dime, quarter, and half showed modest increases. All denominations showed elevated productions from 1939 to 1940, although the Jefferson nickel remained in a swoon compared to the high-water mark set by its introductory issue in 1938, a record that would stand until 1942.

The Lincoln cent saw a proof production of 15,872 coins, a supply still sufficient for today's demand; only ultra high-grade coins are conditionally elusive. The 1940 proof Jeffersons were struck with both the "wavy steps" Reverse of 1938 and the "straight steps" Reverse of 1940. The former is much more elusive, listed in the *Cherrypickers' Guide* as FS-901. Most of the silver proof coins show little to no contrast between the fields and devices. The 1940 silver proofs are generally attractive and well-defined, but Cameo proofs are rare.

Cent PR64 Red. The obverse has a strong copper-orange color and mirrors, but also with a considerable degree of patina for a Red representative. The fields show a degree of haze, and the faint fingerprints visible mostly at the margins must have had an influence on the grade. The reverse has slightly greater variation in color, ranging from lemon-gold to pale violet-magenta.

Nickel (Reverse of 1940) PR66. The sharp, straight steps leading up to Monticello indicate the more readily available Reverse of 1940 variety. At first glance, this Premium Gem proof shows only pale nickel-gray color, but on closer inspection, faint whispers of sky-blue and pastel-yellow also appear, most noticeably in the fields around the dome.

Dime PR65. Light silver-gray toning has settled over much of each side, so that a break in the patina at the upper right reverse field actually appears to be a patch of darker color at first glance. Bold striking definition with attractively mirrored fields that the toning does little to dim.

Quarter PR65. Faintly toned-over in much the same manner as the dime, but with a trifle more color; the obverse has a subtle olive cast to the gray toning, while the reverse shows a touch of yellow. Attractively preserved with excellent mirrors and commendable all-around eye appeal, a worthy Gem.

Half Dollar PR66. The most important piece in the set is also the most overtly patinated, with a splash of bright yellow at the lower right obverse rim. That side has a faint bluish cast to the overall toning, while the reverse combines elements of olive-gold and gray. The well-preserved fields are strongly mirrored, and this specimen boasts a conspicuously bold strike on Liberty's branch hand.
From The Boca Collection, Part I. (Total: 5 coins)

Highly Attractive 1941 Proof Set
All Coins PR65 or Better

2067   1941 5-Piece Proof Set NGC. The Philadelphia Mint produced 15,287 five-coin proof sets in 1941, each containing the five denominations that were in production, from the cent to the half dollar. Actually, each denomination had a different mintage, ranging from the figure above (the proof quarter mintage), up to 21,100 proof Lincoln cents. Examples of all denominations can be acquired without difficult in nearly any desired grade up to PR67 or even PR68. However, the collector who seeks examples with full or partial cameo contrast will face an extremely difficult challenge. Such coins are major rarities in the field of 20th century numismatics.

Many 1941 proof coins are struck from overpolished dies. David Lange explains in *The Complete Guide to Mercury Dimes:* "The proofs of 1941 seem to have been made with a little less care than those from the years immediately preceding. The spike in sales this year may have caught the Mint by surprise, as there is a noticeably higher instance of over polished dies for the 1941 proofs ... this careless die work is symptomatic of 1941 proofs in general."

The most famous of those poorly made pieces from overpolished dies is the 1941 half dollar variety that lacks the designer's initials on the reverse. An informal review of our Permanent Auction Archives reveals that about 75% of proof 1941 half dollars are missing the AW monogram.

One Cent PR65 Red. Brilliant coppery-gold color dominates both sides, blushed with a couple splashes of light red, more so on the obverse. A solid strike leaves bold definition on the design motifs. Devoid of contact marks, with a small toning spot above the 4 in the date.

Five Cent PR66. Tints of orange-gold on the luminous surfaces show up under magnification. A powerful strike leaves sharp definition on the design elements, including six full steps below Monticello's pillars. Additionally, excellent delineation occurs between the pillar bases and the top step. Both sides are completely devoid of noticeable marks.

Dime PR67. Full brilliance greets the observer of this magnificent Superb Gem and an exacting strike emboldens the design features on each side. Close examination reveals no marks or spots of any kind. In sum, this piece generates imposing eye appeal.

Quarter PR66. Whispers of peripheral golden-orange patina are a bit more extensive and deeper in hue on the obverse of this Premium Gem quarter. Well preserved surfaces exhibit impressively struck design elements.

Half Dollar No "AW" PR66. This coin is one of the 75% of 1941 proof half dollars lacking the AW monogram. Walter Breen, in his *Proof* encyclopedia, contends that these are all from the same working die which had been repolished or lapped, "probably to obliterate clash marks." This fully brilliant Premium Gem exhibits crisply defined design motifs. Close inspection reveals no marks on its impeccably preserved surfaces. Interestingly, this piece shows a small degree of field-device variance on the obverse when the coin is tilted slightly under a light source.
From The Boca Collection, Part I. (Total: 5 coins)

A 15% BUYER'S PREMIUM ($14 MIN.) APPLIES TO ALL LOTS.

Six-Piece 1942 Proof Set Including
Both Five Cent Varieties

2068   1942 Six-Piece Proof Set NGC. In 1942, proof coinage continued its twin trends of accelerating popularity and higher mintages; the half dollar, which showed the smallest increase in production by sheer numbers, saw 21,120 pieces struck in 1942 versus just 15,412 specimens coined in 1941. The greatest gains were made by the five cent piece, which famously saw production in two separate compositions, first the 75% copper, 25% nickel alloy that had been standard since 1866, then the 56% copper, 35% silver, and 9% manganese alloy of the "war nickels." Both compositions saw heavy proof mintages: 29,600 representatives for the former and 27,600 coins for the latter.

The same wartime necessities that brought about the two varieties of five cent coins also brought an early end to the rebirth of proof sets that had begun in 1936. While the early history of U.S. proof set production includes the practice's persistence through the Civil War years, circumstances in 1943 were far different: rather than the relative idleness in which the Philadelphia Mint found itself from 1862 to 1865, the World War II-era Mint was struggling to keep up with high coinage demand and other needs. Under the headline "No 1943 Proof Coins Available" was this note in *The Numismatist,* April 1943:

"The Superintendent of the Philadelphia Mint has stated to all inquiries for current proof sets that 'In view of the extremely heavy demand for coinage and service medals, the facilities of the Mint are taxed almost beyond capacity. Due to this fact, the striking of proof coins will necessarily be delayed for an indefinite period.'

"Notice will appear in [*The Numismatist]* as soon as it is learned these are again available."

Proof coins were not struck in 1943, and even the end of World War II did not return them to production. The program did not resume until 1950.

Cent PR64 Red. Strong copper-orange color on the obverse with paler tan elements prominent on the reverse. Exactingly detailed with only a few tiny flyspecks and other flaws present in the fields.

Five Cent Nickel PR66. Light blue and gold tints have settled over each side of this otherwise pearl-gray piece, a strongly struck Premium Gem with potent mirrors. Highly attractive with a touch of frostiness to the portrait.

Five Cent Silver PR66. The faint yellow toning that visits parts of the otherwise silver-white obverse is deeper and more overt on the reverse. Exactingly struck and pleasingly preserved, a rewarding representative of this modern billon issue.

Dime PR65. Light silver-gray color overall with suggestions of crimson and olive near the rims, most prominently at the area of E PLURIBUS UNUM and DIME. The powerful mirrors are key to this Gem's visual appeal.

Quarter PR66. Pale silver-gray patina overall with a touch of golden toning at the margins. Washington's portrait is well-defined for the issue with a whisper of frostiness. A highly attractive piece that represents a clear step up from the average PR65 coin.

Half Dollar PR65. Of the silver denominations, only the quarter would have the same design when proofs resumed in 1950, making this 1942 Walking Liberty half part of the last issue of its kind. A faint skiff of cloud-gray toning drapes the strongly reflective fields, while the devices show little of that patina. A sharp and easily appreciated Gem.
From The Boca Collection, Part I. (Total: 6 coins)

A 15% BUYER'S PREMIUM ($14 MIN.) APPLIES TO ALL LOTS.

Five-Piece 1950 Proof Set
All Pieces PR66 or Better

2069   Five-Piece 1950 Proof Set NGC. The story of U.S. proof coinage restarted officially on May 10, 1950. As the July 1950 edition of *The Numismatist* reports (p. 423): "... President Truman signed the Bill for the striking and sale of proof coins at the Philadelphia Mint. At this writing, June 7, they are not yet on sale nor has the price been decided on. However, our proof makers are working three shifts and collectors can be assured that there will be sufficient 1950 proofs to supply the demand." This feverish production may account for the often-substandard quality of proofs for the year.

Further updates in the August 1950 edition highlighted several changes from the past: rather than being offered as individual pieces, the proofs were offered only as sets of five coins, for $2.10 versus the 91 cents represented by the face value. The 51,386 sets sold more than doubled the most generous possible number of sets sold in 1942, and as future years would prove, enthusiasm for the newly returned proof sets was no fluke.

Cent PR66 Red. The obverse is uniformly pale copper-gold, but the reverse shows more variety. A dot of bright orange appears in the center, and the area of the right wheat stem shows deeper umber color. Great eye appeal.

Nickel PR67. Pale nickel-blue patina overall with the edges partly toned sea-green. Crisply impressed with strong mirrors.

Dime PR67. Lightly toned silver-gray overall with a few streaks of silver-white appearing in the fields. The torch on the reverse assumes a faint golden cast.

Quarter PR67. Bright silver-white reflectivity overall with just a hint of canary-yellow color. A sharply struck and carefully preserved Superb Gem proof.

Half Dollar PR66. Glimpses of violet peripheral toning give way rapidly to near-brilliance. Both portrait and bell are mildly frosted.
From The Boca Collection, Part I. (Total: 5 coins)

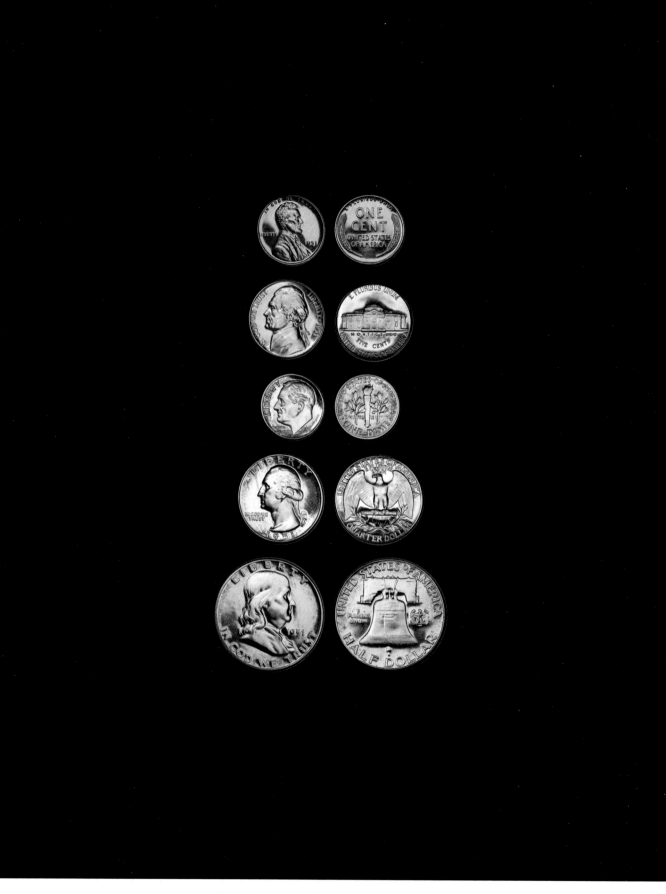

Magnificent 1951 Proof Set

2070   1951 5-Piece Proof Set NGC. In keeping with the experiences of 1936 to 1942, when proof coinages consistently trended up (if by differing percentages), proof strikings increased from 1950 to 1951. The 1951 issue also begins a trend of increased incidence of Cameo strikings, though the Mint habit of using proof dies longer than was optimal necessarily puts a cap on the number of coins that can be claimed as Cameo.

The Mint shipped 57,500 proof sets in 1951, setting records for proof production in a single year for each of the five denominations represented. The previous records had been set in 1950 with the single exception of the five cent piece, which saw 55,200 proofs struck in 1942 between the copper-nickel and copper-silver-manganese alloys.

Cent PR66 Red. Bright copper-gold surfaces display mild contrast between mirrored fields and the motifs when the coin is tilted just slightly beneath a light source. The design features are exquisitely struck up, including all lines and grains in the wheat stalks. Immaculately preserved surfaces reveal no abrasions or unsightly spots.

Nickel PR67. Whispers of ice-blue and champagne-beige make occasional appearances on the brilliant surfaces of this Superb Gem, and a solid strike brings out crisp definition on the design elements that show five Full Steps. Fantastic overall eye appeal.

Dime PR67. Wisps of reddish-gold, sea-green, and cobalt-blue are confined to the margins on the obverse but travel throughout the reverse. Brilliant surfaces exhibit sharply struck design elements that are mildly frosted and yield a degree of variance with the reflective fields. Impeccably preserved throughout, as expected for the designated grade.

Quarter Cent PR67. Blushes of russet, aqua-blue, and purple are slightly more extensive and deeper in hue on the obverse of this lovely Superb Gem. Lightly frosted design motifs are well impressed and stand out against the mirrored fields irrespective of the angle of observation. This well preserved proof exudes magnificent eye appeal.

Half PR67. Freckles of soft sea-green, purple, and sky-blue patina travel over the luminous surfaces of this appealing half dollar. Lightly frosted devices are impressively struck and appear to float over the deep watery fields. Most of the bell lettering is crystal clear, and both obverse and reverse reveal impeccable preservation.
From The Boca Collection, Part I. (Total: 5 coins)

Pleasing 1952 Proof Set, PR66 and Finer

2071   Five-Piece 1952 Proof Set NGC. From 1951 to 1952, proof set production increased early 50%, from 57,500 sets in 1951 to 81,980 sets in 1952. This began an era of exponential growth for proof set mintages: strikings gained at least 50% year-on-year from 1952 to 1957, which was the first year the Mint issued more than a million proof sets.

This rapid development coincided with the middle years of the American "baby boom," and it is not hard to imagine that the tradition of purchasing proof sets for newborns and for children's birthdays became widespread during this time. Whether this or another factor is responsible, it is indisputable that the proofs of 1952, whether singly or in sets, are the most accessible of any up to that time, and with only one further interruption, the years from 1965 to 1967, the story of U.S. proof coinage has been continuous ever since.

Cent PR66 Red. Pale copper color overall with just a touch of deeper gold-orange present at the rims. A sharp Premium Gem proof.

Nickel PR67. The green-gold toning present on each side is peripheral on the obverse with greater field coverage on the reverse. This Superb Gem has impressively mirrored fields.

Dime PR67. Glimpses of gold and pale cloud-white peripheral toning give way to nearly brilliant centers. Boldly impressed and attractive.

Quarter PR67. Golden toning at the margins shows small dots of sage, while the centers are minimally patinated. Great eye appeal.

Half Dollar PR67 Cameo. This Superb Gem's eye appeal is greatly enhanced by its moderate contrast. Both Franklin's portrait and the Liberty Bell show ample frost, and the coin's intermittent green-gold peripheral toning does not interfere with the effect in the slightest. A coin that heralds the greater incidence of Cameo proofs in the following years.
From The Boca Collection, Part I. (Total: 5 coins)

Heritage Auction Galleries Staff

Steve Ivy - Co-Chairman and CEO

Steve Ivy began collecting and studying rare coins as a youth, and as a teenager began advertising coins for sale in national publications in 1963. Seven years later, at the age of 20, he opened for business in downtown Dallas, and in 1976, incorporated as an auction company. Steve managed the business as well as serving as chief buyer, buying and selling hundreds of millions of dollars of coins during the 1970s and early 1980s. In early 1983, James Halperin became a full partner, and the name of the corporation was changed to Heritage Auctions. Steve's primary responsibilities now include management of the marketing and selling efforts of the company, the formation of corporate policy for long-term growth, and corporate relations with financial institutions. He remains intimately involved in all the various categories Heritage Auctions deals in today. Steve engages in daily discourse with industry leaders on all aspects of the fine art and collectibles business, and his views on market trends and developments are respected throughout the industry. He previously served on both the Board of Directors of the Professional Numismatists Guild (past president), and The Industry Council for Tangible Assets (past Chairman). Steve's keen appreciation of history is reflected in his active participation in other organizations, including past board positions on the Texas Historical Foundation and the Dallas Historical Society (where he also served as Exhibits Chairman). Steve is an avid collector of Texas books, manuscripts, and national currency, and he owns one of the largest and finest collections in private hands. He is also a past Board Chair of Dallas Challenge, and is currently the Finance Chair of the Phoenix House of Texas.

James Halperin - Co-Chairman

Born in Boston in 1952, Jim formed a part-time rare coin business at age 15 after discovering he had a knack (along with a nearly photographic memory) for coins. Jim scored a perfect 800 on his math SATs and received early acceptance to Harvard College, but after attending three semesters took a permanent leave of absence to pursue his full-time numismatic career. In 1975, Jim supervised the protocols for the first mainframe computer system in the numismatic business, which would catapult New England Rare Coin Galleries to the top of the industry in less than four years. In 1982, Jim's business merged with that of his friend and former archrival Steve Ivy. Their partnership has become Heritage Auctions, the third-largest auction house in the world. Jim is also a well-known futurist, an active collector of EC comics and early 20th-century American art (visit www.jhalpe.com), venture capital investor, philanthropist (he endows a multimillion-dollar health education foundation), and part-time novelist. His first fiction book, *The Truth Machine*, was published in 1996, became an international science fiction bestseller, and was optioned for movie development by Warner Brothers and Lions Gate. Jim's second novel, *The First Immortal*, was published in early 1998 and immediately optioned as a Hallmark Hall of Fame television miniseries.

Greg Rohan - President

At the age of eight, Greg Rohan started collecting coins as well as buying them for resale to his schoolmates. By 1971, at the age of 10, he was already buying and selling coins from a dealer's table at trade shows in his hometown of Seattle. His business grew rapidly, and by 1985 he had offices in both Seattle and Minneapolis. He joined Heritage in 1987 as Executive Vice-President. Today, as a partner and as President of Heritage, his responsibilities include overseeing the firm's private client group and working with top collectors in every field in which Heritage is active. Greg has been involved with many of the rarest items and most important collections handled by the firm, including the purchase and/or sale of the Ed Trompeter Collection (the world's largest numismatic purchase according to the Guinness Book of World Records). During his career, Greg has handled more than $1 billion of rare coins, collectibles and art. He has provided expert testimony for the United States Attorneys in San Francisco, Dallas, and Philadelphia, and for the Federal Trade Commission (FTC). He has worked with collectors, consignors, and their advisors regarding significant collections of books, manuscripts, comics, currency, jewelry, vintage movie posters, sports and entertainment memorabilia, decorative arts, and fine art. Greg is a past Chapter Chairman for North Texas of the Young Presidents' Organization (YPO), and is an active supporter of the arts. Greg co-authored "The Collectors Estate Handbook," winner of the NLG's Robert Friedberg Award for numismatic book of the year. He previously served on the seven-person Advisory Board to the Federal Reserve Bank of Dallas, in his second appointed term.

Paul Minshull - Chief Operating Officer

As Chief Operating Officer, Paul Minshull's managerial responsibilities include integrating sales, personnel, inventory, security and MIS for Heritage. His major accomplishments include overseeing the hardware migration from mainframe to PC, the software migration of all inventory and sales systems, and implementation of a major Internet presence. Heritage's successful employee-suggestion program has generated 200 or more ideas each month since 1995, and has helped increase employee productivity, expand business, and improve employee retention. Paul oversees the company's highly-regarded IT department, and has been the driving force behind Heritage's Web development, now a significant portion of Heritage's future plans. As the first auction house that combined traditional floor bidding with active Internet bidding, the totally interactive system has catapulted Heritage to the top collectible and Fine Art website (Forbes Magazine's "Best of the Web"). Paul came to Heritage in 1984. Since 1987, he has been Chief Operating Officer for all Heritage companies and affiliates.

Todd Imhof - Executive Vice President

Unlike most of his contemporaries, Todd Imhof did not start collecting in his teens. Shortly after graduating college, Todd declined offers from prestigious Wall Street banks to join a former classmate at a small rare coin firm in the Seattle area. In the mid-1980s, the rare coin industry was rapidly changing, with the advent of third-party grading and growing computer technologies. As a newcomer, Todd more easily embraced these new dynamics and quickly emerged as a highly respected dealer. In 1991, he co-founded Pinnacle Rarities, a firm specialized in servicing the savviest and most preeminent collectors in numismatics. At only 25, he was accepted into the PNG, and currently serves on its Consumer Protection Committee and its Legislation/Taxation Issues Committee. In 1992, he was invited to join the Board of Directors for the Industry Council for Tangible Assets, later serving as its Chairman (2002-2005). Since joining Heritage in 2006, Todd continues to advise most of Heritage's largest and most prominent clients.

Leo Frese - Vice President

Leo has been involved in numismatics for nearly 40 years, a professional numismatist since 1971, and has been with Heritage for more than 20 years. He literally worked his way up the Heritage "ladder," working with Bob Merrill for nearly 15 years, then becoming Director of Consignments. Leo has been actively involved in assisting clients sell nearly $500,000,000 in numismatic material. Leo was recently accepted as a member of PNG, is a life member of the ANA, and holds membership in FUN, CSNS, and other numismatic organizations.

Jim Stoutjesdyk - Vice President

Jim Stoutjesdyk was named Vice President of Heritage Rare Coin Galleries in 2004. He was named ANA's Outstanding Young Numismatist of the Year in 1987. A University of Michigan graduate, he was first employed by Superior Galleries, eventually becoming their Director of Collector Sales. Since joining Heritage in 1993, Jim has served in many capacities. Jim's duties now include buying and selling, pricing all new purchases, assisting with auction estimates and reserves, and overseeing the daily operations of the rare coin department.

Norma L. Gonzalez - VP of Auction Operations

Norma Gonzalez joined the U.S. Navy in August of 1993 and received her Bachelor's Degree in Resource Management. She joined Heritage in 1998 and was promoted to Vice President in 2003. She currently manages the operations departments, including Coins, Currency, World & Ancient Coins, Sportscards & Memorabilia, Comics, Movie Posters, Pop Culture and Political Memorabilia.

Debbie Rexing - VP - Marketing

Debbie Rexing joined the Heritage team in 2001 and her marketing credentials include degrees in Business Administration and Human Resources from The Ohio State University. Debbie has worked across many categories within the company leading to her comprehensive and integrative approach to the job. She guides all aspects of Heritage's print marketing strategies – advertisements, brochures, direct mail campaigns, coordination of print buying, catalog design and production, The Heritage Magazine, and media and press relations.

Ron Brackemyre - Vice President

Ron Brackemyre began his career at Heritage Auction Galleries in 1998 as the Manager of the Shipping Department, was promoted to Consignment Operations Manager for Numismatics in 2004 and in 2009 added oversight of the entire photography operation at Heritage, wherein his department coordinates all photography, scanning and photoshopping. He is also responsible for the security of all of Heritage's coin and currency consignments, both at the Dallas world headquarters and at shows, as well as cataloging of coins for upcoming auctions, coordination of auction planning, security and transportation logistics, lot-view, auction prep and oversight for the entire shipping department.

Marti Korver - Manager - Credit/Collections

Marti Korver was recruited out of the banking profession by Jim Ruddy, and she worked with Paul Rynearson, Karl Stephens, and Judy Cahn on ancients and world coins at Bowers & Ruddy Galleries, in Hollywood, CA. She migrated into the coin auction business, and represented bidders as agent at B&R auctions for 10 years. She also worked as a research assistant for Q. David Bowers for several years.

Mark Prendergast - Director, Trusts & Estates

Mark Prendergast earned his degree in Art History from Vanderbilt University and began his career in the arts working with a national dealer in private sales of 20th Century American Art. Joining Christie's in 1998 and advancing during a 10 year tenure to the position of Vice President, he was instrumental in bringing to market many important and prominent works of art, collections and estates. Having established a Houston office for Heritage, he serves as Director of Business Development, Trusts & Estates, providing assistance to fiduciary professionals and private clients with appraisals, collection assessments and auction consignments in all areas of art and collectibles.

Coin Department

David Mayfield - Vice President, Numismatics
David Mayfield has been collecting and trading rare coins and currency for over 35 years. A chance encounter with his father's coin collection at the age of nine led to his lifetime interest. David has been buying and selling at coin shows since the age of 10. He became a full time coin and currency dealer in the mid-1980s. David's main collecting interest is in all things Texas, specializing in currency and documents from the Republic of Texas.

Jim Jelinski - Consignment Director & Senior Numismatist
Jim Jelinski has been involved in numismatics for more than five decades as a collector, dealer and educator. He started as Buyer for Paramount International Coin Corporation in 1972, opened Essex Numismatic Properties in 1975 in New Hampshire and has held numerous executive positions at M.B. Simmons & Associates of Narberth, Pennsylvania. He works at Heritage as a Senior Numismatist and Consignment Coordinator.

Bob Marino - Consignment Director & Senior Numismatist
Bob Marino joined Heritage in 1999, managing and developing Internet coin sales, and building Heritage's client base through eBay and other Internet auction Web sites. He has successfully concluded more than 40,000 transactions on eBay. He is now a Consignment Director, assisting consignors in placing their coins and collectibles in the best of the many Heritage venues.

Sam Foose - Consignment Director and Auctioneer
Sam Foose joined Heritage Numismatic Auctions, Inc., in 1993 as an Auction Coordinator. He rose to Assistant Auction Director in 1998, and began calling auctions. After a stint serving as a Senior Manager and Consignment Director in other collectible fields, he returned to Heritage in 2002 as a Consignment Director to help Heritage's expansion into other collectibles fields. Besides calling auctions as one of Heritage's primary auctioneers, he travels the nation assisting clients who wish to liquidate their collections of coins, paper money, decorative arts, and sports collectibles.

Katherine Kurachek - Consignment Director
Katherine Kurachek graduated from the University of Mississippi in 1993 as an art major. She came to Heritage in January 2003, working alongside Leo Frese for several years, learning the numismatic wholesale trade. Katherine frequently travels to coin shows to represent Heritage and service her dealer accounts along with her wide ranging duties as Consignment Director.

Shaunda Fry - Consignment Director
Shaunda Fry ran her own textile company for 22 years before meeting Leo Frese while co-coordinating a local school auction. She followed his suggestion to add auctioneering to her list of talents and, after training, worked part-time at Heritage auctions and began to call. She became a Consignment Director and now travels to shows as part of the "Wholesale Dealers Team."

Mike Sadler - Consignment Director
Mike Sadler joined the Heritage team in September 2003. He attended the United States Air Force Academy, flew jets for the military and is a longtime pilot with American Airlines. Before coming to Heritage, his unlimited access to air travel enabled Mike to attend coin shows around the nation, and to build a world class collection that was auctioned by Heritage in 2004. He is known for his tremendous knowledge of rare coins, making him a trusted colleague to many of today's most active collectors.

Chris Dykstra - Consignment Director
Chris Dykstra joined Heritage October 2006. He has held a number of jobs at Heritage including a stint in Wholesale Sales assisting Heritage's dealer clients in locating specific coins and travelling to shows to work the Heritage booth. In August 2008 Chris was promoted into the US Coin Consignments department as a Consignment Director where he now assists consignors in bringing their collections to auction.

Jason Friedman - Consignment Director
Jason's interest in rare coins, which began at 12 and expanded into his own numismatic business, allowed him to pay for most of his college tuition at the University of North Texas, from which he graduated in 2005. He joined Heritage soon after. He is a member of the American Numismatic Association (ANA) and Florida United Numismatists (FUN).

Bert DeLaGarza - Consignment Director
Bert DeLaGarza joined Heritage in 2008, capitalizing on a longtime passion for, and expertise in rare coins from a very young age. Prior to Heritage, Bert spent over 25 years in Landscape Construction and Estate Management having achieved the Texas Master Nurseryman certification. A member of the ANA, Bert is known for his strong knowledge of U.S. coins and an eye for rare U.S. stamps.

Win Callender - Consignment Director & Senior Numismatist
Win Callender has joined Heritage Auction Galleries as a professional numismatist and consignment director. A lifelong numismatist - he found a 1770 Russian 5 Kopek when he was just 5 years old - Callender parlayed his hobby into a fulltime business when he was in his mid-30s, starting his own business in Broken Arrow, Okla., in 1993. He subsequently worked for Carter Numismatics and David Lawrence Rare Coins, working his way up to Vice President in both firms.

Jessica Aylmer - Consignment Director
Jessica joined the Heritage staff as a Consignment Coordinator in 2007, shortly after graduating with a Bachelor's in Art History from the University of North Texas. She was moved up to Consignment Director in 2009, where her main focus is now on working as part of the Heritage dealer consignment team. Jessica has become a familiar face to the numismatic community, attending coin shows and expositions across the country on a weekly basis. Jessica is a member of the American Numismatic Association, Florida United Numismatists and Women In Numismatics.

Diedre Buchmoyer - Consignment Director
Diedre has worked full-time in the numismatic arena for the past eight years buying and selling rare coins, and assisted in several prestigious auctions including the John J. Ford, Jr. Collection. An honors graduate from Hood College in Frederick, Maryland, Diedre received her BA in Art History with a concentration in Archaeology and a double minor in Business Management and Studio Art. She is a member of the American Numismatic Association, Florida United Numismatics, Women in Numismatics and the Industry Council for Tangible Assets.

Mark Van Winkle - Chief Cataloger
Mark has worked for Heritage, and Steve Ivy, since 1979. He has been Chief Cataloger since 1990, and has handled some of the premier numismatic rarities sold at public auction. Mark was editor of Legacy magazine, won the 1989 NLG award for Best U.S. Commercial Magazine, and has won numerous awards for his writing, including the 1990 NLG award for Best Article for his *Interview With John Ford*, the 1996 NLG Best Numismatic Article for *Changing Concepts of Liberty*. He has published extensively and written articles for *Coin World*, *Numismatic News* and has contributed to editions of the *Red Book, United States Patterns and Related Issues*, and *The Guide Book of Double Eagle Gold Coins.*

Mark Borckardt - Senior Cataloger
Mark started attending coin shows and conventions as a dealer in 1970, and has been a full-time professional numismatist since 1980. He received the Early American Coppers Literary Award, and the Numismatic Literary Guild's Book of the Year Award, for the *Encyclopedia of Early United States Cents, 1793-1814*, published in 2000. He serves as a contributor to *A Guide Book of United States Coins,* and has contributed to many references, including the Harry W. Bass, Jr. Sylloge, and the *Encyclopedia of Silver Dollars and Trade Dollars of the United States*. Most recently, he was Senior Numismatist with Bowers and Merena Galleries. Mark is a life member of the A. N. A., and an active member of numerous organizations.

Brian Koller - Cataloger & Catalog Production Manager
Brian Koller has been a Heritage cataloger since 2001, before that working as a telecom software engineer for 16 years. He is a graduate of Iowa State University with a Bachelor's degree in Computer Engineering, and is an avid collector of U.S. gold coins. His attention to detail ensures that every catalog, printed and on-line, is as error free as technology and human activity allows. In addition to his coin cataloging duties, he also helps with consignor promises and client service issues.

Dr. Jon Amato - Cataloger
Jon Amato has been with Heritage since 2004. He earned his Ph. D. from the University of Toronto, and was previously a Program Manager in the NY State Dept. of Economic Development, and an Adjunct Professor at the State University of New York at Albany. He is currently writing a monograph on the draped bust, small eagle half dollars of 1796-1797. He has published numerous articles in prestigious numismatic publications and belongs to many numismatic organizations, including the ANA, ANS, John Reich Collectors Society, and the Liberty Seated Collectors Club, and has made several presentations at ANA Numismatic Theaters.

John Dale Beety - Cataloger
John Dale Beety served an internship at Heritage during the summer of 2004 and started full-time as a cataloger in 2006, immediately after graduating from Rose-Hulman Institute of Technology. In addition to catalog writing and editing, he creates the Coin Monday posts that appear weekly on the official Heritage Auction Galleries blog, heritageauctions.blogspot.com.

Cataloged by: Mark Van Winkle, Chief Cataloger
Mark Borckardt, Senior Numismatist; John Amato, John Beety, George Huber, Brian Koller, Dave Stone
Edited by: Mark Van Winkle, John Beety, George Huber, Stewart Huckaby
Operations Support by: Christina Gonzales, San Juana Gonzalez, Manuela Bueno, Christina Ibarra, Ira Reynolds, Cynthia Pina, Daisy Manhard, Maria Flores, Jose Martinez
Catalog and Internet Imaging by: Travis Awalt, Maribel Cazares, Joel Gonzalez, Colleen McInerney, Sharon Johnson, Nancy Ramos, Jason Young, Tony Webb, Donna Rusnak
Production and Design by: Carl Watson, Mark Masat, Mary Hermann, Debbie Rexing

Terms and Conditions of Auction

Auctioneer and Auction:

1. This Auction is presented by Heritage Auction Galleries, a d/b/a/ of Heritage Auctions, Inc., or its affiliates Heritage Numismatic Auctions, Inc., or Heritage Vintage Sports Auctions, Inc., or Currency Auctions of America, Inc., as identified with the applicable licensing information on the title page of the catalog or on the HA.com Internet site (the "Auctioneer"). The Auction is conducted under these Terms and Conditions of Auction and applicable state and local law. Announcements and corrections from the podium and those made through the Terms and Conditions of Auctions appearing on the Internet at HA.com supersede those in the printed catalog.

Buyer's Premium:

2. On bids placed through Auctioneer, a Buyer's Premium of fifteen percent (15%) will be added to the successful hammer price bid on lots in Coin, Currency, and Philatelic auctions or nineteen and one-half percent (19.5%) on lots in all other auctions. There is a minimum Buyer's Premium of $14.00 per lot. In Gallery Auctions (sealed bid auctions of mostly bulk numismatic material), the Buyer's Premium is 19.5%.

Auction Venues:

3. The following Auctions are conducted solely on the Internet: Heritage Weekly Internet Auctions (Coin, Currency, Comics, and Vintage Movie Poster); Heritage Monthly Internet Auctions (Sports, and Stamps). Signature® Auctions and Grand Format Auctions accept bids from the Internet, telephone, fax, or mail first, followed by a floor bidding session; Heritage Live and real-time telephone bidding are available to registered clients during these auctions.

Bidders:

4. Any person participating or registering for the Auction agrees to be bound by and accepts these Terms and Conditions of Auction ("Bidder(s)").
5. All Bidders must meet Auctioneer's qualifications to bid. Any Bidder who is not a client in good standing of the Auctioneer may be disqualified at Auctioneer's sole option and will not be awarded lots. Such determination may be made by Auctioneer in its sole and unlimited discretion, at any time prior to, during, or even after the close of the Auction. Auctioneer reserves the right to exclude any person from the auction.
6. If an entity places a bid, then the person executing the bid on behalf of the entity agrees to personally guarantee payment for any successful bid.

Credit:

7. Bidders who have not established credit with the Auctioneer must either furnish satisfactory credit information (including two collectibles-related business references) well in advance of the Auction or supply valid credit card information. Bids placed through our Interactive Internet program will only be accepted from pre-registered Bidders; Bidders who are not members of HA.com or affiliates should pre-register at least 48 hours before the start of the first session (exclusive of holidays or weekends) to allow adequate time to contact references. Credit may be granted at the discretion of Auctioneer. Additionally Bidders who have not previously established credit or who wish to bid in excess of their established credit history may be required to provide their social security number or the last four digits thereof to us so a credit check may be performed prior to Auctioneer's acceptance of a bid.

Bidding Options:

8. Bids in Signature® Auctions or Grand Format Auctions may be placed as set forth in the printed catalog section entitled "Choose your bidding method." For auctions held solely on the Internet, see the alternatives on HA.com. Review at HA.com/common/howtobid.php.
9. Presentment of Bids: Non-Internet bids (including but not limited to podium, fax, phone and mail bids) are treated similar to floor bids in that they must be on-increment or at a half increment (called a cut bid). Any podium, fax, phone, or mail bids that do not conform to a full or half increment will be rounded up or down to the nearest full or half increment and this revised amount will be considered your high bid.
10. Auctioneer's Execution of Certain Bids. Auctioneer cannot be responsible for your errors in bidding, so carefully check that every bid is entered correctly. When identical mail or FAX bids are submitted, preference is given to the first received. To ensure the greatest accuracy, your written bids should be entered on the standard printed bid sheet and be received at Auctioneer's place of business at least two business days before the Auction start. Auctioneer is not responsible for executing mail bids or FAX bids received on or after the day the first lot is sold, nor Internet bids submitted after the published closing time; nor is Auctioneer responsible for proper execution of bids submitted by telephone, mail, FAX, e-mail, Internet, or in person once the Auction begins. Internet bids may not be withdrawn until your written request is received and acknowledged by Auctioneer (FAX: 214-4438425); such requests must state the reason, and may constitute grounds for withdrawal of bidding privileges. Lots won by mail Bidders will not be delivered at the Auction unless prearranged.
11. Caveat as to Bid Increments. Bid increments (over the current bid level) determine the lowest amount you may bid on a particular lot. Bids greater than one increment over the current bid can be any whole dollar amount. It is possible under several circumstances for winning bids to be between increments, sometimes only $1 above the previous increment. Please see: "How can I lose by less than an increment?" on our website. Bids will be accepted in whole dollar amounts only. No "buy" or "unlimited" bids will be accepted.

   The following chart governs current bidding increments.

Current Bid	Bid Increment
<$10	$1
$10 - $29	$2
$30 - $49	$3
$50 - $99	$5
$100 - $199	$10
$200 - $299	$20
$300 - $499	$25
$500 - $999	$50
$1,000 - $1,999	$100
$2,000 - $2,999	$200
$3,000 - $4,999	$250
$5,000 - $9,999	$500
$10,000 - $19,999	$1,000

Current Bid	Bid Increment
$20,000 - $29,999	$2,000
$30,000 - $49,999	$2,500
$50,000 - $99,999	$5,000
$100,000 - $199,999	$10,000
$200,000 - $299,999	$20,000
$300,000 - $499,999	$25,000
$500,000 - $999,999	$50,000
$1,000,000 - $1,999,999	$100,000
$2,000,000 - $2,999,999	$200,000
$3,000,000 - $4,999,999	$250,000
$5,000,000 - $9,999,999	$500,000
>$10,000,000	$1,000,000

12. If Auctioneer calls for a full increment, a bidder may request Auctioneer to accept a bid at half of the increment ("Cut Bid") only once per lot. After offering a Cut Bid, bidders may continue to participate only at full increments. Off-increment bids may be accepted by the Auctioneer at Signature® Auctions and Grand Format Auctions. If the Auctioneer solicits bids other than the expected increment, these bids will not be considered Cut Bids.

Conducting the Auction:

13. Notice of the consignor's liberty to place bids on his lots in the Auction is hereby made in accordance with Article 2 of the Texas Business and Commercial Code. A "Minimum Bid" is an amount below which the lot will not sell. THE CONSIGNOR OF PROPERTY MAY PLACE WRITTEN "Minimum Bids" ON HIS LOTS IN ADVANCE OF THE AUCTION; ON SUCH LOTS, IF THE HAMMER PRICE DOES NOT MEET THE "Minimum Bid", THE CONSIGNOR MAY PAY A REDUCED COMMISSION ON THOSE LOTS. "Minimum Bids" are generally posted online several days prior to the Auction closing. For any successful bid placed by a consignor on his Property on the Auction floor, or by any means during the live session, or after the "Minimum Bid" for an Auction have been posted, we will require the consignor to pay full Buyer's Premium and Seller's Commissions on such lot.
14. The highest qualified Bidder recognized by the Auctioneer shall be the buyer. In the event of any dispute between any Bidders at an Auction, Auctioneer may at his sole discretion reoffer the lot. Auctioneer's decision and declaration of the winning Bidder shall be final and binding upon all Bidders. Bids properly offered, whether by floor Bidder or other means of bidding, may on occasion be missed or go unrecognized; in such cases, the Auctioneer may declare the recognized bid accepted as the winning bid, regardless of whether a competing bid may have been higher.
15. Auctioneer reserves the right to refuse to honor any bid or to limit the amount of any bid, in its sole discretion. A bid is considered not made in "Good Faith" when made by an insolvent or irresponsible person, a person under the age of eighteen, or is not supported by satisfactory credit, collectibles references, or otherwise. Regardless of the disclosure of his identity, any bid by a consignor or his agent on a lot consigned by him is deemed to be made in "Good Faith." Any person apparently appearing on the OFAC list is not eligible to bid.
16. Nominal Bids. The Auctioneer in its sole discretion may reject nominal bids, small opening bids, or very nominal advances. If a lot bearing estimates fails to open for 40–60% of the low estimate, the Auctioneer may pass the item or may place a protective bid on behalf of the consignor.
17. Lots bearing bidding estimates shall open at Auctioneer's discretion (approximately 50%-60% of the low estimate). In the event that no bid meets or exceeds that opening amount, the lot shall pass as unsold.
18. All items are to be purchased per lot as numerically indicated and no lots will be broken. Auctioneer reserves the right to withdraw, prior to the close, any lots from the Auction.
19. Auctioneer reserves the right to rescind the sale in the event of nonpayment, breach of a warranty, disputed ownership, auctioneer's clerical error or omission in exercising bids and reserves, or for any other reason and in Auctioneer's sole discretion. In cases of nonpayment, Auctioneer's election to void a sale does not relieve the Bidder from their obligation to pay Auctioneer its fees (seller's and buyer's premium) and any other damages or expenses pertaining to the lot.
20. Auctioneer occasionally experiences Internet and/or Server service outages, and Auctioneer periodically schedules system downtime for maintenance and other purposes, during which Bidders cannot participate or place bids. If such outages occur, we may at our discretion extend bidding for the Auction. Bidders unable to place their Bids through the Internet are directed to contact Client Services at 1-800-872-6467.
21. The Auctioneer or its affiliates may consign items to be sold in the Auction, and may bid on those lots or any other lots. Auctioneer or affiliates expressly reserve the right to modify any such bids at any time prior to the hammer based upon data made known to the Auctioneer or its affiliates. The Auctioneer may extend advances, guarantees, or loans to certain consignors, and may extend financing or other credits at varying rates to certain Bidders in the auction.
22. The Auctioneer has the right to sell certain unsold items after the close of the Auction. Such lots shall be considered sold during the Auction and all these Terms and Conditions shall apply to such sales including but not limited to the Buyer's Premium, return rights, and disclaimers.

Payment:

23. All sales are strictly for cash in United States dollars (including U.S. currency, bank wire, cashier checks, travelers checks, eChecks, and bank money orders, all subject to reporting requirements). All are subject to clearing and funds being received In Auctioneer's account before delivery of the purchases. Auctioneer reserves the right to determine if a check constitutes "good funds" when drawn on a U.S. bank for ten days, and thirty days when drawn on an international bank. Credit Card (Visa or Master Card only) and PayPal payments may be accepted up to $10,000 from non-dealers at the sole discretion of the Auctioneer, subject to the following limitations: a) sales are only to the cardholder, b) purchases are shipped to the cardholder's registered and verified address, c) Auctioneer may pre-approve the cardholder's credit line, d) a credit card transaction may not be used in conjunction with any other financing or extended terms offered by the Auctioneer, and must transact immediately upon invoice presentation, e) rights of return are governed by these Terms and Conditions, which supersede those conditions promulgated by the card issuer, f) floor Bidders must present their card.
24. Payment is due upon closing of the Auction session, or upon presentment of an invoice. Auctioneer reserves the right to void an invoice if payment in full is not received within 7 days after the close of the Auction. In cases of nonpayment, Auctioneer's election to void a sale does not relieve the Bidder from their obligation to pay Auctioneer its fees (seller's and buyer's premium) on the lot and any other damages pertaining to the lot.
25. Lots delivered to you, or your representative in the States of Texas, California, **New York**, or other states where the Auction may be held, are subject to all applicable state and local taxes, unless appropriate permits are on file with Auctioneer. Bidder agrees to pay Auctioneer the actual amount of tax due in the event that sales tax is not properly collected due to: 1) an expired, inaccurate, inappropriate tax certificate or declaration, 2) an incorrect interpretation of the applicable statute, 3) or any other reason. The appropriate form or certificate must be on file at and verified by Auctioneer five days prior to Auction or tax must be paid; only if such form or certificate is received by Auctioneer within 4 days after the Auction can a refund of tax paid be made. Lots from different Auctions may not be aggregated for sales tax purposes.
26. In the event that a Bidder's payment is dishonored upon presentment(s), Bidder shall pay the maximum statutory processing fee set by applicable state law. If you attempt to pay via eCheck and your financial institution denies this transfer from your bank account, or the payment cannot be completed using the selected funding source, you agree to complete payment using your credit card on file.
27. If any Auction invoice submitted by Auctioneer is not paid in full when due, the unpaid balance will bear interest at the highest rate permitted by law from the date of invoice until paid. Any invoice not paid when due will bear a three percent (3%) late fee on the invoice amount or three percent (3%) of any installment that is past due. If the Auctioneer refers any invoice to an attorney for collection, the buyer agrees to pay attorney's fees, court costs, and other collection costs incurred by Auctioneer. If Auctioneer assigns collection to its in-house legal staff, such attorney's time expended on the matter shall be compensated at a rate comparable to the hourly rate of independent attorneys.
28. In the event a successful Bidder fails to pay any amounts due, Auctioneer reserves the right to sell the lot(s) securing the invoice to any underbidders in the Auction that the lot(s) appeared, or at subsequent private or public sale, or relist the lot(s) in a future auction conducted by Auctioneer. A defaulting Bidder agrees to pay for the reasonable costs of resale (including a 10% seller's commission, if consigned to an auction conducted by Auctioneer). The defaulting Bidder is liable to pay any difference between his total original invoice for the lot(s), plus any applicable interest, and the net proceeds for the lot(s) if sold at private sale or the subsequent hammer price of the lot(s) less the 10% seller's commissions, if sold at an Auctioneer's auction.

29. Auctioneer reserves the right to require payment in full in good funds before delivery of the merchandise.
30. Auctioneer shall have a lien against the merchandise purchased by the buyer to secure payment of the Auction invoice. Auctioneer is further granted a lien and the right to retain possession of any other property of the buyer then held by the Auctioneer or its affiliates to secure payment of any Auction invoice or any other amounts due the Auctioneer or affiliates from the buyer. With respect to these lien rights, Auctioneer shall have all the rights of a secured creditor under Article 9 of the Texas Uniform Commercial Code, including but not limited to the right of sale. In addition, with respect to payment of the Auction invoice(s), the buyer waives any and all rights of offset he might otherwise have against the Auctioneer and the consignor of the merchandise included on the invoice. If a Bidder owes Auctioneer or its affiliates on any account, Auctioneer and its affiliates shall have the right to offset such unpaid account by any credit balance due Bidder, and it may secure by possessory lien any unpaid amount by any of the Bidder's property in their possession.
31. Title shall not pass to the successful Bidder until all invoices are paid in full. It is the responsibility of the buyer to provide adequate insurance coverage for the items once they have been delivered to a common carrier or third-party shipper.

Delivery; Shipping; and Handling Charges:

32. Buyer is liable for shipping and handling. Please refer to Auctioneer's website www.HA.com/common/shipping.php for the latest charges or call Auctioneer. Auctioneer is unable to combine purchases from other auctions or affiliates into one package for shipping purposes. Lots won will be shipped in a commercially reasonable time after payment in good funds for the merchandise and the shipping fees is received or credit extended, except when third-party shipment occurs.
33. Successful international Bidders shall provide written shipping instructions, including specified customs declarations, to the Auctioneer for any lots to be delivered outside of the United States. NOTE: Declaration value shall be the item'(s) hammer price together with its buyer's premium and Auctioneer shall use the correct harmonized code for the lot. Domestic Buyers on lots designated for third-party shipment must designate the common carrier, accept risk of loss, and prepay shipping costs.
34. All shipping charges will be borne by the successful Bidder. Any risk of loss during shipment will be borne by the buyer following Auctioneer's delivery to the designated common carrier or third-party shipper, regardless of domestic or foreign shipment.
35. Due to the nature of some items sold, it shall be the responsibility for the successful bidder to arrange pick-up and shipping through third-parties; as to such items Auctioneer shall have no liability. Failure to pick-up or arrange shipping in a timely fashion (within ten days) shall subject Lots to storage and moving charges, including a $100 administration fee plus $10 daily storage for larger items and $5.00 daily for smaller items (storage fee per item) after 35 days. In the event the Lot is not removed within ninety days, the Lot may be offered for sale to recover any past due storage or moving fees, including a 10% Seller's Commission.
36. The laws of various countries regulate the import or export of certain plant and animal properties, including (but not limited to) items made of (or including) ivory, whalebone, turtleshell, coral, crocodile, or other wildlife. Transport of such lots may require special licenses for export, import, or both. Bidder is responsible for: 1) obtaining all information on such restricted items for both export and import; 2) obtaining all such licenses and/or permits. Delay or failure to obtain any such license or permit does not relieve the buyer of timely compliance with standard payment terms. For further information, please contact Ron Brackemyre at 800-872-6467 ext. 1312.
37. Any request for shipping verification for undelivered packages must be made within 30 days of shipment by Auctioneer.

Cataloging, Warranties and Disclaimers:

38. NO WARRANTY, WHETHER EXPRESSED OR IMPLIED, IS MADE WITH RESPECT TO ANY DESCRIPTION CONTAINED IN THIS AUCTION OR ANY SECOND OPINE. Any description of the items or second opine contained in this Auction is for the sole purpose of identifying the items for those Bidders who do not have the opportunity to view the lots prior to bidding, and no description of items has been made part of the basis of the bargain or has created any express warranty that the goods would conform to any description made by Auctioneer. Color variations can be expected in any electronic or printed imaging, and are not grounds for the return of any lot. NOTE: Auctioneer, in specified auction venues, for example, Fine Art, may have express written warranties and you are referred to those specific terms and conditions. .
39. Auctioneer is selling only such right or title to the items being sold as Auctioneer may have by virtue of consignment agreements on the date of auction and disclaims any warranty of title to the Property. Auctioneer disclaims any warranty of merchantability or fitness for any particular purposes. All images, descriptions, sales data, and archival records are the exclusive property of Auctioneer, and may be used by Auctioneer for advertising, promotion, archival records, and any other uses deemed appropriate.
40. Translations of foreign language documents may be provided as a convenience to interested parties. Auctioneer makes no representation as to the accuracy of those translations and will not be held responsible for errors in bidding arising from inaccuracies in translation.
41. Auctioneer disclaims all liability for damages, consequential or otherwise, arising out of or in connection with the sale of any Property by Auctioneer to Bidder. No third party may rely on any benefit of these Terms and Conditions and any rights, if any, established hereunder are personal to the Bidder and may not be assigned. Any statement made by the Auctioneer is an opinion and does not constitute a warranty or representation. No employee of Auctioneer may alter these Terms and Conditions, and, unless signed by a principal of Auctioneer, any such alteration is null and void.
42. Auctioneer shall not be liable for breakage of glass or damage to frames (patent or latent); such defects, in any event, shall not be a basis for any claim for return or reduction in purchase price.

Release:

43. In consideration of participation in the Auction and the placing of a bid, Bidder expressly releases Auctioneer, its officers, directors and employees, its affiliates, and its outside experts that provide second opines, from any and all claims, cause of action, chose of action, whether at law or equity or any arbitration or mediation rights existing under the rules of any professional society or affiliation based upon the assigned description, or a derivative theory, breach of warranty express or implied, representation or other matter set forth within these Terms and Conditions of Auction or otherwise. In the event of a claim, Bidder agrees that such rights and privileges conferred therein are strictly construed as specifically declared herein; e.g., authenticity, typographical error, etc. and are the exclusive remedy. Bidder, by non-compliance to these express terms of a granted remedy, shall waive any claim against Auctioneer.
44. Notice: Some Property sold by Auctioneer are inherently dangerous e.g. firearms, cannons, and small items that may be swallowed or ingested or may have latent defects all of which may cause harm to a person. Purchaser accepts all risk of loss or damage from its purchase of these items and Auctioneer disclaims any liability whether under contract or tort for damages and losses, direct or inconsequential, and expressly disclaims any warranty as to safety or usage of any lot sold.

Dispute Resolution and Arbitration Provision:

45. By placing a bid or otherwise participating in the auction, Bidder accepts these Terms and Conditions of Auction, and specifically agrees to the dispute resolution provided herein. Consumer disputes shall be resolved through court litigation which has an exclusive Dallas, Texas venue clause and jury waiver. Non-consumer dispute shall be determined in binding arbitration which arbitration replaces the right to go to court, including the right to a jury trial.
46. Auctioneer in no event shall be responsible for consequential damages, incidental damages, compensatory damages, or any other damages arising or claimed to be arising from the auction of any lot. In the event that Auctioneer cannot deliver the lot or subsequently it is established that the lot lacks title, or other transfer or condition issue is claimed, In such cases the sole remedy shall be limited to rescission of sale and refund of the amount paid by Bidder; in no case shall Auctioneer's maximum liability exceed the high bid on that lot, which bid shall be deemed for all purposes the value of the lot. After one year has elapsed, Auctioneer's maximum liability shall be limited to any commissions and fees Auctioneer earned on that lot.
47. In the event of an attribution error, Auctioneer may at its sole discretion, correct the error on the Internet, or, if discovered at a later date, to refund the buyer's purchase price without further obligation.
48. Dispute Resolution for Consumers and Non-Consumers: Any claim, dispute, or controversy in connection with, relating to and /or arising out of the Auction, participation in the Auction. Award of lots, damages of claims to lots, descriptions, condition reports, provenance, estimates, return and warranty rights, any interpretation of these Terms and Conditions, any alleged verbal modification of these Terms and Conditions and/or any purported settlement whether asserted in contract, tort, under Federal or State statute or regulation shall or any other matter: a) if presented by a consumer, be exclusively heard by, and the parties consent to, exclusive in personam jurisdiction in the State District Courts of Dallas County, Texas. THE PARTIES EXPRESSLY WAIVE ANY RIGHT TO TRIAL BY JURY. Any appeals shall be solely pursued in the appellate courts of the State of Texas; or b) for any claimant other than a consumer, the claim shall be presented in confidential binding arbitration before a single arbitrator, that the parties may agree upon, selected from the JAMS list of Texas arbitrators. The case is not to be administrated by JAMS; however, if the parties cannot agree on an arbitrator, then JAMS shall appoint the arbitrator and it shall be conducted under JAMS rules. The locale shall be Dallas Texas. The arbitrator's award may be enforced in any court of competent jurisdiction. Any party on any claim involving the purchase or sale of numismatic or related items may elect arbitration through binding PNG arbitration. Any claim must be brought within one (1) year of the alleged breach, default or misrepresentation or the claim is waived. This agreement and any claims shall be determined and construed under Texas law. The prevailing party (party that is awarded substantial and material relief on its claim or defense) may be awarded its reasonable attorneys' fees and costs.
49. No claims of any kind can be considered after the settlements have been made with the consignors. Any dispute after the settlement date is strictly between the Bidder and consignor without involvement or responsibility of the Auctioneer.
50. In consideration of their participation in or application for the Auction, a person or entity (whether the successful Bidder, a Bidder, a purchaser and/or other Auction participant or registrant) agrees that all disputes in any way relating to, arising under, connected with, or incidental to these Terms and Conditions and purchases, or default in payment thereof, shall be arbitrated pursuant to the arbitration provision. In the event that any matter including actions to compel arbitration, construe the agreement, actions in aid or arbitration or otherwise needs to be litigated, such litigation shall be exclusively in the Courts of the State of Texas, in Dallas County, Texas, and if necessary the corresponding appellate courts. For such actions, the successful Bidder, purchaser, or Auction participant also expressly submits himself to the personal jurisdiction of the State of Texas.
51. These Terms & Conditions provide specific remedies for occurrences in the auction and delivery process. Where such remedies are afforded, they shall be interpreted strictly. Bidder agrees that any claim shall utilize such remedies; Bidder making a claim in excess of those remedies provided in these Terms and Conditions agrees that in no case whatsoever shall Auctioneer's maximum liability exceed the high bid on that lot, which bid shall be deemed for all purposes the value of the lot.

Miscellaneous:

52. Agreements between Bidders and consignors to effectuate a non-sale of an item at Auction, inhibit bidding on a consigned item to enter into a private sale agreement for said item, or to utilize the Auctioneer's Auction to obtain sales for non-selling consigned items subsequent to the Auction, are strictly prohibited. If a subsequent sale of a previously consigned item occurs in violation of this provision, Auctioneer reserves the right to charge Bidder the applicable Buyer's Premium and consignor a Seller's Commission as determined for each auction venue and by the terms of the seller's agreement.
53. Acceptance of these Terms and Conditions qualifies Bidder as a client who has consented to be contacted by Heritage in the future. In conformity with "do-not-call" regulations promulgated by the Federal or State regulatory agencies, participation by the Bidder is affirmative consent to being contacted at the phone number shown in his application and this consent shall remain in effect until it is revoked in writing. Heritage may from time to time contact Bidder concerning sale, purchase, and auction opportunities available through Heritage and its affiliates and subsidiaries.
54. Rules of Construction: Auctioneer presents properties in a number of collectible fields, and as such, specific venues have promulgated supplemental Terms and Conditions. Nothing herein shall be construed to waive the general Terms and Conditions of Auction by these additional rules and shall be construed to give force and effect to the rules in their entirety.

State Notices:

Notice as to an Auction in California. Auctioneer has in compliance with Title 2.95 of the California Civil Code as amended October 11, 1993 Sec. 1812.600, posted with the California Secretary of State its bonds for it and its employees, and the auction is being conducted in compliance with Sec. 2338 of the Commercial Code and Sec. 535 of the Penal Code.

Notice as to an Auction in New York City. These Terms and Conditions are designed to conform to the applicable sections of the New York City Department of Consumer Affairs Rules and Regulations as Amended. This is a Public Auction Sale conducted by Auctioneer. The New York City licensed Auctioneers are Harvey Bennett, No. 0924050, and Samuel W. Foose, No.0952360, who will conduct the Auction on behalf of Heritage Auctions, Inc. ("Auctioneer"). All lots are subject to: the consignor's right to bid thereon in accord with these Terms and Conditions of Auction, consignor's option to receive advances on their consignments, and Auctioneer, in its sole discretion, may offer limited extended financing to registered bidders, in accord with Auctioneer's internal credit standards. A registered bidder may inquire whether a lot is subject to an advance or reserve. Auctioneer has made advances to various consignors in this sale.

Notice as to an Auction in Texas. In compliance with TDLR rule 67.100(c)(1), notice is hereby provided that this auction is covered by a Recovery Fund administered by the Texas Department of Licensing and Regulation, P.O. Box 12157, Austin, Texas 78711 (512) 463-6599. Any complaints may be directed to the same address.

Notice as to an Auction in Ohio: Auction firm and Auctioneer are licensed by the Dept. of Agriculture, and either the licensee is bonded in favor of the state or an aggrieved person may initiate a claim against the auction recovery fund created in Section 4707.25 of the Revised Code as a result of the licensee's actions, whichever is applicable.

Rev. 10-20-09

Terms and Conditions of Auction

Additional Terms & Conditions:
COINS & CURRENCY

COINS and CURRENCY TERM A: Signature₀ Auctions are not on approval. No certified material may be returned because of possible differences of opinion with respect to the grade offered by any third-party organization, dealer, or service. No guarantee of grade is offered for uncertified Property sold and subsequently submitted to a third-party grading service. There are absolutely no exceptions to this policy. Under extremely limited circumstances, (e.g. gross cataloging error) a purchaser, who did not bid from the floor, may request Auctioneer to evaluate voiding a sale: such request must be made in writing detailing the alleged gross error; submission of the lot to the Auctioneer must be pre-approved by the Auctioneer; and bidder must notify Ron Brackemyre (1-800-8726467 Ext. 1312) in writing of such request within three (3) days of the non-floor bidder's receipt of the lot. Any lot that is to be evaluated must be in our offices within 30 days after Auction. Grading or method of manufacture do not qualify for this evaluation process nor do such complaints constitute a basis to challenge the authenticity of a lot. AFTER THAT 30-DAY PERIOD, NO LOTS MAY BE RETURNED FOR REASONS OTHER THAN AUTHENTICITY. Lots returned must be housed intact in their original holder. No lots purchased by floor Bidders may be returned (including those Bidders acting as agents for others) except for authenticity. Late remittance for purchases may be considered just cause to revoke all return privileges.

COINS and CURRENCY TERM B: Auctions conducted solely on the Internet THREE (3) DAY RETURN POLICY: Certified Coin and Uncertified and Certified Currency lots paid for within seven days of the Auction closing are sold with a three (3) day return privilege. You may return lots under the following conditions: Within three days of receipt of the lot, you must first notify Auctioneer by contacting Client Service by phone (1-800-872-6467) or e-mail (Bid@HA.com), and immediately ship the lot(s) fully insured to the attention of Returns, Heritage, 3500 Maple Avenue, 17th Floor, Dallas TX 75219-3941. Lots must be housed intact in their original holder and condition. You are responsible for the insured, safe delivery of any lots. A non-negotiable return fee of 5% of the purchase price ($10 per lot minimum) will be deducted from the refund for each returned lot or billed directly. Postage and handling fees are not refunded. After the three-day period (from receipt), no items may be returned for any reason. Late remittance for purchases revokes these Return privileges.

COINS and CURRENCY TERM C: Bidders who have inspected the lots prior to any Auction, or attended the Auction, or bid through an Agent, will not be granted any return privileges, except for reasons of authenticity.

COINS and CURRENCY TERM D: Coins sold referencing a third-party grading service are sold "as is" without any express or implied warranty, except for a guarantee by Auctioneer that they are genuine. Certain warranties may be available from the grading services and the Bidder is referred to them for further details: Numismatic Guaranty Corporation (NGC), P.O. Box 4776, Sarasota, FL 34230; Professional Coin Grading Service (PCGS), PO Box 9458, Newport Beach, CA 92658; ANACS, 6555 S. Kenton St. Ste. 303, Englewood, CO 80111; and Independent Coin Grading Co. (ICG), 7901 East Belleview Ave., Suite 50, Englewood, CO 80111.

COINS and CURRENCY TERM E: Notes sold referencing a third-party grading service are sold "as is" without any express or implied warranty, except for guarantee by Auctioneer that they are genuine. Grading, condition or other attributes of any lot may have a material effect on its value, and the opinion of others, including third-party grading services such as PCGS Currency, PMG, and CGA may differ with that of Auctioneer. Auctioneer shall not be bound by any prior or subsequent opinion, determination, or certification by any grading service. Bidder specifically waives any claim to right of return of any item because of the opinion, determination, or certification, or lack thereof, by any grading service. Certain warranties may be available from the grading services and the Bidder is referred to them for further details: Paper Money Guaranty (PMG), PO Box 4711, Sarasota FL 34230; PCGS Currency, PO Box 9458, Newport Beach, CA 92658; Currency Grading & Authentication (CGA), PO Box 418, Three Bridges, NJ 08887. Third party graded notes are not returnable for any reason whatsoever.

COINS and CURRENCY TERM F: Since we cannot examine encapsulated coins or notes, they are sold "as is" without our grading opinion, and may not be returned for any reason. Auctioneer shall not be liable for any patent or latent defect or controversy pertaining to or arising from any encapsulated collectible. In any such instance, purchaser's remedy, if any, shall be solely against the service certifying the collectible.

COINS and CURRENCY TERM G: Due to changing grading standards over time, differing interpretations, and to possible mishandling of items by subsequent owners, Auctioneer reserves the right to grade items differently than shown on certificates from any grading service that accompany the items. Auctioneer also reserves the right to grade items differently than the grades shown in the prior catalog should such items be reconsigned to any future auction.

COINS and CURRENCY TERM H: Although consensus grading is employed by most grading services, it should be noted as aforesaid that grading is not an exact science. In fact, it is entirely possible that if a lot is broken out of a plastic holder and resubmitted to another grading service or even to the same service, the lot could come back with a different grade assigned.

COINS and CURRENCY TERM I: Certification does not guarantee protection against the normal risks associated with potentially volatile markets. The degree of liquidity for certified coins and collectibles will vary according to general market conditions and the particular lot involved. For some lots there may be no active market at all at certain points in time.

COINS and CURRENCY TERM J: All non-certified coins and currency are guaranteed genuine, but are not guaranteed as to grade, since grading is a matter of opinion, an art and not a science, and therefore the opinion rendered by the Auctioneer or any third party grading service may not agree with the opinion of others (including trained experts), and the same expert may not grade the same item with the same grade at two different times. Auctioneer has graded the non-certified numismatic items, in the Auctioneer's opinion, to their current interpretation of the American Numismatic Association's standards as of the date the catalog was prepared. There is no guarantee or warranty implied or expressed that the grading standards utilized by the Auctioneer will meet the standards of any grading service at any time in the future.

COINS and CURRENCY TERM K: Storage of purchased coins and currency: Purchasers are advised that certain types of plastic may react with a coin's metal or transfer plasticizer to notes and may cause damage. Caution should be used to avoid storage in materials that are not inert.

COINS and CURRENCY TERM L: Storage of purchased coins and currency: Purchasers are advised that certain types of plastic may react with a coin's metal or transfer plasticizer to notes and may cause damage. Caution should be used to avoid storage in materials that are not inert.

COINS and CURRENCY TERM M: NOTE: Purchasers of rare coins or currency through Heritage have available the option of arbitration by the Professional Numismatists Guild (PNG); if an election is not made within ten (10) days of an unresolved dispute, Auctioneer may elect either PNG or A.A.A. Arbitration.

COINS and CURRENCY TERM N: For more information regarding Canadian lots attributed to the Charlton reference guides, please contact: Charlton International, PO Box 820, Station Willowdale B, North York, Ontario M2K 2R1 Canada.

WIRING INSTRUCTIONS:

BANK INFORMATION:
Wells Fargo Bank
420 Montgomery Street
San Francisco, CA 94104-1207

ACCOUNT NAME: Heritage Auction Galleries

ABA NUMBER: 121000248

ACCOUNT NUMBER: 4121930028

SWIFT CODE: WFBIUS6S

Your five most effective bidding techniques:

1 Interactive Internet™ Proxy Bidding
(leave your maximum Bid at HA.com before the auction starts)

Heritage's exclusive Interactive Internet™ system is fun and easy! Before you start, you must register online at HA.com and obtain your Username and Password.

1. Login to the HA.com website, using your Username and Password.

2. Chose the specialty you're interested in at the top of the homepage (i.e. coins, currency, comics, movie posters, fine art, etc.).

3. Search or browse for the lots that interest you. Every auction has search features and a 'drop-down' menu list.

4. Select a lot by clicking on the link or the photo icon. Read the description, and view the full-color photography. Note that clicking on the image will enlarge the photo with amazing detail.

5. View the current opening bid. Below the lot description, note the historic pricing information to help you establish price levels. Clicking on a link will take you directly to our Permanent Auction Archives for more information and images.

6. If the current price is within your range, Bid! At the top of the lot page is a box containing the Current Bid and an entry box for your "Secret Maximum Bid" – the maximum amount you are willing to pay for the item before the Buyer's Premium is added. Click the button marked "Place Bid" (if you are not logged in, a login box will open first so you can enter your username (or e-mail address) and password.

7. After you are satisfied that all the information is correct, confirm your "Secret Maximum Bid" by clicking on the "Confirm Absentee Bid" button. You will receive immediate notification letting you know if you are now the top bidder, or if another bidder had previously bid higher than your amount. If you bid your maximum amount and someone has already bid higher, you will immediately know so you can concentrate on other lots.

8. Before the auction, if another bidder surpasses your "Secret Maximum Bid", you will be notified automatically by e-mail containing a link to review the lot and possibly bid higher.

9. Interactive Internet™ bidding closes at 10 P.M. Central Time the night before the session is offered in a floor event. Interactive Internet™ bidding closes two hours before live sessions where there is no floor bidding.

10. The Interactive Internet™ system generally opens the lot at the next increment above the second highest bid. As the high bidder, your "Secret Maximum Bid" will compete for you during the floor auction. Of course, it is possible in a Signature® or Grand Format live auction that you may be outbid on the floor or by a Heritage Live bidder after Internet bidding closes. Bid early, as the earliest bird wins in the event of a tie bid. For more information about bidding and bid increments, please see the section labeled "Bidding Options" found in the Terms & Conditions of this catalog.

11. After the auction, you will be notified of your success. It's that easy!

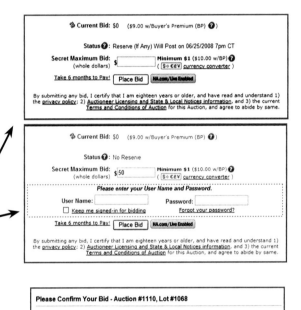

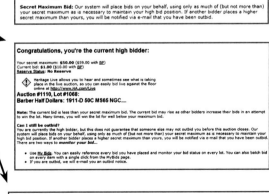

❷HERITAGE Live!™ Bidding
(participate in the Live auction via the Internet)

1. Look on each auction's homepage to verify whether that auction is "HA.com/Live Enabled." All Signature® and Grand Format auctions use the HERITAGE Live!™ system, and many feature live audio and/or video. Determine your lots of interest and maximum bids.

2. Note on the auction's homepage the session dates and times (and especially time zones!) so you can plan your participation. You actually have two methods of using HERITAGE Live!™: a) you can leave a proxy bid through this system, much like the Interactive Internet™ (we recommend you do this before the session starts), or b) you can sit in front of your computer much as the audience is sitting in the auction room during the actual auction.

3. Login at HA.com/Live.

4. Until you become experienced (and this happens quickly!) you will want to login well before your lot comes up so you can watch the activity on other lots. It is as intuitive as participating in a live auction.

5. When your lot hits the auction block, you can continue to bid live against the floor and other live bidders by simply clicking the "Bid" button; the amount you are bidding is clearly displayed on the console.

❸ Mail Bidding
(deposit your maximum Bid with the U.S.P.S. well before the auction starts)

Mail bidding at auction is fun and easy, but by eliminating the interactivity of our online systems, some of your bids may be outbid before you lick the stamp, and you will have no idea of your overall chances until the auction is over!

1. Look through the printed catalog, and determine your lots of interest.

2. Research their market value by checking price lists and other price guidelines.

3. Fill out your bid sheet, entering your maximum bid on each lot. Bid using whole dollar amounts only. Verify your bids, because you are responsible for any errors you make! Please consult the Bidding Increments chart in the Terms & Conditions.

4. Please fill out your bid sheet completely! We also need: a) Your name and complete address for mailing invoices and lots; b) Your telephone number if any problems or changes arise; c) Your references; if you have not established credit with Heritage, you must send a 25% deposit, or list dealers with whom you have credit established; d) Total your bid sheet; add up all bids and list that total in the box; e) Sign your bid sheet, thereby agreeing to abide by the Terms & Conditions of Auction printed in the catalog.

5. Mail early, because preference is given to the first bid received in case of a tie.

6. When bidding by mail, you frequently purchase items at less than your maximum bid. Bidding generally opens at the next published increment above the second highest mail or Internet bid previously received; if additional floor, phone, or HERITAGE Live!™ bids are made, we act as your agent, bidding in increments over any additional bid until you win the lot or are outbid. For example, if you submitted a bid of $750, and the second highest bid was $375, bidding would start at $400; if no other bids were placed, you would purchase the lot for $400.

7. You can also Fax your Bid Sheet if time is short. Use our exclusive Fax Hotline: 214-443-8425.

❹ Telephone Bidding (when you are traveling, or do not have access to HERITAGE Live!™)

1. To participate in an auction by telephone, you must make preliminary arrangements with Client Services (Toll Free 866-835-3243) at least three days before the auction.

2. We strongly recommend that you place preliminary bids by mail or Internet if you intend to participate by telephone. On many occasions, this dual approach has reduced disappointments due to telephone (cell) problems, unexpected travel, late night sessions, and time zone differences. Keep a list of your preliminary bids, and we will help you avoid bidding against yourself.

❺ Attend in Person (whenever possible)

Auctions are fun, and we encourage you to attend as many as possible – although our HERITAGE Live!™ system brings all of the action right to your computer screen. Auction dates and session times are printed on the title page of each catalog, and appear on the homepage of each auction at HA.com. Join us if you can!

Take 4 Months to Pay...

Heritage will Finance Your Purchase

We're collectors too, and we understand that on occasion there is more to buy than there is cash. Consider Heritage's Extended Payment Plan [EPP] for your purchases totaling $2,500 or more.

Extended Payment Plan [EPP] Conditions

- Minimum invoice total is $2,500.
- Minimum Down Payment is 25% of the total invoice.
- A signed and returned EPP Agreement is required.
- The EPP is subject to a 3% *fully refundable* Set-up Fee (based on the total invoice amount) payable as part of the first monthly payment.
- The 3% Set-up Fee is refundable provided all monthly payments are made by eCheck, bank draft, personal check drawn on good funds, or cash; and if all such payments are made according to the EPP schedule.
- Monthly payments can be automatically processed with an eCheck, Visa, or MasterCard.
- You may take up to four equal monthly payments to pay the balance.
- Interest is calculated at only 1% per month on the unpaid balance.
- Your EPP must be kept current or additional interest may apply.
- There is no penalty for paying off early.
- Shipment will be made when final payment is received.
- All traditional auction and sales policies still apply.

There is no return privilege once you have confirmed your sale, and penalties can be incurred on cancelled invoices. To avoid additional fees, you must make your down payment within 14 days of the auction. All material purchased under the EPP will be physically secured by Heritage until paid in full.

To exercise the EPP option, please notify **Eric Thomas** at **214.409.1241** or email at **EricT@HA.com** upon receipt of your invoice.

We appreciate your business and wish you good luck with your bidding.

LONG BEACH
COIN, STAMP & COLLECTIBLES EXPO
Held at the Long Beach Convention Center

FUTURE SHOW DATES

Official Auctioneer

The World's #1 Numismatic Auctioneer

HERITAGE HA.com
Auction Galleries

Feb 4-6, 2010
June 3-5, 2010
Sept 23-25, 2010

Onsite Grading

A Division of Collectors Universe
NASDAQ: CLCT

A Rare Commitment to Numismatics.

NGC
Numismatic Guaranty Corporation

Fun for the entire FAMILY! $$Multi-Million Dollar Exhibits$$! *Daily Gold Prize Drawings!*

Santa Clara
Coin, Stamp & Collectibles Expo
Held at the Santa Clara Convention Center

FUTURE SHOW DATES

April 8-11, 2010
November 18-21, 2010

Bring your Collectibles to our Expos for competitive offers from *America's Top Buyers!*

www.exposunlimited.com

FREE
Kids
Treasure Hunt

www.longbeachexpo.com

EXPOS UNLIMITED

www.santaclaraexpo.com

FREE
Educational
Seminars

A Division of Collectors Universe, Inc. Nasdaq; CLCT
8 West Figueroa Street Santa Barbara, CA 93101
Ph (805)962-9939 Fx (805)963-0827
Email: warreckert@collectors.com